MEMOIRS OF A RIFLEMAN SCOUT

MEMOIRS OF A
RIFLEMAN SCOUT

Major F.M. Crum

Foreword by Adrian Gilbert

FRONTLINE BOOKS, LONDON

Memoirs of a Rifleman Scout
First published in 1950 by A. Learmonth & Son,
'Journal Office', 9 King Street, Stirling.
This edition published in 2014 by Frontline Books,
an imprint of Pen & Sword Books Ltd,
47 Church Street, Barnsley, S. Yorkshire, S70 2AS
www.frontline-books.com

ISBN: 978-1-84832-755-9

For more information on our books, please visit
www.frontline-books.com, email info@frontline-books.com
or write to us at the above address.

Printed and bound by CPI Group (UK) Ltd, Croydon, CR0 4YY

Typeset in 12/14 Times New Roman by MATS Typesetters, Leigh-on-Sea, Essex

CONTENTS

LIST OF PLATES

FOREWORD

'It was in Sanctuary Wood in July that I first made my debut as a sniper enthusiast.' With these words Major F.M. Crum announced his determination to take on the German snipers who dominated No Man's Land in the Ypres Salient during 1915. Crum would become one of the founding fathers of British sniping, initially forming a sniper section in his own battalion before going on to institute training methods used throughout the Army.

As well as being a dedicated officer, who took a keen interest in all aspects of his profession, Crum was also a guiding light in the development of the scouting movement in Britain, having been greatly influenced by Robert Baden-Powell, both men veterans of the Boer War. These two strands form the core of *Memoirs of a Rifleman Scout*, a wide-ranging and engaging story of Crum's career, based on his diaries and the many letters sent to friends and family at home.

On 12 October 1872 Frederick Maurice Crum was born into a Scottish family that had made its money supplying dyes to Glasgow's rapidly expanding textile industry. After attending Eton College, Crum decided not to join the family business but embark on a military career. Passing out from Sandhurst he was commissioned into the 1st Battalion of the King's Royal Rifle Corps (KRRC), which sailed to South Africa in December 1896.

The open plains of the African veldt encouraged the creation of mounted infantry, a tactical innovation designed to improve the infantryman's mobility: he would ride into battle but would fight on foot with rifle and bayonet. The 1st KRRC had formed its own company of mounted infantry, and it was in this unit that Crum opened his military career when Britain went to war with the Boer republics on 11 October 1899.

9

Lieutenant Crum was soon in action, taking part in the battle for Talana Hill on 20 October. Although the British drove off the attacking force, casualties were heavy and they included Crum, shot through the shoulder. 'I realized,' wrote Crum, 'that in the first steeplechase of war, I had come down at the first fence.' To make matters worse, he was captured by a Boer patrol and spent the next six months as a prisoner of war. A Boer rifle bullet has shattered his shoulder, and although the wound was patched up in a basic manner, it failed to heal properly and would cause problems throughout his time in the Army. Rescue from Boer captivity came when a British force overran his camp on 4 June 1900. Eager to resume active service, Crum was back in the saddle in August, taking part in counter-insurgency operations against the Boers. He now commanded his own company of mounted infantry, although ill-health forced him to take sick leave in January 1902, a few months before the end of the war.

Crum was mentioned in Lord Kitchener's despatches for demonstrating great bravery, while his narrative of the campaign in South Africa is one of the highlights of the book. His sincerity and enthusiasm shine through the pages, and although scrupulously fair in his judgments he is not afraid to describe the many British shortcomings that became apparent during the campaign.

Crum followed his battalion to Malta for garrison duty, starting the first draft of his book on the role of mounted infantry. In this he was supported by progressives and Army-reformers, like Lord Roberts, but was opposed by the cavalry school, led by Sir John French, who saw this new arm as undermining the standing of the regular cavalry regiments. Early in 1904 Crum transferred to the 2nd Battalion in India as a brevet-major, a move that gave him an opportunity to work with Gurkhas in scouting operations. His service in India convinced him of the need to improve the Army's poor musketry and field training skills, and of the necessity to instil a sense of initiative in the private soldier. Poor health continued to undermine his efforts, however, and in October 1908 he was forced to retire from active service.

This was a time of crisis for Crum, and by his own admission it was only his strong and enduring Christian faith that saved him from falling into the deepest depression. Combining conscience with practicality, he set about helping the poor of his native Scotland, first working with the Church Army and then the Boy Scout Movement.

The outbreak of war in August 1914 brought these endeavours to an abrupt halt. Securing a reserve commission, he was posted to the 8th KRRC, one of the first of Kitchener's New Army battalions to be sent over to Flanders. The battalion arrived in the trenches in May 1915 to immediately take part in the Battle of Hooge in the Ypres salient. Crum brilliantly captures the sense of shock felt by the troops on encountering this new type of war, which included the first use of mobile flamethrowers by the Germans. He wrote that, 'the whole experience of this extraordinary trench-warfare fighting was so novel and difficult, so different from my mounted infantry experience of the war in South Africa that I found it of intense interest.'

As with all soldiers from rifle regiments, Crum was an exponent of good musketry, but it was only on witnessing German skill in sniping at first hand did he decide to take up this new trench-warfare discipline. 'Sniping was then in its infancy,' Crum recalled. 'The Hun had got the start, and was "Top Dog" nine times out of ten.' In contrast to other sniper devotees, Crum had little practical experience of sharpshooting and was instructed in the basics by a sergeant in the Gordon Highlanders. He was a quick learner, but an initial problem was to convince the Army that sniping should be taken seriously and allocated men, time and resources.

In the period 1915–16, sniping was essentially a private initiative, with the enthusiasts independently developing their own techniques and tactics. They also relied on generous benefactors to send out accurate sporting rifles – including high-velocity large-calibre rifles capable of penetrating German armoured loophole plates – as well as a good supply of telescopic sights and other optical devices. On his first home leave in September 1915, Crum wrote that he had, 'so much to do in London, seeing War Office and gunmaker experts about ideas for sniping, bullet-proof shields, armour-piercing bullet, elephant guns, masks, paint, periscopes.'

Crum's work produced results, and he was encouraged by his CO and brigade commander to develop both sniping and general reconnaissance skills among his men. After weeks of determined effort, Crum described the improved situation: 'It was a great satisfaction to see the victory of our snipers. When we came away not a shot was ever fired by the Bosche sniper, and he had closed and sandbagged all his loopholes.'

In March 1916 the 8th KRRC was withdrawn from Ypres and sent south to Blagny, near Arras, where, once again, Crum and his men slowly and painfully wrested sniper mastery of the front-line trenches from their German opponents. During 1916 the Army began to take an official interest in sniping, having seen the good work of officers like Crum and other such luminaries as Hesketh-Prichard and N.A. Armstrong. In May 1916, Crum established a sniper school at Acq, which gained a reputation for imaginative and effective training methods.

Crum minimised time in the lecture hall and took his students onto a purpose-built training ground, which as well as a rifle range included accurate reconstructions of both British and German trenches. Drawing upon teaching methods learned from his days with the Boy Scouts, Crum and his team acted out potential sniping scenarios to the watching students, who would then take an active part in developing the themes suggested by their trainers. With an emphasis on humour and the unexpected, Crum had little difficulty in catching his students' attention. Confident in his ideas on sniper training, Crum wrote them up as a short book, *Scouts and Snipers in Trench Warfare*, producing 1,000 copies at his own expense and distributing them around the Army. This eventually became 'SS 195 – Scouting, Sniping and Observation', the first official publication on the subject.

In November 1916 – after another period of sick leave – Crum established a sniping school at Aldershot for officers preparing to go to France, improving on the methods first used at Acq. In May 1917 he took up GHQ's request to co-ordinate the training methods of the five army sniper schools then in place on the Western Front.

On his return to Britain, Crum travelled around the country lecturing to officer cadets. When unable to provide open-air demonstrations, he made effective use of lantern slides and even produced his own short films. He recalled how 'many an hour [was spent] in that dark room in Wardour Street, experimenting and working out those films'. His experience with snipers during the war convinced him of the importance of 'teaching officers how to teach', as well as providing formal training in the techniques of leadership.

As the war drew to a close, Crum resigned his commission and almost immediately suffered a total collapse, being sent to a nursing home to recover. This turned out to be a blessing, as a thorough medical investigation revealed the old wound from the Boer War to be the cause of his medical problems. After an operation by the distinguished surgeon Sir Harold Stiles in February 1919 the problem was resolved, with Crum making a good and lasting recovery. The remainder of his life was devoted to scouting, and his activities as a scout leader form the final part of the book.

Published in 1950 – five years before his death – *Memoirs of a Rifleman Scout* is a vivid yet thoughtful account of the life of an officer of the Old Army, one who won his spurs fighting the Boers in South Africa and then went on to make a significant contribution to British success in trench warfare. The publication of this new edition of Crum's classic memoir is to be welcomed, essential reading for anyone with an interest in the history of sniping.

Adrian Gilbert

PREFACE

In these Memoirs I would like to feel myself talking to friends; *not* writing a book.

Having kept a day-to-day log all these years, it has seemed to me wrong not to pass on some word to keep touch with days that are gone, and, maybe, to help in days yet to come.

If, at times, in my story there is too much detail for some, let them skip and pass on; others may like to know more of Scouts and Scout training for Peace or in War.

But my chief wish in writing has been to focus our thoughts on the lead we must give to the men of tomorrow.

As we enter this new danger-zone, the need which is urgent, is ever the same. Survival depends on the Spirit we show.

Away with neglect in our training of Youth to be worthy of Freedom!

Bring on good Leaders.

In a practical way, teach Duty and Honour, Service and Friendship.

Ask for the Spirit which wins.

Whatever may change, God does not change. True Freedom wins through in the end.

[signature]

Kenmuir,
    Rosneath.
       16th November, 1950.

15

MEMOIRS

OF A

RIFLEMAN SCOUT

PART I

PART I.

SOUTH AFRICAN WAR, 1899–1902.

CONTENTS

I. TALANA.

A Lost Diary: Dr. Gunning the Zoo-Man.

It will help me to lead up to my story of the Battle of Talana Hill if I give a few extracts from my diary of 1899. I have it beside me, covered in mud and in places illegible. This diary, after spending some days in the rain and dirt of the deserted British Camp, found its way to Pretoria where it fell into the hands of the worthy Dr. Gunning, a Hollander employed by the Boers as Intelligence Officer.

On my arrival at the hospital in Pretoria in January, 1900, Dr. Gunning came to see me and question me about my diary. He refused to give it me back or even to let me see it. 'All right,' I said, 'the very first thing I shall do when Lord Roberts arrives will be to take it from you.' He laughed, for the very idea of losing the war, to him at the time, seemed a joke. Six long months we had to pass, but, in the end, I kept my word and he gave it me back with a smile. We were quite good friends. In normal life Gunning was Curator of the Pretoria Zoo. At first Officer Prisoners of War were in the hands of Opperman, a bad type of Boer, but when Opperman was sent to the front for stealing parcels and holding back letters, Gunning took his place as our Zooman till a Hollander grocer took his place. Later in the war I sent Dr. Gunning for his Zoo, a monster toad, which astonished us all when we caught it near Middelburg. He was pleased, and sent me its Latin name and measurements which I forget.

To return to the diary – As I look at it now, some 50 years later, I see it is just the day-to-day log of a young officer, with much still to learn but intensely keen on his profession. It is full of details of ponies and polo, racing and sport; these were of no great interest to Dr. Gunning, but, as we were often in touch with Lord Milner's

Staff, and Army and Navy Headquarters circles, I see there were indiscretions. All these had been awarded blue-pencil crosses by him!

At the Cape.

The Boer War did not come on us at the Cape as a surprise. In December, 1896, when the 1st Batt. 60th Rifles sailed from Bombay for the Cape in the 'Warren Hastings,' three years before war was declared, already then, such catchwords as 'Roll on Kruger's doom,' and 'Pulling old Kruger's whiskers,' were common in barracks.

On December 28th we arrived at Cape Town. The 'Warren Hastings' went on and was wrecked, but that is another story (a story all Riflemen are proud of).

At the Cape we soon settled down. At Cape Town we joined in all that went on – jump races and flat, polo, cricket, and various functions; and, further afield, we hunted the Jackal with hounds and made friends with Dutch farmers all over the district. Many a time we slept seven or eight officers in one huge Dutch bed and enjoyed hospitality. But, for all our energy in training ponies for polo and jumping and races, we knew very well there was trouble ahead. Our one set purpose was to train ourselves for war.

Under Sir William Goodenough and Sir William Butler we trained specially in skirmishing and shooting, and, later, in mounted infantry duties. All talk of 'Boer War' was tabu; there was to be no provocation. It was to be called 'South African Warfare.' These two Commanders were distinguished Generals in their day, and we were keen to learn. It must be remembered that smokeless powder, Lee-Metford rifles, and Maxim guns were new and untried factors in warfare then.

Training at Muizenburg.

A few notes on our training may be of interest to-day, though, at the time, they did not interest Dr. Gunning.

We had finished a long and thorough course of musketry training. We left Barracks and moved into Camp at Muizenburg, and here, for a month, we went through our Company Field Training.

Muizenburg, on the coast, is like St. Andrews, with sands and sea-air, sea-bathing and sun. Its sand-dunes and the unlimited space inland for manoeuvres, and no golfers to consider, made it an ideal training ground. As we marched out each morning from camp and saluted the guard in passing, at the head of our column was always the bugler, armed with a football as well as his bugle. There were taunts – 'Good old "B" Company, off to play football again!' In those days such a thing was not orthodox. But it paid us in the end, for the length of the game depended on progress made in the training, moreover it added to 'esprit-de-corps.'

Here are two extracts:–

'Men worked well, but when left to themselves seem quite hopeless, surely some sense will dawn on them when the real thing comes. Some didn't even know on which side of a hill to take cover.'

Later – 'A real good morning's work, put each man individually through skirmishing, felt had improved a lot.'

Sir Wm. Butler.

Then came the day of Inspection. What would our new General ask us to do? Most Generals have some special hobby. As it turned out Sir Wm. Butler had come, not to drill into us any special notion of his own. He had come to make us think for ourselves. He called on each Company Commander to lecture his men on some given task, for instance, attacking some given ridge, or defending some bridge. After that the men were sent off to *do* whatever it was. Then followed helpful advice. My men played up and we got a good mark. The football had paid!

Natal.

In May, 1899, the clouds of war grew darker. We moved to Natal. At Maritzburg all ranks were united in a feeling of great keenness. This was inspired by the conviction that war was coming. For four months we lived in a continual state of suspense. We rushed to the papers each day. When it looked like peace there was gloom; when war seemed more likely our spirits went up. No wonder our Zoo-man thought us 'war-mongers' and blue-pencilled such entries as these:–

Rumours of War.

May 7 – 'Chamberlain protests to Reitz – excitement. Ultimatum?'

" 8 – 'Results of Conference for peace – quite depressed.'

June 22 – 'Sir P. Symonds and H.E. dined, 40,000 Troops coming.'

" 26 – 'War scare not so strong. Kruger climbing down.'

" 28 – 'Chamberlain fine speech, looks more like war.'

Aug. 12 – 'Rumours more like war than ever.'

" 15 – 'War seems very likely.'

" 18 – 'More peaceful news made everyone depressed. Stables, etc., as usual. Watched 'B' Coy. draw with 'F' in football final. General dining.'

" 20 – 'Saw two Tailor birds, got a Shrike and skinned it. C. had an interview with Kruger, reports him saying 'war inevitable.' K. says the Transvaal is like a pretty girl. England in love for long time. As couldn't marry her, was going to kill her. Boers openly say they will occupy Laing's Nek.'

" 30 – 'Rumours of peace and Kruger's climb down, everyone quite down.'

" 31 – 'Bored with suspense.'

There are plenty of other such entries all with blue pencil crosses. One goes right back to April 9th at Cape Town. It tells of a petition 125 yards long, from 21,000 Uitlanders demanding the vote, and to be forwarded to Queen Victoria. 'While H.E., Lord Milner and Staff were examining it on the lawn at Government House, Dr. Leyds from Pretoria called.'

Training under Gen. Sir Wm. P. Symonds.

On our arrival in Natal we had come under command of a third Sir William – the gallant Penn Symonds, who came with a great reputation for musketry and Indian Frontier Service. In June we had our first field-day under him.

In the light of after events it is of interest to give a few items scribbled in haste at the time and not intended for Dr. Gunning – just a subaltern thinking aloud to himself –

June 29 – 'Big Field-day. Two Coys. M.I. take up position and whole Garrison attacks us. Grand position and view of proceedings. Cavalry scouting much too slow, one dismounts, t'other holds his horse in full view. He would have found out more by cantering round us. Infantry attack would have been another Laing's Nek and great slaughter. The General ran the whole show himself and made his whole force keep within 200 yards limit. Every shot from us would have hit five or six men. General seemed quite pleased. Knocked about polo ball p.m. Turned out Guard 11.45 p.m. Wellington boots and overalls most uncomfortable.'

Aug. 2 – 'Another extraordinary attack. Four waves heaped together at 800 yards á la Gravelotte, then a charge. Must be mad. Kruger still obstinate but Cabinet seems against war.'

,, 9 – 'Mounted infantry Field-day. General himself took command of our two Coys. and stormed a hill held by 5th Lancers. Much pleased. On the way home Dublin's M.I. told to gallop away. 5th Lancers pursuit with lances. Stampede of "Dubs." At pow-wow told they were like "Wild Irishmen." Lonsdale indignant.'

,, 16 – ' "General dining." It was on this occasion that some approached him expressing doubts as to his methods. He was always approachable. He liked to dine in the Mess and sit next to a subaltern, or any one else. He made friends with us all and we felt him to be a very gallant Leader, but we preferred the tactics of General Butler.'

Visits to Laing's Nek.

In July and September, with others, I visited Ingogo and Majuba. We had made our own maps, for these were scarce, and we had read all we could about the first Boer War. With two Natal Mounted Police we rode all over the ground. This formidable Pass on the frontier, with its rail and tunnel, seemed to be a key position. Our guides were splendid fellows but had a difficult job with their sixty-mile rides round very hostile farms within our borders. There were rumours of prepared gun-positions and magazines and dynamite stored at farms to blow up the tunnel. As we rode along the Nek from Majuba to the Buffalo River, we came on three Boers. 'Here come the biggest rebels in the district,' said the Sergeant. Certainly old Akerman and his two big sons did *not* seem friendly. It was said they openly boasted they would be the first to shoot an Englishman.

On the heights we had wonderful views and many talks with those who were left in Charlestown, about all things Boer.

Before leaving I took a ride, on my own, over the border, round Volksoust but saw nothing of rumoured redoubts.

Move to Ladysmith.

On Sunday night, the 24th September, the General came in while we were all at Mess. We all stopped talking. We felt something was up. He said we were all to move to Ladysmith next day. The Ladysmith Troops were moving to Dundee. At last it was business.

It took us no time to move, we were off next morning early, the Battalion by train, and we marching up with the 5th Lancers. The enthusiasm was tremendous. What cheering there was as we, in fine fettle, passed the crowded teams of British refugees escaping from Jo'burg!

In those days there were a few, but very few, who shook their heads and said we were too confident. We did expect to have a hard fight, perhaps two, and we realised that with modern weapons there must be many casualties. But we were not going to make the blunders of 1880. We were dressed in khaki now, and well trained. We would be in Johannesburg by Christmas.

Ladysmith.

We reached Ladysmith October 2nd and found it as bad as reported.

Officers had been known to resign their commissions rather than serve there. We arrived on a typical afternoon. Dust, a black grimy dust, was ankle deep. For the first half of the day, strong hot winds blew clouds of dust in one direction, then, at half-time the wind would change and blow it all back again.

The flies were in clouds, you could not eat without swallowing them and the heat was oppressive. Very glad we were when on

October 4th orders came to March to Dundee next day.

Our last night was bad. All tents had been struck and packed on the wagons, and we were sleeping in the open, when a storm and whirlwind of dust carried off boots, helmets and kits into the darkness. As we started before daylight, much kit was lost.

There were rumours of 16,000 Boers round the frontier. Full military precautions were taken, our Company doing its first real active service scouting for the Battalion. On October 7th we arrived at Dundee without adventure.

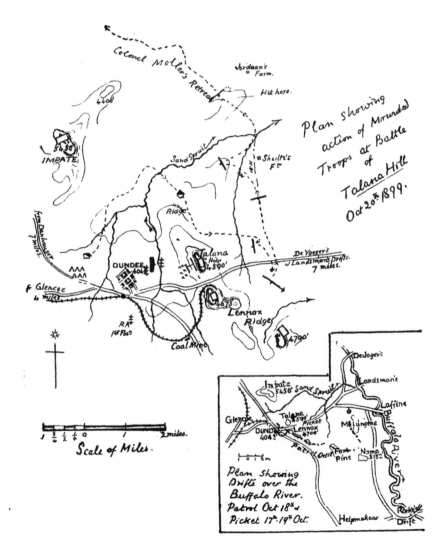

Dundee.

Dundee, with its beautiful climate and scenery, was welcome after Ladysmith. The shops were still open and the people were going about their ordinary business, while a military band played regularly each afternoon.

On October 10th General Symonds arrived to take command, and all women and children were sent down country.

Then, on October 11th, Kruger, on his own birthday, sent in an Ultimatum and, at last, on October 12th (my birthday) we heard that war was declared. Shots were fired close by and large numbers of Boers were reported advancing to our front and on both of our flanks.

At the time, though so long expected, the fact came as a shock.

I sat up with a start. So it had really come!

From the 12th to 19th, scouting by day and pickets at night kept us hard at work.

Night Patrols.

On these patrols we were sent out further than was thought wise later on in the war. However, we came to no harm, and even the night picket of 12 men of the Dublin's M.I., under Grimshaw, which was rushed at 2 a.m. the morning of Talana had only one man wounded. They were able to fall back and warn the General of the attack.

Two nights before I had been on this same picket, it was three miles out from Dundee, watching the road from De Yagers and Landsman's Drifts on the Buffalo River.

What would have happened if the Boers had come on our night?

In a small notebook I find this sketch and report:–

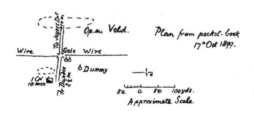

28

Picket 3 miles E of Dundee, October 17th, 1899 (to give warning of any advance). 'Arrived on the ground in good time to look round, with 2 men out took good look round with Cpl. Oglesby. At foot of rising ground to our front was a barbed wire fence running at least a mile in each direction, across our front. Only one gap at gate on road to Drift. Posted two men behind fence at gate, lying down behind ant heap – orders to watch sky-line to their front, especially where road crossed. To be alert for sounds of men getting through wire. If approached to challenge quietly. One man to slip back quietly and warn picket, the other, if satisfied it was an enemy, to get back to picket without firing. A dummy was rigged up with helmet and coat on our side of fence, but a bit to our right, to draw the Boers to give themselves away. Horses in hollow 150 yards in rear, one man on look-out, one watching horses. All slept with great-coats over them, *not* in them, to be ready at once. In case of alarm men on picket to creep up some 50 yards, extending to cover the gate, order to fire from Cpl. Oglesby or myself. To let some get through gate first. We rehearsed all this, every man knew what to do.'

Patrol to Buffalo River Drifts.

On October 18th I was out from 4 a.m. to 6 p.m. on a long reconnaissance with a patrol of seven, four picked men of M.I., one Natal Carabinier, Spencer, a good man who knew the district well, and a Trooper of local Police. We were sent to watch the De Jaeger, Landsman and Laffina Drifts over the Buffalo River, about 12 miles from camp. To do this we had stalked up by Fort Pine to the top of Moma Mountain, 5,152 ft., and then worked our way along to Malmgave Range, fully expecting to come on a party of 30 Boers daily in those parts. There were none, however, that day. What a clear view we got of the Drifts! It was 3 p.m. when we started home. On arrival I reported to the General. He had word that the Boers were all round us, intending to attack us next day. He seemed relieved at my report.

The long reconnoitring upset me and I spent a bad night. I had to remain in bed with fever the following day, and was very glad that the expected battle did not come off just then.

On Friday, October 20th, the Troops fell in at 5 a.m. awaiting an attack. I lay awake on my valise listening and praying for another day to get fit in. Dr. Julien passed my tent and told me on no account to get up. I told him the plaster he had put on me had made me so sore, and the fever had left me so weak, that I didn't think I should do the Boers much harm, but if they did come, I should certainly have a try. At 5.15 a.m. all our fellows came back much disappointed, saying the battle was 'off' again. The troops had been dismissed and it looked like another day of 'armed peace.'

Surprise of the Camp.

Presently I heard a rumour that Grimshaw's picket, on the road to the Drifts, had been rushed.

Next I heard men outside saying – 'What's them 'ere blokes on that bloomin' hill?' and some discussion as to whether they were Boers or Fusiliers. Going out of my tent I saw them staring at the hill above Piet Smith's Farm, which is about two miles East of the Town.

I saw crowds of men on the sky-line and something very like guns. The whole camp had turned out to look at them.

I knew at once they were Boers and rushed into my tent, and forgetting my fever and plaster and everything else, bundled on my clothes as fast as I could. I had got one puttee on, and was putting on the other, when there was a loud, sharp report from the hill. A noise like a rocket, then a kind of explosion which sounded at the next tent.

Never did I spend less time in dressing, and yet, I forgot none of the things I should need for a long day's fighting – my difficulty was to find them. Every jacket but the right one seemed to come to hand. Another shell – Hurry up! And I nearly 'made do' with Northey's jacket, but just in time, I spotted my own at the bottom of everything. 'Where are my field-glasses? My watch, knife, whistle, helmet?' More shells tell me not to waste time. Luckily there is my haversack ready with all the outfit needed, and my sword-belt, but of course, this is buckled up and takes a lot of undoing. 'Shall I take my sword? No, it won't be much use against Mausers. Spur, too, can go to the devil. Well, here goes,' and I bolt across to the M.I. lines.

The camp has been surprised. There is much confusion, but all are doing their best to get right.

Shells are landing all over the camp – there goes one into a span of mules, but they don't seem to get killed.

My own men are saddling up as quick as they can, some calm, some excited. 'Can I help you there? Your horse don't seem to like shells, but that's no reason for putting the bit in upside down, and that strap first – there – that's right, up you get.'

What a lot of loose horses! hope mine are not loose. 'Faulkner! Oh, there you are! Well done you!' The good Faulkner with 'Ronnie' and 'Fiddlehead' nearly ready – as cool as when saddling up at the paddock for a race, just a 'soupçon' of mutual excitement, as he tells me my rein is twisted. 'The Mounted are going in that direction, Sir, I don't know what their orders are.' 'All right, Faulkner, come on,' and away we go.

As I rode through the tents of our Battalion I saw the men huddled behind their tents, and just as I passed C/Sgt. Davies and B Coy., one shell seemed to land in the middle of some of the men, and yet no one seemed to get hit! The aim was very straight, how bad it would be if they fired shrapnel!

I felt a bit of a deserter as I rode away leaving my old Company.

At first, I am told, there was some confusion, but with Officers like 'Johnny Campbell' and 'Jack Pechell' and others, and with men who had faced death calmly on the 'Warren Hastings,' all were soon sitting tight, hoping for luck and waiting for orders.

The Mounted Infantry and 18th Hussars and Transport were ordered to get under cover under a rocky slope on the north side of the camp.

It must have been about 6.15 a.m. when all the mounted troops were formed up. In our Company, Northey was in command, with Jelf, Majendie and myself as subalterns and about 80 men. We went round and saw that each man had his ammunition, his magazine charged with ten rounds, and food in his haversack. All the men were ready and keen. 'Keep cool and shoot straight' was the order.

As we had no orders, I got leave from Northey to ask the General what our orders were. The Artillery duel had begun.

Our guns had got a bad start. All the horses were away watering, so that they could not choose their positions. They opened fire from where they were. But they were grand batteries, every shot that they fired was a good shot, and while giving confidence to our waiting men down below, was a blow to the nerves of the Boers on the hill.

Orders from General Symonds.

I found General Symonds and his staff standing at his tent near the guns when I galloped up. Shells were landing here too. The General signed to me not to gallop and asked, 'Well, what is it?'

I told him the Dublin's and 60th M.I. had no orders.

He said, 'You are to go with the 18th Hussars. Go and tell Col. Moller that he is to wait under cover – it may be one or two hours – I will send him word to advance. but he may advance if he sees a good opening. Go quietly. Don't gallop.' That hint as to calmness was good. I repeated the order clearly, to make sure I had it right. I saluted and trotted away to where our men were. I told Lonsdale, on my way to Northey, who sent me on to Col. Moller. The whole lot then dismounted.

Reconnaissance towards Impate.

The early mists had not yet cleared from the Impate hills, on what was now our left flank. While we were waiting, I got leave to go with one man (Swaine) to scout in that direction. We went some distance and found all clear. It was from this direction that Joubert attacked next day.

From this reconnaissance I got back about 8 a.m., coming on Col. Moller first, reported to him. He told me our M.I. had gone with Cape and his Maxim gun, so I cantered on after them.

We soon sighted them working their way down the Sand Spruit Valley, and getting round the Boer right. There was also one squadron of 18th Hussars.

The Boer guns on Smith's Kop (Talana Hill) had spotted this move and opened fire on this moving target. As Swaine and I drew nearer the Maxim and escort, we got nearer the shell fire. I said to him, 'Don't ride beside me, there is no reason we should both get hit.' He said he could not hold his bally horse, so I took a pull at mine, and let him shoot ten yards ahead. Immediately a shell whistled past between us and struck the bank of the spruit close to

32

us. I had had hardly time to say 'By Jove!' when another, and then a third, fell all so close that it seemed a matter of inches.

Pom-Pom Fire.

This was the quick-firing gun, afterwards known as a 'pom-pom.' It had got the range, if not the direction, of our Maxim gun.

When I got up to the Maxim I found only Majendie's Section of 22 men had been detailed as escort to Cape and his gum.

The rest, my own Section included, had been sent to escort the two Batteries firing at Talana Hill. (As it turned out later, I had 'missed the bus' for the Seige of Ladysmith.)

Meanwhile the 18th Hussar Squadron had gone on in front, and we got orders to follow. As we advanced there were many fences to cut. Once round the Boer flank the firing grew less. One had more time to look round. To our front, all seemed clear, but the heights to our left were still shrouded in mist and might have held an Army Corps. We found the tendency of horses and men under fire was to get too close together, so we divided the escort, each of us taking half, we then advanced in two small sections. From this experience I should say that 12 men is a limit for one man to supervise under fire.

We pushed on down the left bank of the Spruit, through two farms and a Krall, and more barbed wire; then, turning sharp to our right, we re-crossed the Spruit at a bad place, and came right up towards Talana to the cover of a ridge of stones and boulders.

Here we found the advanced squadron of the 18th Hussars.

Soon afterwards we were joined by the remaining 2 squadrons 18th Hussars and the whole of the Dublin's M.I. under Lonsdale.

These too had been heavily pom-pommed on their way. Here there was cover for all, we dismounted and waited.

A grand position.

I crept up to where Col. Moller was, and asked leave to peep over the ridge. It was grand. Here we were, with all the mounted troops, hidden in an ideal position on the Boer's right rear. Not 2,000 yards away, with a Maxim and 120 rifles, and a whole Regiment of Cavalry. The Boers were about 500 feet above us. Peeping over the crest, I counted some 500 ponies and many Boers. What was the range? Major Greville thought 1,200 yards. I put it at more. We called for a range finder, but it had been left behind. No matter, we should soon get the range when firing began. We had only to wait and keep out of sight.

The ground all round our ridge was bare and open and by shifting a few rocks and boulders we soon had a strong position.

It must have been about 11 a.m. Our guns seemed to have silenced their guns, and the time for action seemed right, when the Colonel sent out a squadron towards Shultz's Farm, and soon afterwards took the Maxim gun and the whole of the rest of his force, in that direction – what his reason was, I can't say – it was a sore disappointment to me.

We went on, cutting fences as we went, about two miles, till we came to the Landsman Drift Road. There the M.I. were told to dismount and extend at right angles to the road facing the rear of the Boer position. We were now right behind the centre of their position and about 2½ miles from it.

The country was open undulating veldt, covered with thousands of ant-heaps. We lined out across the road, each man behind his own ant-heap, our whole line about half-a-mile long. Our horses were in a slight hollow 400 yards in rear.

Here we lay for an hour doing nothing. What our object was in coming I do not know. Hidden on a flank, these few rifles might have been some use when the Boer retreated, but what was the use of planting 120 men across the line of retreat of 4,000 Boers?

The pawn says 'Check' to the Queen.

While waiting, I had a wonderful view of the Boer position and movements. What a chance of sending word back to our gunners.

There were three distinct hills: On their right Talana. In the centre a similar hill, slightly higher and joined by a neck – this was a spur of the Lennox Hill – the highest of the three. There were large groups of Boers and ponies on all these hills.

Looking at Talana from my position I could see a farmhouse with a huge Red Cross. This was the Boer Hospital to which I was taken later. It was full of Boers and ponies moving about the farm.

I watched our shells bursting over the top of this hill and could not make out what was happening. On the centre hill, and Lennox

Hill, there seemed to be on each, some 2,000 Boers and ponies, like flocks of sheep and goats on our side of the hill. I longed to direct our guns on those targets, and almost sent a messenger round with a sketch on my own.

A Unique Opening.

On the Lennox Hill a large force was collecting; they seemed to have transport. What were they up to?

After an hour or so, we changed position, still further to the Boers' left, and lined out facing Lennox Hill.

About 2 p.m., I should say, I saw much movement on Lennox Hill, also the Boers seemed to be leaving Talana and making for Lennox Hill. I suppose this was part of their coming retreat, at the time it puzzled me. It was a long way off.

Then I noticed a party of some 200 Boers mounted and advancing down a water course from Lennox Hill in a straight line for us. Later the whole of the 2,000 on Lennox Hill also took this line: Evidently now they were retiring, Commandos, baggage, and all, but at the time I sent Faulkner to warn Col. Moller they were going to attack us.

We moved our line up a bit to a better position. I felt we were now in for our first experience of Mauser fire.

Passing down our line, I cautioned each man not to waste a single round and keep his magazine for an emergency.

Someone called to me 'They are firing on our left, Sir' and looking towards Lennox Hill, I could see the whole of that lot heading towards us.

The Dublins opened fire but they seemed to be still out of range, however, it was a big target, so we fired a few volleys, before they were lost sight of in the donga.

But the advance party of Boers were much nearer now. Bullets began to whistle and the men were taking every advantage of cover. 'Shoot whenever you can see anything to shoot at,' I yelled, 'No Hythe words of command now.'

Baptism of Fire.

The Maxim was blazing away, and the Dublins were having a great fusilade and Boer bullets grew more plentiful, but I could see nothing to fire at, and even popping up quickly, I could only occasionally catch sight for a second of some Boer creeping towards an ant-heap. A good many horses were galloping about loose. Our men were cool and steady.

The fire was getting very warm, very straight.

I was not the least afraid of those in front, but they were bound to work round us in time, and our horses in rear were quite exposed enough already. I found one man lying behind his ant-heap, more bent in cover than shooting. I took his rifle and fired a shot or two and told him he must keep up the fire.

I knew that the Boer liked bullets no more than we did, and would hesitate to come nearer so long as we kept up the fire, but was anxious all the time about my right.

The Dublins and Maxim on our left retired.

We hung on a bit. 'Keep up the fire' – then, after a space, 'Now,' I shouted, 'one volley along the ground. *Volleys*! *Fire*! *Retire*!'

There was a lull in the Boer's fire, and then a perfect hail of bullets as we ran back and mounted our horses.

Wonderful, no one seems to get hit, I thought, when Greenfield's horse carried him past me, hit in the back and done for. Here two other riflemen were also hit.

The Dublins and Maxims were well away so, telling my men to follow them, I made for the Colonel to ask for orders.

He pointed out Shultz's Farm, and said, 'Go and hold that ridge and cover my retirement.' The Cavalry had been doing nothing all this time – 'Good God,' I thought, and almost said – 'Cover your retirement! Why don't you charge all those Boers and their transport in the open,' I may have been wrong, but, however that may be, what Moller did do was utterly wrong.

It was soon after this that Cape was cut off with his Hussars and Maxim gun in a spruit. They put up a great stand. Four were killed, the rest all wounded.

When I left Col. Moller, passing Lonsdale on the way, I shouted my orders to him. I took for granted our object must be to get back to the ridge and strong position we had held early that morning, and should never have left so prematurely. I felt that once there we could hold any number of Boers, whereas, if they got there first, we were quite cut off.

When we got to the ridge as ordered, we dismounted and held it, but not for long, a strong party of Boers was heading us off, and we were under fire from other directions.

But Col. Moller now led the retirement, bearing more and more in the wrong direction, making towards Impate to our right.

The retirement had a bad effect. It was all Majendie and I could do to keep our men steady and together.

They began to think they were being chased, whereas the Boers, having now got us clear of their line of retreat, were noticably getting fewer and fewer. There was every minute less object in retiring.

Covering Moller's Retreat.

After galloping a mile or so, we halted behind a ridge, one mile from Jordan's Farm. We dismounted and faced about, and advanced in extended order, the 'Dubs' on our right, while Moller headed away north. I suppose there were some 30 Boers firing at us now, but Boers are so clever that there might have been only two or three.

There was nothing now to stop us from returning to camp the way we had come.

It was here that I took my knock. I took two men on our left, and with them, crept round the flank of the only two Boers I could see. We got well round them. I took a rifle from one of my men, and crawling up, took a good aim at a Boer not 50 yards away, when from another ant-heap another man fired and got me plump in the right shoulder.

The rifle dropped with a thud. 'Take the bally gun and shoot' I said to my companion. I got back to Faulkner who had my pony in rear. As I went the pain was great. It was a curious feeling. I thought my arm had been shot clean off, and was only hanging by a few khaki threads. I seemed to be carrying in my left arm an enormous heavy bolster. The fingers were twitching and dancing and seemed far away. I caught at them and said good-bye to them affectionately, and I realised that in the first steeplechase of war, I had come down at the first fence.

I am sorry to own, for the time, I thought more of myself and my arm than I did of my men – but they got on all right. (No

Boers ever came any further) and when I next met the man I deprived of his gun he forgave me all right. Of this I am sure, had I *not* been hit, they would have shared no further in Moller's disgraceful retreat.*

The good Faulkner soon got his field-dressing and tied up my shoulder as tight as he could pull. I was feeling giddy and sick.

The doctor was soon on the scene, a real good doctor was Hardy. He got me under an ant-heap, and, disregarding cover himself, cut off my jacket and shirt and dressed the wound. The rest retired leaving me with Hardy and his orderly (José, 18th Hussars).

When Hardy had patched me up he went off elsewhere helping British and Boer alike, while José got me somehow to Jordan's Farm.

Here we found a most unsympathetic Dutchman. At first he seemed to have no intention of taking me in, but as I had neither the ability to go a yard further, nor any intention of doing so, and as José ordered him to get some rugs, I was soon lying on his kitchen floor.

Soon a trooper of the 18th Hussars was brought in. He, too, had a broken arm, also some internal wound. He seemed very bad. Under José's instructions he was put on the floor next to me, and so close that a touch gave great pain.

There were besides Jordaan, Madam Jordaan, a grown-up Miss Jordaan, and two small children. None of them could talk English.

The family did nothing but stare at us, but the little chap, called Hans, about six years old, was very good in fetching water for us, and we spent our time in drinking water and vomiting most of the afternoon.

My arm began to bleed again; there was no one to stop it for me. I began to feel very week.

It was dark and raining when Hardy turned up. He had commandeered a 'Spider' and six mules and a Boer driver. He had with him Ernest Reade and C/Sergeant Davies and some riflemen. The first question I asked was how the day had gone, and it was a great joy to hear we had turned them out of that hill, and that the

*Major Knox and two squadrons of 18th had already left him.

38

Boers had retired across the Buffalo. But what losses! So many good friends.

Rescued by Hardy and Reade.

There was so much to hear – how the General had assaulted and carried the hill with over 20 killed and wounded; how our guns, after smothering the Boers with shrapnel, had later shelled our own foremost troops by mistake, and then been forbidden to fire on masses of Boers, guns, and wagons retiring in great confusion, in the open and well within range, while the Cavalry were heading the wrong way.

Trooper Masters and I were got into the cart somehow. It was raining hard and very cold and a five-mile drive to the Boer Hospital on Talana Hill. The driver walked himself and drove his mules at a walk. He drove well and did all he could to save us, but the road was bad, and we both felt it a lot, groaning and vomiting at every bump.

Crossing the spruit, where we saw the bodies of the Maxim gunners, the cart nearly upset and we were cannoned into each other.

Hardy rode just in front, picking out the best road. It must have been 10 p.m. when we got in and a place was found for us both on an out-house floor.

The Boer Hospital.

There were three other men sleeping here. Irishmen of a low type, with Red Cross bandages on their arms.

The doctor told them to look after us. My feet were very cold; one man took off my boots and rubbed my feet for which I was most grateful.

The only other attendance we got was brandy and water, of which I was very glad too. There seemed a liberal supply of brandy, and the 'hospital assistants' did themselves well. The night dragged on, it seemed to have no end. The Irish assistants turned in and had a snoring match. Poor Masters seemed to be dying and kept calling for water, but I couldn't help him.

At last day came, they said the ambulance and carts would soon come for us, but no carts came.

The place was full of men with red crosses, loafers who knew no ambulance work and were only there for their own safety. They ate all the food intended for the wounded. There were about 60 wounded Boers and a few British, Cape and one or two other Hussars. Many wounded Boers came and looked at us. They shook their heads gravely as if it was all up with us. Some came and talked to me; all were kind and sympathetic. Our shrapnel, they said, had done terrible work and we all agreed that modern war was not 'ghoot.'

The Boers kept leaving in large numbers, with rifles, ponies, and wagons. All seemed agreed that they did not want to fight any more.

They had come from Vreiheid, Utrecht, and Krugersdorp, under Lucas Meyer, 'the Lion of Vreiheid,' about 4,500 of them.

They had crossed the Buffalo mostly by Jaeger's Drift and occupied Talana after a long quick night march.

At the farm still the time dragged on, and we seemed to have been forgotten. The arm, and the thought of being deserted, made me feverish. About noon some Dundee Town Guard turned up, surprised to find us. One of them rode back for an ambulance. By this time the Boers had all cleared out except a few badly wounded.

About 1 p.m. the ambulance turned up and at last we got away. Dr. Hardy, who had turned up again, put Cape and me into the same wagon. The jolting was bad and I don't know how I should have stood it but for Cape holding my shoulder for me.

We got back to our old camp about 2 p.m. We shared a hospital bell-tent, no beds or mattresses, so many had been wounded.

General Symonds was in the next tent, hit in the stomach.

The ground was wet and muddy. Someone, however, got my valise and a rug. The troops were away somewhere, we could hear firing.

In the Camp Hospital.

About 3 p.m. we had got more settled, when, from the Impate ridge, about 4,000 yards away, there came a bang and then the now familiar sound of a Long Tom shell whizzing over in our direction. It exploded some 200 yards away. Another and another. They were shelling our camp. One shell sent mud splashing all round our tent, an unpleasant experience. About 20 shells and it ceased. It left an uneasy feeling – Why did our guns make no reply?

Next day came rumours of Elandslaagte Victory. Sir George White was coming to shift old Joubert and his Long Toms from Impate. But soon the truth leaked out. General Yule was retiring from Dundee.

I lay in that camp for forty-eight hours. The Army Doctors were busy; they never dressed my wound or looked at it. The attendance was very bad and we called for hours before we got any attention.

The Swedish Mission.

Under these circumstances I was glad when at 2 p.m. on October 22nd I was transferred in a dhoolie to the Swedish Mission in the town.

Now it seemed that the Boers had a special down on me, for only one shell was fired from Impate that day and this landed quite close to my dhoolie. I was being carried by four Indian bearers. They pulled up short. I thought they would drop me and run. I caught hold of the pole above me, with my left hand ready to break the fall. I shouted 'Chelo!' (go on) 'Hospital log (people) will be safe,' and I cheered them on with 'Shabash!' (well done!).

No more shells were fired. We arrived safe, if not sound, at the Swedish Mission of the good Pastor Noranius.

This Hospital, organised by Dr. Galbraith, the local doctor, and highly qualified at Edinburgh and Dublin Universities, was originally meant for the Dundee Town Guard wounded. After the battle, however, it was filled with our wounded and wounded Boers, and was put under Colonel Daly, R.A.M.C.

What a difference it made on arrival, to be lifted by experts with science and skill and placed so gently into a wonderful bed! For a month I had not been under a roof. With the kind attention of Mrs. Galbraith and others, at once I felt ever-so-much better.

Boers Enter the Town.

After a good look at my arm Dr. Galbraith cheered me still more by saying he hoped to save my arm.

Soon after this, when we had all been seen to, and had got settled down, I heard yells and shouting and a loud clatter of horses coming down the street towards our hospital. I heard the Italian lady, as she rushed to the door, exclaim in French – 'Ce sont les Hollanders!' I could not move to look, but I knew she was right. The Boers had arrived in the town.

'Well,' I thought, 'these are the chaps who have been threatening to shoot the first "roineck" they see. These are the people who shell our hospital. How will these ignorant Boers deal with us?' I had visions of Boers coming in at the door and pointing their rifles at us. Elated by success, no doubt, jumpy, and under the impression that there were still British troops in Dundee, some 200 Boers rode up with rifles cocked and ready to shoot the first 'Roibatche' they met. It was at some risk Mrs. Galbraith went out to meet them. She told them the British had left, that this was a hospital. The wounded, both British and Boers, were on no account to be disturbed.

It was not till later, when the Boers used to come and sit on my bed and fill my pipe for me, and show me other attentions, that I came to know more of the Boers and see their side of the quarrel.

A Relapse.

For the first three weeks I felt comparatively well, and was able to talk to the others before they were moved down to Ladysmith. I was also able, by holding my wrist with my left hand, to scrawl my story up-to-date, while fresh in my mind; but on November 13th my temperature went up to 105 deg. and remained there, or thereabouts, till November 20th. During this time erysipelas added to my troubles, so that I could neither sleep nor breathe freely, and was mostly unconscious. All through this crisis Dr. and Mrs. Galbraith fought hard for my life and won through.

On St. Andrew's Day, November 30th, some bits of bone came out of the wound. That was a turning point. I felt better at once.

Then as time went on I began to sit up and take note of things I had seen as a far-off dream. How did I come to be there? What did it all mean? That bullet did more than stop a young Officer dashing about the veldt – it halted him to look a lot wider on life. Why were we fighting these decent fellows at all? How did it come that in the compound outside that Dutch Viercolor flew flaunting over my head? Had we let down the British Union Jack?

42

I can hardly call it a prayer, and yet my thoughts were focused on one central wish to get well, and so, as a soldier, play my part in upholding the Union Jack.

Here was something to live for. It had not yet dawned there are more ways than one of saluting the flag, and upholding its honour mast high.

2. PRISONERS OF WAR.

I remember some years ago, after the Boer War, a friend at the War Office showed me the new 'Field Service Regulations.' It was just out. I asked him – 'What about Surrenders?' We turned up the index in vain. In my earlier training the very thought of 'Surrender' had never even been mentioned, and yet, later on, I felt that some guidance was needed.

Surrenders.

While shut up in Pretoria, wondering how so many good men came to be there, I collected personal accounts, and now, some 50 years later, on re-reading these, I see inexperience, mistakes, and misfortune, but never lack of courage. This one perhaps should have left that wounded man and got on with his job; another, maybe, should have been more ruthless about that white flag, but nine times out of ten, he was merely carrying out his orders. Someone above him may have blundered. Often the victim deserved the V.C. and no blame.

It was a new kind of war. The invisible, galloping, crack-shot Boer, with the modern quick-firing long-range rifle, was thoroughly at home, and bravely defending his own home-land, with all its rocky Kopjes and Krantzes, its tricky spruits and dongas; while we, to make up for our slowness of movement, often had to make long and exhausting night marches over difficult ground.

These new conditions were not yet fully understood.

Thus it was that when in June, 1900, 150 officers and 3,000 men were released at Pretoria, there were those both at the front and at home who openly said – 'We must put a stop to all this surrendering. It is a disgrace.'

Court of Enquiry.

When it came to my turn at the Court of Enquiry in Pretoria, I stated my case. The President then asked me – 'Why didn't you resist?'

'Because I was wounded, unconscious and under the Red Cross flag,' I answered – but these three good reasons seemed to carry no weight with the President. So also in other cases explanations did not seem to matter. Two weeks later we heard that this same Colonel had himself surrendered with all his men, only a few miles out from Pretoria. He got no sympathy from us.

It must be owned that we officers did not look our best in all sorts of odd clothes, and as for the men who had not fared so well, it was touching to see the poor fellows, mostly in rags and few with boots, some so pale and starved-looking – a ragged, untidy mob, carrying bundles and coloured Kaffir blankets, a good side-show for a war-correspondent to describe; and yet, so pleased to see their officers again and keen to get on with another chance. It took one who knew them to know their true worth. In this connection an incident comes to mind. Our men were refitting and drawing equipment. The officer-in-charge had his own rather complicated system of distribution. The men were to wind their way in and out through a maze of piles of socks, shirts, boots and what not. While this was going on I heard the officer in charge shout at one man – 'No wonder you were taken prisoner!' he said. This was too much for me; I went up to him, saluted, and said – 'This man, Sir, was taken because he was wounded, and for no other reason.' The officer apologised handsomely.

'No Surrender Bullock' at Colenso.

From the many accounts of captures I will only take one as a sample and give only the gist of a long report which shows how such things may happen to the best of us.

It is the story of Colonel Bullock, commanding the Devons. He was one of the large force under Sir Redvers Buller, which met with a big reverse in attempting to cross the Tugela at Colenso, December 15th, 1899.

At the time the Colonel became well known as 'No Surrender

Bullock.' On his capture some of the Boers, mistaking the names, thought they had captured Sir Redvers himself and that the war was as good as won.

In the wide battlefield of Colenso, the point at which this incident took place was near the scene of the loss of our guns. The story of the V.C.'s won that day, in gallant attempts to recover the guns, is an epic outside my province. I will only say that Col. Bullock, with his Devons, had already been launched as reserve of an attack in a different part of the field, when he was diverted towards the scene of the loss of the guns. This loss took place about 8.30 a.m., the guns were exposed and disabled and completely commanded from the Boer position.

It was 10 a.m. when the Colonel was ordered in that direction. He was given discretion to do what he could in the confused situation.

At 10.30 a.m., hearing heavy and increasing fire, he moved part of his force in that direction. As it turned out this firing was the covering fire in a general retirement ordered by H.Q. No word of this had reached him.

From this point I give his own story. We find him in a donga near the captured guns–

'We were now isolated. About 3 p.m., the Boers creeping up the dead ground to our right, captured the gunners in a detached donga to our right. This was unknown to us. About this time the British Ambulance came along the railway line and a Stretcher-Coy. came up to our donga. About 3.30 p.m. we lined the edge of our donga and opened fire on the Boers approaching our right. Heavy fire was coming from our front and left. Then a Boer in front shouted something about the wounded, and, as at the same time, some Boers were removing their wounded and also attending some of ours, I stopped the firing and went forward.

A Difficult Position.

'They shouted to me to surrender and I shouted back that we would not surrender and would fire if they did not clear out.

'The Boers said they would shoot all the wounded if we did not surrender. The Doctor went out to explain, but while this went on the Boers kept creeping on. Just then a Boer came up on my left

46

with a flag of truce and I interviewed him and pointed out how they were advancing. The Boers had now actually reached our trench. I went to the leader and told him to clear out. While I was speaking a young Boer knocked me down. Even then the donga might have been cleared, but only for a short space. The position was untenable.'

The Officers' Zoo.

I do not propose to go into detail of the days we spent as prisoners of war in Pretoria. To have been a prisoner of war was then a novelty. To-day it is not so, but I think some account of our final release may be worth recording.

We were housed, 150 of us, crowded in a long low barn of corrugated iron which had been built to receive the Ladysmith garrison! It was dark and draughty with a mud floor.

There were four rows of beds not one yard apart. There was no privacy. Washing and lavatory accommodation were bad. The nights were cold and a chorus of coughing went on day and night. We were young and we stuck it somehow.

One advantage was our position, high up overlooking the town, with a fine view of the surrounding hills and forts.

A Change of Guard.

About March the Zarp Police Guard was sent to the front and a kind of Home Guard took their place. They had far more men but efficiency was lacking. One only of the 200 men showed sign of martial bearing – an ex-Prussian Guardsman, who entertained us by clicking his heels with short spells of goose-step.

The others amused us, too, when they started drills in full view and followed it up with somewhat erratic musketry practice. But in the end they answered their purpose and foiled more than one desperate venture.

The German Guardsman later proved himself an efficient and friendly waiter after Lord Roberts' arrival.

Towards the end of May, the ups and downs of rumours good and bad, were trying. Depressing delays, and hopes deferred, made time seem long.

47

Panic in Pretoria.

Then one day, with the wind to the South, a heavy bombardment seemed just over the hills four miles away.

The U.S. Consul came that night and told of panic in the Town. Kruger had left and the Foreign Legion were drunk and looting the Town. The British might come any time now.

The grocer Commandant appealed to us all to be good boys and promised that when the time came he and his army would change places with us. That night we sang 'God Save the Queen' as never before.

Then came a hitch. Botha had stayed the stampede. Fifteen thousand Boers were said to have sworn to hold the heights and win or die, and we were to be moved to the East.

On the 4th of June, from 9 a.m. on, we had a front seat view of shell after shell bursting along the high ground to the South. At 3 p.m. we saw a British balloon about 15 miles away. We gave it a cheer. Then great lyddite shells burst on the forts. Then came clouds of dust, Commandos and waggons retiring. We turned in that night in good cheer.

A Disturbed Night.

About 1 a.m. I woke up. The Commandant had switched on the lights. As he walked down the rows of beds he was shouting – 'Pack up, gentlemen! Pack up! We start at 3 a.m. and march six miles.' 'Why?' 'I do not know,' was the answer, 'but those are my orders.' 'Where to?' we asked. 'To the East and then by rail,' was the reply.

It was evident, something had to be done. The Commandant was disarmed and told to sit down. He was told that not one of us would move. Presently his assistant arrived to learn the cause of delay. He, too, was disarmed. We now had two hostages – with two of our biggest men on guard, each armed with a revolver.

Outside was a mounted force which had come to escort us away.

We Refuse to Move.

After some delay the Hollander Commandant offered to go and see the Boer commander and explain and try to persuade him not to move us. Our Dutch-speaking Officer from Natal went with him. I followed to listen.

An excited and exciting scene followed. I did not like the look of that crowd, all shouting and angry. In the end they galloped away, their leader cursing the – Hollander, and shouting that he would soon be back with more Boers and a Maxim gun.

Then followed an anxious time for us. It was frightfully cold. Some more serene went back to their beds and kept warm. Some hid in the roof and in other impossible places. Some started digging for cover. Personally I went with a friend and tried to square a likely looking sentry – we asked him to look the other way when the time came. We would put in a good word for him when Lord Roberts arrived.

From that time on we strained our ears to hear and our eyes to see with the coming of dawn.

Would it be 'Bobs' or the Boers?

As daylight came the sky-line seemed quite clear of movement. We waited and watched in suspense.

By 8 a.m. we could see far away, large bodies moving East. Was it a Boer retreat or General French on the move to cut off retreat? Briton or Boer? We could not tell.

Then at 9 a.m., up galloped two men in felt hats and khaki, and still, even up to 100 yards we were doubtful. Then the leader took off his hat and waved. A yell, and as one man, we rushed to the gate.

Who was this young man? I will leave you to guess. But here is a clue – Forty years later, by both Briton and Boer, he was hailed as the hero of 'Britain's Finest Hour.'

3. FREE AGAIN!

Vredefort Road in the Free State.

When in June, 1900, Lord Roberts had hoisted the Union Jack in Pretoria, people at home began too soon to say the war was over. Very soon our long line of communications was in trouble. Constant raids on the railway line became the order of the day, and the end was indeed a long way off. Personally, having spent long months in hospital and as a prisoner of war, I must confess that with recovered health and freedom, I was far from being war-weary.

In the general scramble for clothing, arms and equipment we got off with a good start. My ambition was to join the Mounted Infantry under General Hutton in the big coming advance, but the result of our energy and keenness was that we Riflemen found ourselves sent post-haste to Vredefort Road, a harassed point in the Free State, about 100 miles South of Pretoria.

But for us the great thing was that at last we had got a job – 50 good men, well-mounted and keen – What a grand thing it was that first ride, cantering off in the keen morning air of the open veld, taking in health and spirits at every breath. What a glorious feeling of freedom!

And with returning health a great keenness seized me. Every morning, long before dawn, we used to ride out some 5 to 10 miles, and arriving at some vantage point we waited and watched for Boers with varying success. Very soon, with captured ponies and Cape-carts, we had a very mobile miniature column.

Here is the story of one incident, with a sketch, as reported at the time:–

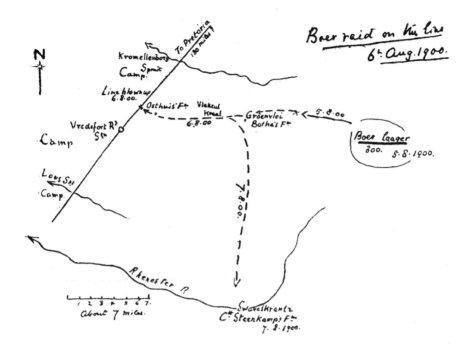

N

Boer raid on the line
6th Aug. 1900.

Kromellenborg
Camp.
Spruit
Line blown up
6.8.00
Osthuis' Fm
Vlakeul
Kraal
6.8.00
Groenvlei
5.8.00
Botha's Fm
Vredefort R?
Sta
Camp
Boer laager
300. 5.8.1900.

Lous Sta
Camp

30 m to Pretoria

Rhenoster R?

1 2 3 4 5 6 7.
About 7 miles.

Swavelkrantz
Cd Steenkamp's Fm
7.8.1900.

Sunday, August 5th, 1900.

Hearing that a Commando of 300 Boers had just left Botha's
Farm at Groenvlei, 12 miles away, I went out with 15 men to bring
in Botha, the farmer. I cautioned my men before starting that
though the Boers were said to have gone, they were to behave as if
the Commando was still there; so we went out cautiously, arriving
about 9 a.m. We put men well out, to watch all round the farm. As
I rode up, two men came out, old Botha himself, and his son, a
fine-looking chap of about 30, with his Sunday-best on.

I rode straight past them round the farm, looking in at the
windows and doors, and then came back to see Botha.

Caution Needed.

The women, about six of them, were standing together at the
door and all looked very anxious at our visit. Though I noticed
this, it did not arouse my suspicions at the time. I told old Botha
(a great big man with a shifty look) through my Kaffir guide,
'Klass,' that he was to inspan at once and come to Vredefort to

see the Intelligence Officer. I said I wanted two horses at once. There was no protest which struck me as unusual. The old man got into his Cape-cart and his wife with him, and his son willingly pointed out two good grey ponies which he said were riding horses. Eight others were hobbled and grazing near the farm. We left about 9.45 a.m. and I sent Klass to a Kaffir kraal to ask for news of the Boers. I sent old Botha back on his own. From Groenvlei we rode to Vlackeul, and Klass came galloping up to say that 200 Boers had just had breakfast at Botha's farm and had only just left when they saw us coming. He said that old Botha had only two horses, the rest belonged to Boers who must have been in the farm while we were there. I did not go back to search the farm as I thought the 200 might be watching us and we might get into difficulties.

I went to Vlackeul where the Kaffirs confirmed the report. They also said that the Commando had crossed the line near Osthuis' Farm, having failed to join De Wet, and that Osthuis had been heard to boast that a road was always open at this point. He also said that the Commando intended to come back that night.

I went to Osthuis' Farm, which had a large white flag over it, and there I found a couple of long-legged Boers and a large family having dinner. I told the whole family to hurry up and finish their dinner and come in to Vredefort. My idea was to remove the whole lot and come back and entrench and loop-hole the farm and await the Commando that night with 50 men.

Plans for an Ambush.

The family Osthuis gave a lot of trouble, the two men were very cheeky. We inspanned the only two horses, one had never been driven before but we managed. Men were left to watch the farm and we brought the family Osthuis in to the Intelligence Officer who detained them for the night. He thought well of my plan.

But, alas, to my utter disgust, I found an order awaiting me – to go to Rhenoster with 30 men and stay there that night.

It seemed there was no way out of it, so off we went at 4.30 p.m., in marching order, a well equipped party. There was a good moon and we arrived at Rhenoster (12 miles) by 7.30 p.m. There we bivouacked. I was not best pleased to find our mission was only to burn two farms and that these were nearer our camp than Rhenoster.

On Monday, 6th August, we went with Intelligence Officer Liebman (a fat German covered with medals) to burn the farms where the Boers had, in spite of their oath, taken up arms again.

Burning Farms.

After a very painful removal of the families and their household goods, we set fire to what was left and returned to Rhenoster with two men as prisoners of war. I disliked this job very much and was glad to see my men did too. Eventually we got back to Vredefort earlier than expected, but too late, for our ambush plans had been cancelled.

At 3 a.m. I was woken by the line orderly who reported four explosions in the direction of Kromellenborg Spruit. I quite expected trouble in that direction, but as the infantry picket was nearer the scene than we were, I thought they would be sure to report. I decided to save our horses and men meanwhile, but to go out half-an-hour earlier before dawn. Trains did not run at night. Taking two men, at 5.30 a.m., I came on the scene of the four explosions, 2½ miles up the line. This was just as expected, at the nearest point to Osthuis' Farm. Eight rails had been damaged. I sent off a man at a gallop to report and stop any trains. We waited and watched a party of Boers hanging about with evil intent.

Line Blown Up.

Eventually we got back to camp. The infantry picket had reported nothing. Later information came that 200 Boers, under Steenekamp, had come from Botha's Farm in the night, and passing Osthuis' Farm, had blown up the line, returning back to Steenekamp's Farm. It was a great disappointment. We had missed a great chance.

It was not long before the G.O.C. was on the spot in his armoured train and gave orders for the burning of Osthuis' Farm, which dirty duty fell to us soon after.

With as much consideration for the wretched women and children as possible, we carried on, leaving them their waggon and tarpaulin and pots and pans, but we left them a sad broken-up home. The old Dutch vrou, with her head buried in her lap and an innocent little girl of three or four, smiling at the effects of the bonfire. A little chap of 12 was manfully doing his best to arrange what was left, as we escorted Old Osthuis back to the line. Such is war and it is a very sad side of it.

Old Osthuis does not want to fight. His lanky, slim-looking, eldest son does not want to fight. But De Wet comes, along with rifle and threats. The Osthuises break their oaths and give information to their brother-burghers. The line is blown up a mile from their house, yards of fuse are found in the farm. The farm is burned and the family ruined.

It would take a better man to say what should be done.

The old Colonial says – 'Destroy them like rats.' The Britisher just out from home says – 'Give the poor devils a chance.'

Both are wrong. Perhaps some day Education will help to put things right, but I fear it must take a long time before Briton and Boer pull together, though I do feel some day the time will come.

4. ATTACK ON LORD KITCHENER'S TRAIN.

A Restless Mood.

I see from my notes that after some time at Vredefort Road I began to get restless. Certainly time did not drag. In August on one occasion the line was blown up on three nights in succession. This brought both the G.O.C. Lines of Communication and the Commander-in-Chief to the scene. When General Chermside came he congratulated us on good work done. I pointed out the disadvantages mounted men had in patrolling the line in the dark and suggested bicycles, but when he informed me that these 'did not grow on mulberry trees,' I did not press the point.

Then just as the great K. of K. arrived in his special train, the line was blown up for the third time. One of my men came galloping in at midnight. To save time, I sent him at once to report to Kitchener's Staff direct. I remember calling him back and cautioning him to practise Baden-Powell's advice and keep calm by whistling some favourite tune, suggesting that 'In the Midnight Train' would be a suitable air.

At this time I began to feel that there was a local lack of enterprise. A column with guns and infantry would go out a few miles in slow time, in broad daylight, and accomplish no more than we could do with a few mounted men by sudden raids in the dark. Was I discontented or homesick? Of course I was longing for home but I think it was chiefly nostalgia due to a longing to see black buttons again! We never seemed to see a Rifleman among all the troops passing through. What a poor kind of Army it would be without the Rifleman!

In the end I got my way but it meant much importunity. It took me two months hard-going to get back to my Battalion in Lydenburg, and it was not till November that we got our Vredefort

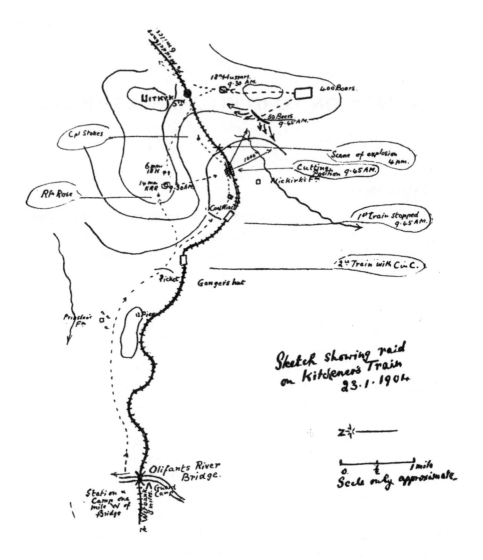

Sketch showing raid on Kitchener's Train 23.1.1901.

Scale only approximate.

Riflemen back. I now found myself in command of our reunited veteran company, guarding the line in the Transvaal at Olifant's River. It was here that on January 23rd, 1901, a determined attack was made on Kitchener's train.

The Story of K. of K.'s Train.

In the small hours of January 23rd, 1901, a cypher message arrived to say that the C.-in-C. at Pretoria would visit General Lyttleton at Middelburg that day, and extra precautions were to be taken.

Accordingly, I sent out a sergeant and eight extra men to the West which was less exposed, and started myself at daybreak with all available men to the East towards Uitkyk where the ground was more tricky.

At Uitkyk, some six miles from Middelburg, the 18th Hussars had 50 men. Expecting long delays and a quiet day, I took my little collector's gun and bird-skinning set in hopes of securing a sugar-bird I wanted. I had also my Mauser pistol in case of bigger game and took every precaution.

Leaving pickets at important points, we got in touch with the Hussars at a point some seven miles from our camp and eight from Middlelburg. At 9.30 a.m. I was talking to a Hussar sergeant. We saw the trains reach Olifant's River. Then, in the other direction, towards Uitkyk, we heard shots. With my glasses I saw some 300 men in close formation galloping hard towards Uitkyk. At over a mile I could not be sure what was up, for I had never before seen Boers manoeuvre like cavalry.

Now Subalterns do not like halting Commanders-in-Chief without good cause, but so far as I knew there were only 50 Hussars. They must be Boers. All the time the two trains were drawing nearer. I had only 14 men with me. The leading escort train was quite close and within range of the Boers. I sent a man galloping back to stop the train, saying I would let them know more as soon as I was certain. I then galloped forward myself with my men to a cutting, a good position between the Boers and the train. Yes, they were Boers all right. When they saw the train stop, 50 or more came galloping straight for the train and for us con-cealed in our kopje.

Leaving Sergeant Ross in charge, with orders to shoot for all they were worth, I galloped my pony, stumbling and shying at rails and sleepers and wires, 600 yards down the line to where the advance train was.

I told the officer in charge that there were fully 300 Boers about and asked him to get both trains back as quickly as possible, saying I would do what I could to keep them off. He seemed sceptical, but I left him to it. I was in a hurry.

Galloping back to my men I was relieved to find that the Boers, not knowing our strength, and having had several saddles emptied, had for a time been held back. We pushed on cautiously trying to see what was doing. Within long range we could see fully 200 Boers at Uitkyk buzzing about like bees disturbed.

Sergeant Ross to the Rescue.

Leaving Corporal Stokes and one man hidden here to observe, with orders to fall back on us if Boers began to get round him, I sent back Rifleman Rose to report that the Boer were now in possession of some two miles of line near Uitkyk, and retired myself to a better position further back. Later, thinking the position seven miles from Olifant's River was too isolated and hearing shots on my left where I had men out owing to the ground, I retired to a strong position 1000 yards back. Before retiring I sent two men to call in Corporal Stokes, but they came back under fire, without having found him. They reported Boers, as usual, creeping, forward round our flanks. I had no option but to retire and trust that Stokes would not be caught napping. We retired none too soon for the Boers sneaking round by a donga would soon have had us in difficulties. We had just reached our new and very good position when three of our men came galloping in under a heavy fire. Sergeant Ross, unknown to me, had gone forward a mile between two fires and brought both back to safety.

Rifleman Rose.

Then came firing from our left (as we faced the Boers). It turned out to be Rifleman Rose who had been sent back to me with an order from 'K. of K.' himself. Trying to find me, he had seen a man in khaki like me, also riding a grey, he had exchanged our private signal, and had only seen his mistake when, within 30 yards, three Boers had fired from the saddle and missed him. Also I had forgotten to give Rifleman Rose Baden-Powell's advice, for when he reached me, he was so full of his own adventures and so out of breath, that it took me some time to find out what the original message had been.

The order was that a column was coming out from Middelburg, that I was to watch the Boers and report when clear.

A Young Hussar.

We took up a position five miles from Olifant's River and felt our way forward occasionally but there were too many Boers for us. About noon we saw a man sneaking forward and thinking him a Boer, gave him a volley: he dropped, apparently dead. About 12.30 we pushed forward again and coming up to where the man fell, we found him lying as low as a young plover, but well and alive. A fledgeling Hussar just out from home, the Boers had found him easy prey and relieved him of his horse and saddle, rifle and bandoliers.

We pushed on and got touch with the 18th Hussars once again and sent men along the line to see if any damage.

About 3 p.m. the Boers seemed to have retired three miles South of the line. We could see them near Triciard's Farm. I sent to report. Then the two trains came on again, the leading escort train had passed us and was puffing noisily up the winding slope, when there was a loud explosion and the train came to a halt. 'That's bad,' I thought to myself, 'after reporting all clear.' However, only an expert could spot a hidden mine and moreover it was beyond our section of the line. I sent back word to the C.-in-C.'s train, but he brought his own train on, right up to the disabled one. After seeing to pickets round the two trains, we went to have a look at the famous chief. I had never seen him at close-quarters before. He got out of his saloon, a tall, fit-looking man, and went straight to inspect the damage. Then, seeming much annoyed at the delay, he gave some order, and went straight back to his carriage. He never seemed to notice us, or even to look in the direction of the Boers, where our old friend Trichard was still in view. He left it to us to see to such details.

While waiting here I met two good Riflemen friends, Congrave and Watson, on Kitchener's Staff. Luckily the explosion had missed the engine and troop trucks, only an empty waggon had had it.

The column came out from Middelburg and drove the Boers away. It was found that repairs would take 24 hours, so the Chief went straight back to Pretoria.

It was not till 1906, in Simla, when my wounded shoulder had again had to be operated on and I was offered a post as his A.D.C., that I came to know more of the great 'K. of K.'

Again, in 1915, I saw more of him as one of 'Kitchener's Army.' A stern-looking man but a great one, admired and respected by his A.D.C.'s. Though I was not one of them, I know that in that inner circle, they had their jokes and fun, and loved him because they knew him well.

5. ERNEST READE.

From among my old papers I would like to rescue some word of Ernest Reade. He was one of those lovable ex-public school boys who seem by their happy natural ways and strong sense of duty, to be cut out from the start for leadership. Full of boyish enthusiasm, he joined us at Dundee on the eve of the Battle of Talana Hill, October 20th, 1899.

His letters give graphic accounts.

'The first thing we knew was that there, up above us, at some 3,000 yards, there were about 3,000 Boers. The next thing was shells landing all over our camp down below.' Young Reade was soon in the thick of the fight. Wading through the spruit, and wet through for a start, they crossed the open space beyond. He was so taken up with steadying his men and keeping direction, that 'the bullets as thick as an ordinary hail-storm' were hardly noticed, but, 'men were falling thick all around . . . the groans of the poor fellows were terrible.'

Then came the wood, then on and up through the wood, to that fateful three-foot wall, the scene of such losses. Here at this wall, for over an hour, our men were delayed, exposed all the time to an accurate cross-fire.

In those days, with their cross-belts and swords, officers were conspicuous targets. Soon Reade sees his own captain fall, then his colonel (Bob Gunning) and Jack Pechell and many others.

He seems himself to have been very active, helping to keep touch, getting and passing orders, trying to find out what was going on and what to do next – the wonder is that he did not get hit.

Then at last came the order to advance. They were itching to get on and tackle the final cliff.

'Up the steep slope our fellows went; when almost at the top, out rushed 20 old Boers, who, standing on the skyline, not ten yards off, shot down our leading men. Every one of these Boers was wiped out by our fire.' (He gives great credit for their courage.)

'This stopped the charge for a time.'

It is probable that this incident, seen from a distance, misled our gunners. All day they had backed up our infantry magnificently. Then came the tragic mistake.

'Then,' he says, 'Our Battery, by a dreadful mistake, showered shrapnel on the brow near the top. . . . Then we charged again.' Very few officers were now left. Three very young officers and 70 men. Reade was one of these.

'Up and up we went, revolvers and swords, with all the morale of a victory charge, passing dead comrades and fully expecting the brow of the hill to be lined with Boers. But when we reached the top, not a Boer at close quarters, and there, retiring below us, at 800 yards, a long black huddled mass of fleeing Boers. Oh, what a glorious feeling of victory! We were just about to fire, when up came a staff officer yelling – 'Stop firing! There is a flag of truce.'

It was only after all this excitement that young Reade, having had no food, realised that he was hungry, wet through and tired. All the more then do I owe him a word of thanks, for it was he who at some risk, with the good Doctor Hardy, Colour Sergeant Davies and two or three riflemen, ploughed their way through the mud with a cart, and brought me and a wounded Hussar, five difficult miles in the dark, back to the Boer Hospital on Talana Hill, where a crowd of Dutchmen lay wounded, groaning and dying, the whole of a very long night.

Then followed anxious days. General Symonds and most of his Staff had been killed. From Impate to the North, Joubert attacked with his long-range guns, and after exhausting marches and counter-marches, the whole Dundee force set out on its desperate forced march back to Ladysmith.

The Retreat to Ladysmith.

Here I will give just a few extracts.

October 22nd.

'Sounds of great cheering when Elandslaagte results became known. This put heart into the men and we set off in the direction of the Boer big guns. The going was very heavy. Impate was shrouded in mist. All at once the fog lifted and then the Boer Long Tom spoke out, sending shells right over our heads into our artillery beyond. We lay down in a hollow and I for one, and many others, went fast asleep, we were so done out. . . . At 7.45p.m. Major Campbell* told us it had been decided to try and reach Ladysmith.

'With wonderful skill (due mainly to him), in pitch darkness, the whole column was got together. . . . It was a wonderful march and completely outdid Joubert. . . We were, of course, dog done. We started at 9 p.m. and halted at 4 a.m.'

October 24th.

'Promised a good rest, but a thunderstorm drenched us all and upset calculations.'

October 26th.

'Last night was, I should think, the worst ever. We started footsore and very much in want of sleep, have had practically none for a week. We had already done twelve miles that day. A terrible thunder-storm. Six inches deep in soft sticky clay – it rained the whole time as we tumbled, and stumbled along. It was so dark that we had to put anything white we could get on the man in front so as not to lose touch. At one time with constant checks, it took us three hours to cover a quarter of a mile.'

But I will not enlarge on this nightmare of a march, nor will I write of the Siege of Ladysmith, I will only say here that Reade came safely through all these experiences and emerged a veteran in experience. He was also mentioned in despatches for good leadership.

* Later Sir Wm. Pitcairn Campbell.

With the Mounted Infantry.

It was not till fourteen months later that I next came in touch with Ernest Reade, when he joined the Mounted Infantry Company from our 1st Battalion, which was then on block-house duty in Cape Colony.

At that time all our ex-prisoners-of-war and our Zululand detachment had both rejoined our Ladysmith men, and it was now my good fortune to command these reunited men, 125 of the best, well-mounted, efficient and keen, with great esprit-de-corps. For the time we were employed in helping to guard the line at Middelburg.

Reade was at Pan with 30 men. Lynes was at Witbank (the place where Winston Churchill lay hidden during his escape) and I with H.Q. was at Olifant's River. At all these points Trichard's Middelburg Commando kept us busy.

It was a time of transition. While the British troops were preparing, the Boers grew bolder. They delivered a series of determined night attacks on our garrisons all along the line. Occasionally they were successful. To meet this new phase each garrison looked to its defences. We built stone sangars and dug where we could and collected every available yard of barbed wire. Sentries were doubled, and though Kaffirs and dogs were added to relieve the strain, it meant long hours. We slept with one ear awake. By January, 1901, our position was strong and we hoped they would come. Meanwhile we were given the hint to save our horses so far as we could. General French would soon be wanting us all for his coming big drive to the Swazi border.

In those days each little garrison with its infantry and guns, its mounted troops and Q.M. stores, was a self-contained unit in which morale would vary according to the imagination of its intelligence officer or the leadership of its commander. At Olifant's River we were lucky. With Major Guthrie Smith of the Artillery in command and with troops who were all old friends and comrades since the early days of the war, our garrison was a happy family, a good efficient team.

At Pan, Reade was less fortunate. I have now torn up the reports I received from him at the time, but even to-day it makes me indignant to see the harm bad leadership can do. Thus when the order came to quit Pan, to rejoin our company and serve once again under Colonel Campbell, it was with great joy that Reade found himself back among us.

In French's big Eastern drive it had been intended that nine columns should join hands and sweep the Boers to the Swazi border. But at the last moment two strong columns were called off to attend to the elusive De Wet.

Thus it was that Colonel Campbell's small column was left to fill the wide gap, and so, for a time, had a stormy passage.

His column, some 1,200 strong, was made up of old Natal comrades. The 18th Hussars (now under Colonel Knox), with our M.I. attached, Corbyn's Battery and Poole with his pom-pom, and the trusty Leicesters, old friends since Cape Town days. The faith of all ranks in their own 'Johnny Campbell' was a factor worth double the numbers.

On February 1st we moved South from Middelburg.

Next day we moved on and soon after starting the 18th Hussars clashed with parties of Boers. By now these Hussars were armed with rifles, not carbines. We used to tell them they skirmished nearly as well as riflemen, and they honoured us by calling us their D Squadron. Covered by Corbyn's guns the Hussars cleared several ridges. My company was 2,000 yards in rear with the pom-pom.

Presently I saw some 18th Hussars come under fire and was told to send a section to reinforce them. As I launched this section, I cantered part of the way with Reade on one side and Sergeant Burton on the other, explaining what was wanted. I then returned to Poole and his pom-pom where a few stray shots were whizzing past.

From this point it was hard to make out what was happening. I saw Reade's party met by an officer and then dismount.

An Ambush.

Then the 18th seemed to advance and soon there was heavy firing. It seems that time was not given for Scouts to get well out; anyway, Reade with his men dismounted, suddenly came under a heavy fire; his horses in rear were well under cover.

Reade shouted 'Advance!' and with 12 men, got down and fought gallantly. All his men were hit. When hit, he called to his men to retire and Sergeant Burton repeated the order. Five of his men fell back fighting, to their horses, which were now also under fire.

The moment we saw that our men were in difficulties, Sergeant Allan galloped his section half-left and dismounting, worked his way round Reade's left, and at 50 yards shot three Boers and drove off the rest who were looting the dead and wounded. Then we got orders to advance.

What a shock it was. Passing two dead Hussars and a rifleman I had known since 1895, I came on another good rifleman, just a boy, in great pain, gave him a drink and a word and passed on. Fifty yards on I came on Reade and Burton and Freeman, all still alive but badly hit. I could not stop, we had to make good the ground beyond.

After posting some men I came back. Reade was hit in both arms and one hand, with the good Dr. Hardy attending him. Sergeant Burton was lying dead with one arm round Reade whom he had been helping when hit. Ten yards to the left was Freeman, our Matabele-Medal man. He had eight wounds and was in great pain. He called for water but died as he spoke. Ten yards more to the left I turned over a body. It was Rifleman Parnham, one of those who had shot a Boer when with me in the Free State.

I went back to Reade with a heavy heart. He was quite conscious and asked if he had done right. He was thirsty. We cheered him up and gave him cold tea. He was wandering and said it was not hot enough. Then he said – 'Well, anyway, this is better than Pan.' The Leicesters now came up. I was terribly cut up, but I had to go on. I was on duty ahead.

After this mishap we pushed right on, covering a wide front, and camped that night at Roodeport Farm where we remained two nights. It was a satisfaction to hear that we had given our troublesome Middelburg neighbours a hard knock.

Next time I saw Reade, Hardy was attending to him. It was strange that we three should be together once more under similar conditions. Reade seemed easier. 'Last time we met,' he said, ' you were hit and Hardy and I were looking after *you*.'

At Roodeport we buried five Hussars, Sergeant Burton and three riflemen. Next day we had to move. The pity was that we had to bring our wounded along in jolting transport. We were isolated and had to get in touch with other columns.

At 5 a.m. we left on a 15 mile march to Bosman's Pan. We expected trouble. Before the start, Colonel Campbell had his leaders up. He explained all about expected trouble and made his intentions clear. He seemed extra cheery. We were ready to take on all comers. As it turned out the march was not so difficult as expected.

By now the Boers had learned respect for our small column, so when we bumped into a new Commando under Chris Botha with his long-range guns and pom-pom, we just went straight ahead, ignoring his guns and sniping. It was here some Canadian Scouts appeared from the blue and said we had the 'Tidiest little outfit' they had seen so far.

That night when I got into camp, sad about our losses, and tired after a long day, I went with Colonel Campbell to see how Reade had stood the journey. Alas, he had died ten minutes before we came. I had got so fond of the boy. The last silent look was one of those moments one does not forget.

The Boers were shelling and pom-pomming the camp. There was sniping all round us. The question was where to bury Ernest Reade. About 400 yards from camp I found a spot above Bosman's Pan Lake. His own men, coming in off picket, rode as escort to the grave. In the dusk the Colonel himself read the service. Little we cared for a few sniping shots – our thoughts were with one of the best.

*NOTE ON COLONEL CAMPBELL.

A good story was told of Colonel Campbell at this time. At the height of our troubles, with waggons stuck and sniping all round us, the Colonel had sent an urgent message to the Q.M.G., Pretoria, for more transport. The answer came back by helio to our isolated and harassed column.

It read:– 'Re your X.Y.Z date, time, place, etc., your indent for bullocks received – stop – See King's Regulations page, para., section, Appendix II., etc., etc.'

To this the Colonel replied: 'Damn your Appendix II. – stop – We want bullocks.'

Armed with this answer the indignant Q.M.G. headed straight for the C.-in-C. On his way he showed it to more than one distinguished General. But each of them laughed so loud and long that the Q.M.G. changed his mind. Anyway, we got our bullocks.

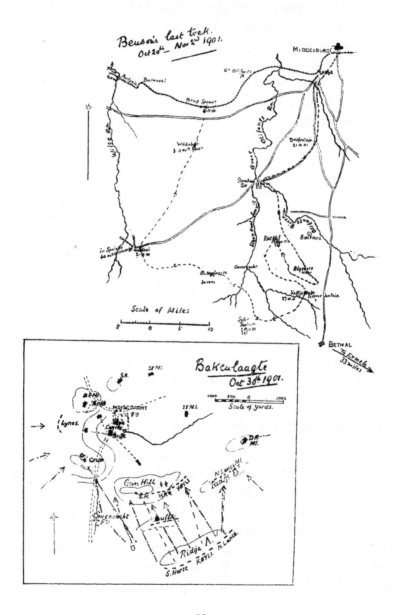

6. BAKENLAAGTE.

Benson's Last Trek.

The engagement at Bakenlaagte, 30th October, 1901, stands out in the story of the Boer War for many reasons:– First, it is a historic example of success in a charge by mounted riflemen. Secondly, it was a clear-cut clean-fought duel between two fine leaders of men. Then again, to a rifleman, it has this special interest, that never before or since have four companies of the 60th Rifles been brought together and formed into one battalion of Mounted Infantry (25th M.I.). Their conduct on this occasion is proudly recorded in the chronicles of that famous regiment. Finally, Bakenlaagte for me is not only a landmark in war, but also stands out a mile-stone in my life.

To make my story clear I will draw on the 'Times History,' then I will give my own story from a log kept at the time.

Events Leading up to Bakenlaagte.

By April, 1901, a new phase of the South African War had begun. The opening battles were over. Lord Roberts and Sir Redvers Buller had gone home and the great 'K. of K.' (Lord Kitchener of Khartoum) was in command of huge guerilla operations, with thousands of men spread over thousands of miles.

At the time we tell of, French had just finished his Eastern Transvaal drive. He had dispersed the Boers right up to the Swazi border and it had been thought that, at least for some time, Botha would keep quiet. But no, not a bit. Very soon after, suddenly Botha threatened Natal with over 2,000 Boers.

Pursued by eight columns he gave them all the slip, and by October was back again in the High Veld country where the elusive Transvaal Government was in hiding.

The conditions of rain and floods and mud had been trying for all concerned (Botha included) and the eight British columns which had been in pursuit were now back on the railway resting and refitting.

Now, while Botha was away in the South threatening Natal, a new war-leader had come on the scene.

The High Veld country was ringing with rumours and news of the exploits of Colonel Benson, 'A born guerilla leader,' who, with Wools Samson as his intelligence officer, by constant bold and long night-marches, was capturing and harassing the Boers in all directions.

Benson Isolated.

On returning from raiding Natal, the High Veld Boers, seeing the panic and havoc wrought in their absence, were full of bitter resentment. Here was their chance. Here was the 'Mad Englishman' at his old game of raiding their homeland – here, while the other columns were resting, Benson was isolated.

Botha, in spite of his recent losses and hardships and narrow escapes, did not take long to strike. Keeping his own movements absolutely secret, while Groebler was harassing Benson's column, Botha suddenly concentrated every man within reach, and covering 70 miles at a stretch, launched his well-aimed well-timed blow at Benson's isolated column.

Let us now turn to Benson. His column consisted of the Scottish Horse, 3rd and 25th M.I., The Buffs (6 Coys.), four guns of 84th R.F.A., and two pompoms. There were 350 vehicles of which 120 were ox-waggons. His system of working was for the mounted troops to make long marches at night followed by raids at dawn, while the infantry and heavy transport acted as a movable supply depot.

On October 20th, 1901 (some 2,000 strong), he left Middelburg to clear the country South of the line. From the start there was stiff opposition, nevertheless, quite unperturbed, Benson went about his business, and after collecting 50 Boer prisoners, he decided to return to the line, 35 miles North.

At 4.30 a.m., October 30th, the long trail of ox-waggons moved off in a mist, followed at 5.30 a.m. by the rest of the column, each

70

with its own safety precautions.

It was a difficult country in which to hold off any attack on a long convoy of waggons. The open veld with its undulations and difficult contours allows of unseen approach and it takes a trained eye to see how to act. In rain and mist the difficulty is doubled. From the first the rear-guard was pressed hard, but the 3rd M.I. were old hands. Anley handled his men with skill and kept determined attacks at a distance.

On both flanks and away in front there was also considerable trouble.

Up till 9 a.m. fair progress was made, then a difficult drift caused a delay of several hours. The ox-convoy, after crossing the drift, was halted some distance on, and the rest closed up, till the two convoys became one.

A Difficult Position.

Up till 1 p.m. all had gone well in spite of mist and rain and Boers. Then two carts got completely bogged and the rearguard was halted again at a point some four miles from the new camp. The transport was then arriving in camp.

It was here, while delayed by these two carts, that Anley first realised clearly that large reinforcements of resolute Boers had now joined in. At 1.15 p.m. he sent an urgent message to Benson, and abandoning the two carts, he retired in good order to a ridge (marked 'A' in the plan) about 1,000 yards further back.

Between this ridge 'A' and the camp, about half way, there was the rising ground later known as 'Gun Hill.'

On hearing from Anley, Benson sent two guns to Gun Hill, with a section of Rifles, M.I. under Ashfield as escort. He also sent one gun to me on supporting high ground some 1,500 yards S.W. of camp. Benson himself with the Scottish Horse joined Anley on Ridge 'A.'

Under ordinary circumstances, with these precautions, all would have been well – but this was no ordinary occasion. Botha had timed his arrival to the minute. With over a thousand more Boers he had covered some 70 miles, and making full use of the ground and the mist, he brought them up hidden and ready to launch at Benson's camp and rear-guard.

Botha's Charge.

When Benson joined Anley on Ridge A, he grasped the position at once. Leaving sections of 3rd M.I. and Scottish Horse to hold Ridge A, he ordered a retirement back to Gun Hill. Suddenly swarms of Boers appeared on the misty skyline. Botha had seen his chance and ordered a charge. Soon the rearmost party was swamped in a gallant defence, and soon it became a race with the rest for Gun Hill.

Here the guns were already unlimbered, with the rifleman escort waiting and ready. Our galloping rearguard dismounted and hurriedly facing the Boers formed an irregular line on each side of escort and guns. As the Boers came on, other Commandos joined in, and soon for a mile and a half there were galloping Boers, shooting, shouting, outflanking as they came.

Reaching a hollow of dead ground, here ponies were left to stand where they were and the Boers stalking and shooting pressed on as only Boers can, right up to within 30 yards of the guns and their gallant defenders.

For a space they were halted, but it could not last long. Here and there, behind his ant heap, some gallant survivor kept up the sniping – fifteen minutes perhaps, then, four or five deep, the whole Boer line rose as one man and poured in their fire on all that still moved on the ridge.

Of Benson, hit three times, yet cool and active to the last, of that great last stand, a grand record is given in the 'Times History' – a wonderful story well told.

Diary of Benson's Last Trek.

And now having given a general outline, here is my personal story:–

October 12th, 1901. – At Leydenburg received urgent orders that the newly-formed 25th M.I. (4 Coys. 60th K.B.R. M.I.) were to concentrate at once at Middelburg and join Colonel Benson's famous column.

This was the best news I could have on my birthday. We were off next day, and doing double marches, reached Machadodorp in three days and Middelburg in three more. 'The weather was glorious and with our companies brought together for the first time, we all enjoyed that march.

Very little time at Middelburg. By October 18th all ready, my company as strong and well turned out as I have seen it in the five years I have known it. We have three officers and 130 men. The Battalion under Eustace, 350 strong. The column about 2,000 strong. Printed 'Standing Orders' in this column and everything much stricter, still, if we know what is wanted, we shall get on all right.

October 20th. – Celebrated Talana Day by starting with Benson's Column. Did 15 miles to Driefontein, S.W. of Middelburg. Dined with Murray (Black Watch) who was at Talana on General Symonds' Staff and is now in command of Scottish Horse.

October 21st. – Driefontein, collecting information – a busy day, found five pickets three miles out and two night posts.

October 22nd. – Colonel Benson went on overnight with 3rd M.I. and Scottish Horse, while we moved seven miles to Steenkool Spruit. Benson returned with 37 Boers, cattle and sheep. His information through Wools Samson splendid and he acts promptly and successfully. The Boers call him 'The Mad Englishman' and say nothing simpler than to dodge other columns, but Benson's Column frightens them, and they won't sleep within 30 miles of it knowingly. Terrible storm about 4 p.m., hail-stones as big as racquet balls, stampeded horses, luckily ours were knee-haltered and grazing near us, so we got them all back. The others lost 100 between them. A wet night, very uncomfortable as most of shelters blown down.

October 23rd. – Went with S.H. collecting horses, some stampeded as far as last camp.

A Typical Raid.

October 24th. – An easy day. At 5 p.m. notice of night march. Baggage and infantry to come on next morning to Rietkuil, 17 miles S.W. Left 6.30 p.m. A clear, moonlight night. The idea – to round up 200 Boers said to be 20 miles off. Rode all night, mostly at a walk, occasionally dismounted to halt or lead. Moved in sections, undulating over the veld and avoiding sky-lines. At 1.30

a.m. we halted and those who were not too cold, slept, while our native Kaffir scouts went on.

About 3 a.m. we pushed on again, and as day dawned, about 4 a.m., we broke into a trot; then forming a long line – one Coy. Rifles, one 3rd M.I., and one Scottish Horse, the remainder of the Corps in support – we galloped about five miles, but the Boers had heard of our coming and cleared.

It was a long gallop after a long march, but our horses kept up well. I did not quite like the risk of letting men get out of hand till I could see what was going on. The 200 Boer were there right enough, but we did not get to close quarters. We had a few casualties including our doctor (Robertson), only just arrived in the country.

The Boers Follow Up.

We halted till about 8 a.m. at Witbank, eight miles from our new camp. We could see the Boers waiting and watching on the high ground. I felt pretty sure they would bother the rearguard, so when we were told off for that duty I knew we were going to be tested in the eyes of our new leader. My company and Lynes' were the two rearmost companies. The moment the guns left, the Boers came on at a gallop. Our men and horses came under fire from the very first. Not to make a long story of it, we kept on holding positions and retiring, while the Boers thrust gallantly, some firing at us, and some always working round.

Our men did splendidly, the chief difficulty being to get them to retire when the right moment came. In these shows it is the getting away that needs attention as much as the lighting. Often one wants to hang on and shoot at Boers coming on in the open. It is then we have the advantage, but always their turn comes, when they have the advantage. We had many exciting retirements but our luck was good. We only lost eight horses and one man hit twice, but not dangerously.

Unfortunately Bircham's Company got into difficulties and Troyte and Crichton were hit. Troyte and three men were left in the hands of the Boers, so we don't know yet if badly wounded.

These Boers were under Groebler and had collected to attack Benson at night, and our scouts had apparently met. Whoever they were, they came on with great boldness and both Benson and Murray agreed they had never seen Boers attack in the open so boldly. We were pleased that they gave our men great praise. Got back to camp 5 p.m., having had nine hours' rearguard fighting over eight miles of country, and that on top of a long night march. Very tired. Slept jolly well.

October 26th. – A welcome day of sunshine and rest. Troyte being well cared for by Boers. Boers tell our doctor, they had bad time of it yesterday.

Rifleman Egan.

October 27th. – An early start. On right flank with half company, Seymour and Watson left flank. Camped Kaffirstadt. On arrival heard Seymour had had nasty time. One of his scouts, Rifleman Egan, saved them from a clever ambush. Egan shot through the stomach and three horses hit. All seem to have done very well, especially Seymour. Corporal Brindly and Egan, who with his horse killed, stuck to his rifle and ran back, in spite of his wound, 100 yards, just in time to give warning. In afternoon farm-clearing, so we had a long day.

Went to see Egan who was very bad but plucky. Told him he had saved his section. He said – 'Someone must stop the bullets, Sir, and I'm glad.' 'Kushi,' I think he said. This was the second time he had been hit. A man you could trust. We are on rearguard and to-morrow and certain to be worried, the Boers seem all round us.

October 28th. – Left Kaffirstadt for Syferfontein relieving outposts at 4.15 a.m. At first it was very difficult to make out what our direction of march was to be. We were spread out over five miles, and I had a lot of hard work getting all the men in right positions and making it clear to each one, when and how to retire, all the more as there was a difficult spruit in our way, and I was not too clear myself where they could cross. Boers visible from all our posts. Luckily they did not press us hard at first. A delay from a wagon breaking down would have been awkward. Three miles on we got stopped, luckily in a fairly good position, as the wagons were sticking at a difficult drift. A lot of Boers, some 200, came on boldly to my right rear. We had to hang on a long time. They got to pretty close quarters. Lucky again, only one horse hit. A few followed right up into camp, the rest went off towards Bethel. The only way to cope with these Boers will be to have a lot of columns under one good man, and work them into a corner of block-houses.

Got into camp 3 p.m., a bit tired. Heard poor Egan was dead. Chose a place for grave and made a sketch to mark the spot. Had to read the Service myself, a new experience for me. Poor Egan, one of the best, you had only to look at him to know it.

October 29th. – Remained Syferfontein. Glad of rest. Some of our horses are done up and all the men have had hard work. At 5.30 a.m. the day-pickets lost 4 men and some 200 Boers had to be driven off. Evidently they had hoped to follow us up again on the move, but we did not oblige and gave them what for.

October 30th. – Ox-convoy under Eustace left 4.30 a.m. with Lynes and Bircham, 3 Coys. Buffs, 2 guns and a pompom as escort.

At 5.30, remainder under Col. Benson, started with: 3rd M.I., 2 guns and a pom-pom as rearguard. The rest with Convoy and on the flanks. Lynes and Crum were between the two convoys available as required. There was mist and rain.

After 2½ miles a bad drift gave trouble.

By 5 a.m. our rearguard had been hotly engaged. We could hear their pompom and musketry fire.

Confusion in the Mist.

At the same time I could see there was something going on about 2 miles away on our right flank. Both the right flank guards were doing a bit of shooting and galloping about. They were on one of those undulating ridges which it is often difficult to know whether to hold or not. In this case it was held, but weakly.

I said to Watson and Rowat, 'Surely those are Boers,' but they did not think so. The mist came and went and it was impossible to be certain. Presently there was a good deal of shooting and some of the leading right flank guard came galloping in. One man, rather excitedly, told me that Bircham was wounded and his section had been driven in. I had no orders from anyone, so I sent Watson with half the Company to report to Eustace, telling him at the same time that I had no orders from Benson to do so. I let Col. Benson know at the same time.

Deceived in the Mist.

About 7 a.m. rain and a very cold wind came on, and a thick mist.
They were shooting on all sides and it was altogether unpleasant. I
went up to Eustace to find out what was going on, and found him as
much in the dark as myself. He asked me to reinforce a height to our
left where there seemed some hesitation. It was an important point
as the convoy was halted below. I was to try and find out what was
happening and let Eustace know. When I got there, dismounting
most of the men to hold the hill, I pushed on with a few Scouts and
found all clear, but beyond, some 150 Boers were moving slowly and
unconcernedly away in two groups about a mile off. This was, as I
found out later, the same party we had seen and discussed earlier on.
They had swooped down in the mist and collared a few of Lynes'
scouts and crossing our front were now on our left. Dressed in our
calvary cloaks and slouch hats, they had got right up, shouting
'Stop!' before the mistake was seen. Eyre had his horse shot and a
narrow escape. Lynes got his men to a farm and gave them a warm
reception. His horse was killed and he himself slightly wounded.

While I was watching the two small groups of Boers moving
away on our left flank, Col. Benson, who seems to have been
everywhere he was needed, came up with a pompom. I told him
what had happened. There was no doubt now that there were a
great many Boers all round us.

The mist grew thicker and the wagons were struggling at the
drift behind us. It was a difficult position, but it did not seem to
worry Benson the least. I admired that man. He halted and got his
wagons together on the high ground, while we all waited and got
very cold and wet.

When we did advance, it was the Infantry he sent out in the mist
to the front, while the mounted troops were drawn in.

Anley Hard Pressed.

Meanwhile Anley's rearguard, having to wait for two bogged
waggons, was having a difficult time.

By 11 a.m. it began to clear. By then we had covered about six
miles of our journey.

At this time the Scottish Horse were sent to help the rearguard and our No. 1 Section under Sergt. Ashfield was sent as escort to the guns, while I with the rest of the Company was sent to support the Advance guard.

We had advanced about a mile, when I saw some of Lynes' men in front of me, dismount and shoot from a ridge, so I galloped up at once with a section and coming up on their right, we were in time to receive and give back a few long-range shots at some 60 Boers who retired in the open.

We were now on a hill which was destined to become a very warm spot, and the scene of hard fighting.

At the time of our arrival, about noon, we were on the left of the advance guard. Eventually, at sunset, which found us still there, our position had become the right rear of the column at a distance of 3000 yards.

Eustace came up soon after I had got there and said, 'We are going to camp near here. You are to hold this hill, while I take Lynes to that hill further on.' He left one gun with me. I was to keep it there till the other two guns in rear took its place. Luckily this gun got away.

The Cockpit.

There was on the top of our hill a cup-shaped hollow with a commanding view, an ideal position for one of the pickets round the camp, which we should, in the ordinary course of events, have had to find. We made a note of this at the time.

As I searched the ground round this post, the Boers I had seen before seemed to be clearing off.

Then, a bit later, looking towards our rearguard, I saw there was something important going on, what it was I could not make out.

About 1½ miles half-right as I faced the rearguard, there were over 300 mounted men making slowly towards Onvervacht Farm. I rushed to the gun and told the Sergeant to shoot, which he did, the shell falling just behind them. Then I saw what were certainly our men, further away than those we had fired at, so, thinking I had made a mistake, I told the Sergeant to stop. There was the greatest difficulty throughout the day in distinguishing our men from Boers, and this difficulty was greatly increased by the use of these beastly slouch hats and cavalry cloaks.

Suddenly there was heavy firing in rear. The 300 men at the farm shot out and extended at a very fast gallop, joining hands with at least 700 mounted men to the rear, all shouting and shooting and thrusting.

The Charge.

There must have been 1,000 of the finest Boers in the country charging our rearguard. Soon I saw this flood mix with our dismounted men and come right on and on up to the guns a mile in rear and below me. My gun kept firing away, but seeing the flood still coming on, I sent it away and lined out my men in the best positions available, pointing out what to fire at and telling them we must hold our hill at all costs. They were coolness itself.

There were besides the hollow mentioned, one or two good excavations of the same kind, but smaller. Someone, I think, had been prospecting for gold: anyway, he had our blessing.

Wonderfully soon we were ourselves under a heavy fire, and were shooting back steadily and hard. It did one good to see how steady the men were. The Boers who had originally retired in front of us were now coming back, so on three sides of us they were firing.

I joined Watson and Sergeant-Major Rowat and 5 men in the hollow. Quoting Lichtenburg, of the 18th Hussars, I said – 'Now, men, we are in a jolly tight hole, but a jolly good hole, and we'll make the most of it.' I should say this was about 12.30 p.m.

At first we fired a lot, but very soon the Boers had got our range and the least exposure was dangerous. Very soon, to my great grief, poor Rowat, the best N.C.O. in the Army, fell back, hit through the head and apparently done for. While we were attending to him several shots came right in and we had to keep down. Every shot that we fired was a stealthy shot at some bit of a Boer occasionally seen on the slope slightly below us. Soon Cherriman was hit in two places. Curiously enough, he had been hit the same day two years ago, at Lombard's Kop.

A Cool Rifleman.

Rifleman Livesay was splendid, marksman too, shooting and talking to the Boers he fired at – 'Would you?' 'I see you my friend,' 'Take that!' and such-like comments.

About an hour later, reinforcements came up, Seymour bringing up more of the Company. Right well they faced the fire. It was here we lost two more valuable riflemen.

Reggie and Beauchamp Seymour and 3 Riflemen joined us in our hollow. There was hardly room for us all now, but we were glad of their ammunition. Very soon Reggie and Corpl. Oglesby were hit. We cut Seymour's coats open (I never saw a fellow with so many clothes on) and were relieved to find it was a clean wound, arm broken, but a clean wound. Livesay set the arm with two scabbards. All this time we kept up an occasional shot and accounted for more than one horse or Boer.

Ammunition Runs Out.

The time went quickly, but the ammunition went quicker, and after two hours it began to give out. We had been throwing what we could spare, tied in handkerchiefs, to a party close to us.

About this time Casey, Pedrick and Baker came up with ammunition, the two former flat on their stomachs. Casey came right in to us, Pedrick lay flat under the crest close by. Baker came on at a run, upright, and drew a hot fire, dropping, hit as I thought at the time, beside Corpl. Rowles, who was doing great things in a small hollow some six yards away.

We had lots of ammunition now. At one time it looked as if the Boers were retiring and we fired more and with less need for caution. But soon their firing increased again. We resumed our former tactics, keeping well down and firing carefully.

Shelled by Our Own Guns.

The Boers kept coming back in twos and threes. We thought they had been for ammunition, but later we heard that they were being urged back by Louis Botha. The incessant crack of their rifles was very loud. It seemed so close, though really some 20 yards. About this time our guns from camp opened fire on our ridge where the Boers were, a bit too close, and then to our dismay our pom-pom joined in. One shell in our cock-pit would have sent the whole 14 of us to glory. Pedrick was still lying under the crest some 20 yards away; I sent him to crawl back and tell them it was us they were firing at. Later, I sent Rowles to say I could hang on, but wanted food, ammunition and water, and that there were quite enough Boers to rush us if they tried it, also that I had 4 wounded. While these two were away, the pom-pom placed 4 shells just to our left, just where Rowles had been, then 4 just to our right, and then a lot in the middle. What a row they made!

There was a groan from the good Livesay and he fell back with a lot of blood about his head.

I got my field dressing and to my great relief found it was only three splinters and that the wounds were not bad. I tied him up. So now we had 5 out of action.

There were still B. Seymour, Watson, 5 men and myself.

We started to burrow with sword-bayonets. What I dreaded was shrapnel.

Assault Expected.

It was growing dark. We had been in our cock-pit the whole afternoon. The Boers were collecting in growing numbers and evidently wanted our hill. I was sure they would rush us at dark. But this hill commanded the camp. I gave out that if they advanced we would let them come right up to within six yards and then shoot all we could.

I had two rifles, one carbine, and my Mauser pistol, all full-cock and loaded, so that I could not complain of my battery.

Orders to Retire.

At this crisis Pedrick got back to his old place and shouted – 'Major Eustace says you are to retire at once, and he will cover you with guns.' At first we were against leaving our wounded, but remembering they knew the wounded were there we decided to try it.

Now retiring was no easy matter. We had to get out of our cockpit, and however flat we crawled, we were bound to be seen and shot at.

The first three got away unnoticed, probably owing to the failing light. We said goodbye to Seymour and others and then took our turn.

I crawled flatter than any pancake and wriggled along at a pace, bullets spattering or singing past me. Just behind, I heard a cry; it was poor Scrimshaw bowled over. Watson got up and ran, and I said to myself, 'If a long-legged chap like that don't get hit, why should I?' So up I got and ran like the wind, with 'crack! crack!' all round me. I was delighted to find all the party, except Scrimshaw and two others cut off beyond us, were safe.

When the Boers saw what we were up to, they stood right up and fired, any number of them. Seymour said they were on him the moment we left. We had taken all the bolts out of spare rifles, so we did not leave much. But I left my haversack and in it printed notes of my own on rearguard fighting. Botha will smile when he sees them. He has taught us a bit about rearguards to-day!

It was dark when we got into camp. We guided the Ambulance to our wounded and they were brought in about 2 a.m.

We now heard for the first time that it was Louis Botha and over 1,500 men that we had been up against, also that Benson and Murray, Guiness and Lloyd, and many others were killed. Sergeants Ashfield and Weyman, Corpl. Brindley and seven others of the escort all killed and many more wounded, besides two guns taken.

Digging in.

On the top of all this, Louis Botha was expected to attack our camp. It was dark and a terrible storm came on, we were wet and cold, but had no time to be depressed. Myself, somehow, except for anxiety about Rowat and our sad losses, I felt easy in mind and confident. Collecting 40 of our men, we slushed our way in the dark towards the camp. At various points we came on men who exhorted us not to speak above a whisper for fear of drawing fire. With nervous fingers on more than one trigger, our return had its risks. About 9.30 p.m. it cleared and the moon gave us light to find spades. With these we worked in relief, all night and by dawn had good cover for 40 men. By 9 a.m. we had a splendid trench, a regular fort. Luckily the Boers had missed their chance. It is said that Louis Botha did collect 1,400 men for a night attack, but at 3 a.m. they changed their minds.

By 10 a.m. we were ready for all comers and hoped they would come. Colonel Wools Samson, now in command, came round and was pleased with our fort.

October 31st. – The whole of the 31st our Column lay low. We seemed like a man staggered by a blow, game to fight again, but glad of a pause for breath. It had been a heavy blow. Benson, the brilliant leader, was dead. Besides two guns we had lost 280 killed and wounded. In my Company we had 10 killed and 14 wounded.

Sergeant Ashfield.

Of Ashfield's gallant escort to the guns only 3 escaped. These were holding the horses and had to be ordered back twice before they would leave their comrades.

The crowded hospital was a sad sight and the doctors had more than they could do. Many men died of wounds and among them we buried, near Colonel Benson, Rifleman Tew, a good soldier.

November 1st. – With October our anxieties ended. Louis Botha went back whence he came. The country for miles was clear of Boers and by noon, helios flashed from many directions – Allenby, De Lisle and Barter had reached the scene.

November 2nd. – Next day our wounded made their painful way to Springs, 40 miles East, while we trekked back 35 miles North to Brug Spruit, arriving November 5th.

Return to the Line.

Having had more trouble with my teeth, I got leave, and riding on ahead with the advance Scouts of the advance guard, arrived just in time to jump into a train for Pretoria. Here I enjoyed a very short spell of civilisation, returning to Brug Spruit November 8th.

After five hectic days refitting, time was called, and the Column, scarcely recovered from shock, was launched again into the arena. There is nothing like work to distract men's minds from their troubles, and yet, I could not but feel that our men had deserved some pat on the back, and, were missing that word of 'Well done!' which a leader like Benson would surely have given.

Conclusion.

And now my story is done. We set out again in good heart, and the Column did well, again and again, for many months more, right up to the end of the war.

But why, have I dealt at such length with this mere incident in a war which itself, after two great wars, seems so small and so far away?

Why have I thought it worth while to pass on the log of a mere boy of 28?

It is this (and I want to say it as simply as I can): Looking back on these days I see a young fellow in dangerous days constantly and with confidence asking God for guidance. In a very private letter, dated 'Officers' Club, Pretoria. Nov. 8th, 1901,' I see that this day was to him a landmark in Faith.

There have been many landmarks since then. World War I for instance, and World War II, with great days of National prayer and thanksgiving.

Is God to grant us our prayers and we do nothing about it? To-day, with our Faith itself being threatened, what are we going to do?

What About It?

In the name of all the good fellows we lost at Bakenlaagte, in the name of the millions of men we have lost in war since then, in the name of all that we fought for, and may have to fight for again; I say it is time to declare our Faith in God and to ask for the Spirit to make ourselves as a Nation more worthy to stand for right against wrong.

The call is for Leaders, Leaders with faith and grit to face hardships in finding the way, and glad would I be if this story of mine were part of the call.

7. RIFLEMAN JOYCE.

It is difficult for a Veteran going through old papers to know what to destroy and what to pass on.

Take for instance these two old letters from Rifleman Joyce. For me, as I read them, I see a young Rifleman, keenness and 'esprit-de-corps' bubbling out in every expression and in all his actions; and the scenes he tells of, while vivid to me, may mean little to others at this long interval of time and changed ways.

Bakenlaagte, 30:10:1901.

First, he is writing of Bakenlaagte, in its way a historic event, when the Boers galloped in and shot down gunners and escort, the General and most of his Staff.

As one of the escort he writes:–

'As Sergt. Ashfield gave the order to dismount and the guns were unlimbering, our No. 3 called out, 'Oh, Joyce, I'm hit.' I lifted him up and got him off to camp. Then we formed a half-moon in front of the guns. Poor Ashfield was killed, and very soon too the guns were beaten down by an overpowering fire.

The Assault.

'The Buffs on our left, poor devils, they too were for it. I took cover behind an ant-heap but it did not stop a bullet through my left arm, just a sharp twinge, that's all, not enough to stop me firing whenever I could get my man.

'They were now within 50 yards. I had visions of them rushing us and felt for my sword-bayonet. I had left it behind – the only time I had ever left any kit behind. A 'Regimental entry?' What a distraction in front of an enemy rush!

'However the loss of my sword saved my life, for I know that

85

with it, I would have stood up to attack.

'When the rush came I met an old fellow clean in the stomach and fell to the ground with a prayer for God's mercy.

'Then came the fire of our own men: it was worse than ever.

A Good Turn.

'While the fight went on a young Boer gentleman came and squatted by me. I told him I longed for a smoke. He lit his own pipe and gave me a puff. All the time the fight went on. He told me he had graduated at Cambridge and that the ground we were on was his father's farm. On leaving he said – "Well, Tommy, you have a saying, 'One good turn deserves another.'" I said yes but I was in no position to return his goodness. He told me I was – all he wanted was for me to take a note to the woman's laager in our camp with this message – "All well. Piet van Nieman," which I did in the dark on my way to the dressing station.'

On Outpost Duty.

The second letter was written some 30 years after the event, but even so, though 20 more years have passed since then, still I hesitate, for it shows our friend caught napping.

'I had been on outpost duty the night before, and had done an extra turn of sentry-go for one of the picket who had dysentery.

'Daybreak came. We returned to camp, and soon were saddled up again, and away we went on a new day's adventure. What clear sunny mornings now, after all that long spell of mist and rain and mud and flies and short rations.

'We had now left the endless rolling veld and had come to the edge of beyond looking towards the drifts and heights on the Swaziland border.

'Our job was to watch a drift where the Boers were expected. The Corporal posted me on a rock some way down, and away from the rest.

'The dizziness of scanning the distant ford, the quietness of my position, the blazing sun and my very weariness from that long watch the night before – I did not intend it, nor do I remember ever fighting against it, but went off into the deepest sleep I ever fell into, and, worst of all, was fast asleep till you placed your hand on my shoulder, called me by name and told me that the Company had ridden over a mile before I was missed.

'Full of shame and regret at my own Captain finding me so un-rifleman-like, yet the tone you addressed me in, told me more than ever words could have done, that you knew me and did not condemn.'

8. GEORGE ROWAT.

A RIFLEMAN WHO DID HIS DUTY.

Any memoirs of mine would be quite incomplete if I left out some note of the very best Rifleman I ever knew.

George Rowat was an Evangelist, who by his sincerity, tact and example, won the respect and affection of all those with whom he served, throughout a long and distinguished career.

In his earlier days he tells us he was 'not too good.' One day, however, his whole outlook was changed. He went straight home, burned his cards, his pipes and tobacco, and all his gambling gear; in a word – he became what Riflemen called a 'Bible-thumper.'

Not content with one good step, he decided to take another. In 1899 he joined the 1st Battalion, 60th Rifles, remaining with that Battalion all his service.

Whatever difficulties Rowat may have had in his missionary work among soldiers, he certainly received every encouragement from his Officers, who fully valued his good influence. His Colonel, for instance, the beloved 'Johnny Campbell' (later Sir Wm. Pitcairn Campbell) wrote of him that he had done more good to the British soldier than anyone else he had known in the Army.

Service in India.

In this connection Rowat tells a typical story of his experience in one of his four Indian Frontier campaigns. After the fighting was over at the Malakand, Major Dwane, the Quartermaster (himself a great character) had, as usual, been first to secure a few tents. Getting wind of this, Rowat was early on the scene, and with some misgivings as to how he would be received, he boldly tackled the Quartermaster and asked if he might have a tent for a prayer-room. 'Well, Rowat,' said Dwane, 'the men have a tent to drink in and swear in, I don't see why they shouldn't have one to pray in.'

On active service and in barracks, in the hills and plains, through cholera and fever epidemics, Rowat stuck to his work, a model cheery Rifleman and a good Missionary all the time he was in India.

But it was the South African War which brought him out and proved the truth of the words of Gustavus Adolphus, 'A good Christian makes a good soldier.'

In South Africa Rowat served with the Mounted Infantry Company of his Battalion. After Talana, he took part in the nightmare retreat back to Ladysmith.

Retreat to Ladysmith.

What a march it was! Pitch dark nights, shocking mountainous roads and drifts, rain and mud up to the knees, waggons bogged and man-handled out of the bog; constant checks and halts, progress often not one mile an hour, sleeping and stumbling as they trudged on; and all this, on the top of their Dundee troubles. After three ghastly nights and days, the Column, exhausted man and beast, got safely through without the loss of a single man or waggon.

*'The victors of Talana had rejoined Sir George White, who, at the time can hardly have hoped ever to see them again.'

It was during this march that a Sergeant tells us how, as he staggered along in the darkness, Rowat came up, put his hand on his shoulder, and said a few words which inspired him with courage.

Ladysmith.

It was not very long before the Dundee troops were at it again. Some 23,000 Boers were closing in on Ladysmith. On October 30th came 'Black Monday' and the failure at Lombard's Kop. In this action we find Rowat on rearguard helping a wounded man in the retreat.

By November 2nd some 13,000 British troops, with 51 guns, were

* Annals of K.R.B. Vol. iv. p. 202.

encircled and a siege began which dragged on for four trying and anxious months. The Boers were strong in long-range guns which could reach any part of the defence from the surrounding heights. What with this, and constant sniping; with whirlwinds of dust, with flies and heat, with very disheartening news, and with dwindling rations, it was indeed a great test of pluck and endurance.

Wagon Hill.

Rowat's job throughout the siege was that of Quartermaster to his unit, stationed on Wagon Hill, three weary miles from the Town. This duty entailed a daily journey of 13 miles with mules and rations, dodging Long Tom shells and sniping. He never missed a single day. In addition, when men were short, he was often needed to go out on tricky scouting patrols. No wonder he soon lost a stone in weight. Then on January 6th, 1900, came the critical night assault on the key positions of Wagon Hill and Caesar's Camp. It covered 2 miles of front, and lasted right on to next day. It was the climax in the siege. There are many good accounts of this ding-dong night and day fight. Desperate courage was shown on both sides. I will only say here that our friend did his share, and was specially commended for gallantry at Wagon Hill.

For his services throughout the siege he later received the D.C.M.

Religious Meetings.

When we think of all that these men went through, and see an entry in Rowat's log – 'Pain in stomach, off and on, the last three months' it is surely a marvel that during all those 119 exhausting and anxious days of siege, never once did the longest day's work, or the hardest day's fighting ever interfere with Rowat's religious meetings.

It might be, just 2 or 3 'Brothers' gathered together for 2 or 3 minutes of prayer, at 2 or 3 a.m. – or it might be the keen-eyed little Sergeant standing up boldly on some table or cart, cheering and exhorting his hearers in his best parade voice. He tells us he had to work hard preparing his talks. As the siege wore on and candles and oil ran out, Rowat continued his services in the dark, reciting readings he knew by heart, from the Psalms or St. John or St. Paul, and leading in Sankey hymns. Later when the Columns moved on trek, his wagon was known as 'Spurgeon's Wagon,' and many a good soldier from many a corps, Gunners, Hussars, High-landers, Dominion Troops – all kinds came, and many were not ashamed to come again.

Buller's Advance.

By February 25th Buller had relieved Ladysmith. On March 12th, after an all-too-short rest to recoup and refit, we find Rowat, now promoted Sergeant Major of the M.I. Coy., off again on Buller's long march to the North. Langs Nek and Majuba, on over the High Veld, and crossing the railway, on into the mountains, 8000 feet, on up to Pilgrim's Rest and beyond. And not, even then, was there rest for our Pilgrim.*

With his base 500 miles away at Durban, Buller's progress was slow. The strong position at Majuba had to be turned. At Amersfoort in July some 2,000 Boers with 5 guns made a vigorous stand, and in between, there were constant skirmishes in which the Boers proved past masters in retreat.

A few extracts from Rowat's log may help to picture conditions. I do not give them always exactly in his own words.

From Rowat's Diary.

Amersfoort, July 24th. – 'A day to remember. Heavy shell fire. 18th Hussars and M.I. approached Boer trenches, rather warm, retired at a gallop, pom-pom shells thick, changed position, ordered to take hill. Enemy rifle fire terrible. I crawled on my stomach till it was sore and got to a forward position where it was impossible to move for some time, bullets so thick, however we took the position in grand style. The best work the Battalion has done. Marvellous escapes recorded on return to camp. Cold intense. As I write am shaking all over, teeth chattering with cold. For the last three nights wet blankets to sleep in.'

August 17th. – 'The whole of the troops moved off towards Amersfoort. On the way M.I. took two kopjes under heavy fire, our Company being well spoken of. We had a hard time of it as the

* Entry from Diary, May 13th: 'I am now in hospital with jaundice and look like a Chinaman. Doctor says seige – in a few days should be right.'

grass being burnt caused our eyes to get filled with black dust and become sore. The country since we left Ingogo has been one mass of burnt grass.'

August 19th. – 'Company mentioned in despatches for Amersfoort.'

August 21st. – 'Some hard gallops after the enemy, but when we get near they drop from their horses and set fire to the grass to delay us. Our casualties about 30. When approaching a farm with white flag flying, the Boers fired, killing one and wounding six.'

August 22nd. – 'On outpost duty 2½ miles from camp, at Boer farm. A family of ten, no husband of course. After a little conversation with the good woman of the house, she gathered her family round her and sang a few hymns, which we enjoyed very much. She was very sorrowful, the "Roineks" having taken her firewood, etc., and left her with little food. I gave her some of my rations and coffee, and to repay me she brought down from the roof a little "biltong."'

August 25th. – 'Artillery and musketry all round us, too usual to notice. Our Battalion had 22 casualties yesterday. More horses died this morning. Saw a dead man brought in. It proved to be Clark, the Doctor's orderly with a red-cross on his arm; missing three days, was found shot through the breast. Only a few weeks before I had pleaded with him, but his answer was – "Not to-night."'

Another entry is in lighter vein – 'I had volunteered to do the accounts for a Colour Sergeant who was unwell. A whirlwind came and carried away all my papers, up into the air, scattering them half a mile: so, after packing up the remaining books, I said – "Now I will have a walk. It's just what I wanted to stretch my legs." "Well, I never!" exclaimed a Sergeant, "Anyone but a 'Bible-thumper' would have cursed and sworn." So God spoke in the whirlwind!'

Bergendal.

By August 26th Lord Roberts and Buller and French were closing in on Louis Botha, East of Pretoria, beyond Belfast. Botha had still some 7,000 men and 20 guns. It was at Bergendal that the Boers made their last stand as an army; after that, for close on two years, it was all guerilla warfare. Here are some extracts from Rowat's log:–

August 27th. – 'Roused 5 a.m. Saddled up and moved off at 6.30 a.m. We look like negroes owing to the scarcity of water and the burnt grass. Our poor horses are suffering, it is now 30 hours since they had a drink. Heavy firing, we are ordered to the front, off we go at a gallop, shells and bullets, we take up a position near the railway line, and there I witnessed a sight I shall never forget. The roar of artillery is deafening. My Company opened fire at the retreating enemy. As we returned to camp, we passed over the battlefield where dead and dying were lying in all directions. They were mostly Rifle Brigade who had won right up to the Boer trenches where the Johnnesburg Police had made a great stand. It was midnight before we could have our word with the Master.'

Pursuit to Leydenburg.

On September 1st, the dogged Buller set out to pursue the equally dogged Boers, to the North, forcing his way right into the heart of precipitous mountains and gorges round Leydenburg and beyond. It was very hard going for all concerned and there were many casualties. The Boers, now some 2,000 strong, made full use of their long-range guns to cover their skilful retirements, the wonder was how they could get their big guns away.

With the transport difficulties, rations and blankets for men and mules and horses often went short and all suffered from cold and privations. But the country with Spring coming on was beautiful reminding our pilgrim of happier days in Hill stations in India.

Crocodile Valley.

In the Crocodile Valley our men had a gruelling time, and round the camp fire there were wonderful yarns and many proofs of narrow escapes, which gave our hero his openings. 'One man came to me while the shelling was on, and said, 'This is the time, Sergeant Major, to pray. If ever I prayed it's to-day.' But as soon as the firing ceased he had said goodbye to his prayers. When invited to our meeting on the veld, he declined. 'The Troops would laugh at him,' he said.'

There are many such yarns in Rowat's log. It might well become tedious if I gave them all, and in his own language; but always, as an old comrade in arms, I see at the back of it all, the twinkle of fun and the business-like look of the man as he spoke.

One more example to show that Rowat also had his successes.

The troops had fought their way through mountains and cold and exposure. They came to a beautiful valley. 'No snipers or shells, so we could admire the lovely wild flowers and the clear water of the Sabie River, wending its way in and out of huge mountains, a magnificent waterfall made one giddy to look up at it. We all hope to stay here a few days.'

A Conversion.

Here in this camp, Rowat speaks of 'many new faces' at their meeting. 'Some were moved to tears. One man rushed away in tears.'

Two days later a Staff Sergeant walked some distance to see him. Did Rowat remember five years back, in Chitral, 1895, how he had tackled him, the Staff Sergeant, about his soul? Rowat did not remember, but it seems that from that day, off and on, the Staff Sergeant had been troubled about his way of life. He had come to Rowat's meeting and seen the Light.

Buller's Departure.

On return to Leydenburg, after all their battles and treks there was a general feeling of 'going home' in the air. Some had earned it and some had not, but all were agreed that no one had earned it more than their veteran leader, Sir Redvers Buller. On leaving he paid a glowing tribute to his men and wished them good luck and God speed. As he left the troops lined the road and gave him a wonderful 'send off.'

'Never,' says General Sir Stuart Hare, 'Never, through the worst of his failures, had he lost for one moment the confidence and affection of his Troops. Never did the most successful of Generals receive a more touching and heartfelt ovation than did he on his departure for home.'*

Yes, I know this is true. I arrived just in time to see the enthusiasm, it was tremendous.

* Annals of the King's Royal Rifle Corps, vol. iv. p. 298.

Rejoining the Regiment.

It was a great day for me on October 5th when I rejoined the old Battalion and its Mounted Infantry Company. So many old friends and Colonel Campbell in command. Over four years before, I had helped at the start of the Company at the Cape. What veterans they now were! It was good to be back. Scratchley was in command, with Lynes and Johnson as subalterns, the good Rowat also was there, cheery and keen as ever. Many tough old warriors too, all joined in giving me a good welcome. I found all ranks a bit war-weary. They wanted to hear that the war would soon be over, but I, having come all the way round from Pretoria by the Free State, the Cape and Natal, had found along the whole route small local Commandos each causing its quota of trouble. As a matter of fact the war had yet to run nearly two years.

On October 6th we moved from Leydenburg, under General Lyttleton, seven marches South West to Middelburg.

It was mountainous country and there were plenty of Boers. The horses were still in poor condition, but thanks to good management there were still 80 men mounted, out of 115. Our 1st Battalion was also with us. It was good to be back with old friends.

The Dulstroom Rearguard.

On October 12th, 1900 (my birthday) we left Dulstroom, on rearguard, Col. Campbell, with our 1st Battalion and guns, in command.

By daybreak we had got our mounted screen spread out in an arc about 2 miles out. With Lynes on my left and Johnson on my right, I took the centre. Scratchley in rear, in support.

As dawn broke I was standing on rising ground behind some rocks with Corporal Parkes. We were waiting and watching.

It would be some time before the convoy got clear and our turn came to retire. Boers were soon in evidence in the distance. We knew their old game and had our retirement planned.

Then I noticed a mounted Boer scouting towards us. 'Shh,' I whispered to Parkes and pointed. We crouched down and watched. In a whisper I asked – 'Are you a marksman, Parkes?' 'Yes, Sir,' he whispered. 'Then take a good aim,' I whispered. 'To-day is my birthday!' The Boer came on peeping round and alert, but quite unaware of our presence. I should say at some 2 yards Parkes fired. Bang went his gun but away went the Boer! Arms, elbows and legs galloping hard for dear life.

Bugler Douglas.

We had a long wait after that. Then our turn came to retire covered by Lynes and Johnson on each flank. There had not been much sniping so far. As we retired I came on Bugler Douglas who had been sent to me with a message. His horse was badly bogged. Telling my Section where to go, I went back to Douglas. But his horse from fear and exhaustion lost heart and sank deeper and deeper. Rowat now joined me from the blue! We packed Douglas off to the next position. The Boers had now got our range, a good target we were at some 500 yards, so we shot the horse, destroyed the saddle and came away quickly. Poor Douglas had a long run, for on reaching the next position, before long he had to retire again. Helped by Rowat and Scratchley he got back unhit. (This good man was later killed at Bakenlaagte.)

From daybreak till noon the Boers in increasing numbers followed up boldly. We had a hot time but, knowing each other and knowing our job, we worked as a team and all went well. We covered each other and held them off, and always when things got tight, the Colonel was there with his guns to keep them at bay.

'Our Colonel,' says Rowat, 'met me as I was taking up ammunition, badly needed, and told me to inform Captain Scratchley that M.I. Coy. had done exceedingly well in their rearguard action. Of course there were narrow escapes, but no one was killed.'

It was late that night when we got into camp in the dark in a drenching storm, with lightning flashes and deafening crashes of thunder, echoing round the Dulstroom Hills.

We made no attempt at comfort and lay down where we were. An early rise before us and rumours of trouble ahead.

So ended my 28th birthday.

Middelburg.

On October 15th we arrived at Middelburg to rest, recoup, and refit, and for a few days we lived in peace, drawing stores and remounts from Pretoria.

On October 17th Scratchley went home and passed his mantle on to me. On leaving he sent in a special commendation of Rowat – 'A first-class accountant and good horse master,' 'had trained 50 raw horses and many new hands,' 'most conscientious in all his duties,' 'gallantry July 24th, and again on 30th,' 'I can not speak too highly of him.'

The reader perhaps will grow tired of all this commendation, but remember, I have cut out a lot, and that each new commander had always more praises to add.

I will now pass quickly over events many of which I have mentioned elsewhere.

On October 23rd, 1900, Kruger had left for Holland.

From that time on for nearly two years in guerilla warfare, the infantry's job was chiefly defence of the railways or block-house lines, and of the transport columns. The mounted troops were chiefly employed on patrols or on drives to round up the Boers. For three months we helped in guarding the line round Middelburg. Then for three months we served in Colonel Campbell's column, had many adventures, and won a good name.

Well-earned Leave.

On January 11th, 1901, Rowat was given a well-earned month's leave to rest and see his family at Cape Town, not having seen them for 16 months. It was not till April that he rejoined us at Piet Relief and glad we all were to get him back.

It was here that he received a personal telegram from Lord Kitchener:–

'The Residency, Pretoria, April 25th, 1901.

'I congratulate you on your D.C. Medal.'

Leydenburg.

After this, followed five months of duty in Leydenburg till on October 12th, 1901 (my birthday again) we got welcome orders to join Colonel Benson's famous Column.

On October 20th (Talana Day) we moved off.

Of all this I have given some account elsewhere.

There is just one more incident I wish to record before I come to a close.

Benson's Column.

On October 24th Benson had just done one of his long night marches, ending up with a five-mile gallop at dawn.

The time had come to return to our new camp. Two of our Companies from our 4th Battalion were on rearguard. The Boers were more pressing than ever. Bircham, Troyte and Crichton and several men were wounded. It was during this trouble that a young Rifleman with his horse hit, was seen to be in trouble. It was Captain Dalby who saw the incident and recommended Rowat for the V.C.

Recommended for V.C.

Rowat seems to have specialised in such ventures. Once again he appeared from the blue and with Rifleman Parish rescued his man. He did not mention it to me at the time and thought little of it. In the evening, just before stables, the young Rifleman came over to our lines and thanked Rowat sincerely for having saved him that morning. 'That's all right,' said Rowat, with his cheery laugh. 'We saved your body, now go and groom your horse for all you are worth, then come back after Stables and tea, and we'll save your soul too. Prayer meeting at half-past seven!'

Rowat Wounded.

A few days later Rowat's career as a fighting soldier came to an end, for among the many good men who fell, dead or wounded, with their splendid leader at Bakenlaagte, Rowat was one.

Day by day, for over a month, many an anxious friend received the same report – 'Sergeant Major Rowat is still dangerously ill from a gunshot wound in the head.' There seemed no hope, yet Rowat refused to die. After a week of pain most patiently borne, he recovered slowly, and was able to be moved down to the Coast. In December, 1901, he was invalided home. In July, 1902, he retired with a pension, with a broken head and stone deaf, but his stout heart intact.

1905. In a Sheffield paper, 1905, was the following notice – 'A happy incident was witnessed, when an unassuming man in plain clothes, was conducted up to H.M. King Edward VII. His Majesty received him with a smile, shook hands with him, and bending down, for the man was evidently deaf, asked him several questions in a loud voice. The man was George Rowat, a Sergeant Major of the Rifles Mounted Infantry, whose latest honour is to receive from the King the Royal Victorian Medal.'

Yes, it was 'Brother' George Rowat whom the King delighted to honour, and as the veteran left the dais, muttering over and over again to himself, 'Who could have thought of such an honour?' – 'Now,' he said, 'all Riflemen will see what may come to them if they do their duty.'

A few years more this gallant old soldier lived on in South Africa where he went for his health, but now he is gone.

Conclusion.

To-day, some 50 years later, as I read this long-forgotten story, I see how lucky I was to have such an expert in horses and men and accounts as my right-hand man at such a time. A picked all-round man, standing out in a Corps which abounds in good men and is second to none.

And as I read his diary, which is now out of print, its language in places is foreign to me, but in those days, all of us knew, some more and some less, all of us knew that Rowat lived a good life and did what he did, and was what he was only because of his absolute Faith in God.

Dear little Rowat. He lived very near to The Way, The Truth and The Life. Such contacts are precious and few.

9. AFTER BAKENLAAGTE.

When I read the story of our wanderings over the veld by day, and more often by night, during the last stages of the war, I see I shall have to be careful not to inflict more than just a suggestion of the boredom and hardships entailed in those long weary marches.

And yet, lest my memoirs should end too abruptly, I think it is right to close with some side-lights certainly not to be found in any official account of the war.

General Bruce Hamilton's Columns.

After Benson's reverse at Bakenlaagte, Kitchener was quick to retaliate. In two weeks he had collected 15,000 mounted men, in twelve columns under well-known leaders, with Bruce-Hamilton in command.

His object was to crush Botha in the High-Veld country round Ermelo. New block-house lines, and advanced bases were established and the intelligence Service under Wools Samson was greatly strengthened. By a combination of drives and long night-marches, it was hoped to succeed where so often before we had failed.

The wonder is that in the end Botha not only evaded the large forces pitted against him, but more than once, dispersing his men, was able by sudden concentrations, to inflict minor reverses.

Results.

After six weeks of constant night raids, it is true that the moral effect went far towards ending the war, but only some 700 Boers had been captured. Botha was still at large, his scattered Boers too wary to be surprised, yet still in the field an ever-possible danger.

Night Marches.

The successes of Benson's night raids were chiefly due to the novelty and surprise of his free-lance methods, but later, the Boers grew more wary. With the use of larger numbers, risks were reduced, but mistakes in the dark were more frequent.

With Colonel Benson night marches had been a speciality. Before starting, each man was told the object of the march and all started keen.

At every drift, wire fence, or obstacle, there was always a Staff Officer to supervise. The column was frequently halted and straggling was reduced to a minimum. Touch was kept up systematically. No dogs, no talking, no smoking, no rattling of wheels or accoutrements.

But when we joined this large force, and precautions were all the more needed, it seemed an unwieldy force. Often there was considerable confusion.

Our first night march is an illustration of this.

We had specially trained our men to work at night as connecting files, opening out or closing like an elastic band, to keep touch in the dark.

'There were many drifts. The leading column forged ahead without waiting. I constantly had my whole Company strung out as connecting files and we had great difficulty throughout.

Stray men from columns in rear kept pushing up from behind.

At one check, men from all columns crowded up and soon there was chaos. Men were shouting out loud 'Hello! Who are you?' 'What Corps is this?' 'Where are the Greys?' 'Have you seen the 18th Hussars?' 'Who the devil are you?' and so on, and it was not possible to right the confusion before dawn, just the time when good order was needed.'

Or again:–

'Another night march. Ground difficult. An extra dark night, but the Column being anxious to surprise a laager, did not make halts in front. At a boggy spruit I waited to supervise and send out connecting files. This done, I cantered on up to the head of my connecting files and found the Corps in front had suddenly galloped on and touch had been lost. I galloped off into space and was lucky in finding the troops about half-a-mile in front.

(Half-a-mile on the bare veld in the dark may be quite a long way.)

I got the leading file in touch, but just then, my old grey galloped into a barbed-wire fence and came head over heels on top of me, doubling me up and rolling on me in that position.

The Doctor came up and helped me, but there was no ambulance, so that when the rear of the column came up, I had to decide between being left on the veld ten miles from Carolina, or riding another twenty miles. It took me four days to recover.'

Here is another entry:–

'At 11 p.m. the moon had set and it grew so dark it was impossible to tell whom one rode next to.

At dawn our men and the 3rd M.I. and Scottish Horse got all mixed up, but I managed somehow to get mine together and soon after dawn came the order to trot, then gallop, and before I could stop it, a stampede and chaos. I followed the stampede, using strong language, to a farm where there was shooting in all directions and no one knew what was going on.

We had surprised Smit's Commando near Lake Bannagher, after a 37 mile march. I could not help feeling that we in rear, as organised reserves, would have been more use. However, all were happy. Our latest hooroosh had been a success!'

Another Night March – An Unfortunate Incident.

'As we started in daylight I asked for, and got, permission to smoke. Then as it grew darker, I passed down word to my men – 'I will give you five minutes more to smoke.' My Company was at the rear of our Column. Colonel Fortescue's Column, some 600 mounted men, was coming on behind us.

By some mistake the order reached Colonel Fortescue – 'You may smoke.' Later he told me that though a bit surprised, he was quite pleased, so he lit a cigarette, and passed on the order to his men, who, having no scruples in the matter, promptly lit up.

The column was coming down a slope, and, turning round, I saw, with an uncomfortable feeling, the whole hill-side ablaze like a prairie fire. It was not very long before this fireworks display attracted Colonel Mackenzie's attention. He had all the Officers up. There was a row. However, all was forgiven in the light of after-events.'

Capture of a Convoy.

On another occasion:–

'We had hoped for a rest, but at 9 a.m. we received orders to start at 9.30 a.m. with stripped saddles, no transport; we were to be back before long, so they said.

Luckily we were Advance-guard.

About 11.30 a.m. we sighted a Boer convoy six miles off. I felt we would get it all right, but the horses must suffer. We moved quickly, trotting and leading alternately till we got to the point where the convoy was first sighted. A few Boers shot at us. I was told to reinforce and push on. This we did, and were soon on the rearmost waggons. A few shots did not delay us. We pushed on and spread panic. The Boers galloped off, leaving families and cattle to their fate.

We galloped on and on, past gesticulating families, isolated waggons, and Boers waving their arms excitedly, anxious to surrender. We left all these to be dealt with in rear and pushed on. Once on the run, keep them on the run.

At last, however, after a nine-mile gallop, my pony was about done, and only four men up with me, so, planting ourselves on a ridge between the escaping Boers and their convoy, we waited till more came up. Soon more men came up under Eustace. They pushed on. There were only six capecarts now left with the escaping Boers. Eustace pushed on well and got all but two of the carts and a few more prisoners.

I could see some 60 Boers escaping as they deserted their carts, quite enough of them to make it hot for Eustace with his 25 men on beat horses, so we sat down and lit our pipes and watched. We should be more use in rear with rested horses than in front with beat ones if the Boers gave trouble.

It was about 3.30 p.m. when I had pulled up; we had covered near 40 miles. Many horses were quite done.

Seeing Eustace returning unmolested, I rode back some three miles and found Colonel Mackenzie very much pleased. Everyone was happy!

We recovered our own cart with three days groceries, to say nothing of chickens, turkeys, ducks, and sacks of mealies and

MEMOIRS OF A RIFLEMAN SCOUT

coffee. I found men attired in top hats, frock-coats and Sunday-best suits. It came on to rain, with a plague of mosquitoes and sandflies. There was some confusion. Kaffirs had bolted. Thousands of cattle and sheep had to be got back to camp with only surrendered Boers to drive them; however, in spite of darkness and rain, by 8 p.m., we got back to our new camp at Lillieput. It had been a strenuous time, but hardships, along with success, count 100 per cent less.'

25th M.I. are Commended.

Order 24.12.06. Colonel C. Mackenzie.

The O.C. Column congratulates all concerned on the operations of 21st inst., resulting in the capture of the Standerton Convoy. The 25th M.I., under Major Eustace, and particularly captain Crum's Company, contributed in a marked way to the day's success.

'To the fact of moving with stripped saddles, though it entailed hardships for two days, it was due that over 30 miles were covered after a 30 mile march in only five hours.'

Total bag – 23 Boers, 20 waggons, 20 carts (and others destroyed), 2,000 cattle, 1,000 sheep, and many good ponies.

Mobility.

Whatever may be said of results, there is no sort of doubt that we did get over the ground those days, and we often had greater success than we knew at the time.

On December 30th we were off at short notice, 6.30 p.m. We had no idea why or where we were going. We marched all night. By now the Southern stars were old friends of mine, so I knew our direction was E.S.E. We continued our march till 12 noon next day. The transport got in at 3 p.m., having done 34 miles in 19 hours, a very big march for waggons. It was only later we heard we had been a big success in blocking the Umpilosi drifts, while other columns had captured Erasmus and over 100 Boers.

Looking back, I think that, in spite of our numbers, a 'Monty' would have worked up our keenness better, and cheered us along, by telling us more.

Storms.

On our first day out we had a bad storm. Three Cameron High-landers were killed by lightning in their guard tent. I had also seen a horse killed by lightning not one hundred yards from my tent, but for me the storm of January 9th at Carolina stands out as a kind of special departing salvo.

'It had been very hot all day in camp. At 3 p.m. it was clear that a storm was coming, so we got our horses in early from grazing. We had just watered them and tied them up in the lines when there came a sudden blast of wind and dust. Then lightning, thunder, hail and rain.

'I ran to the lines and got some men out to stop the horses stampeding. We stood by them for a bit trying to quieten them but the storm was too much for us. Hailstones and rain came down harder and harder, and for longer than I had ever seen.

'I never got such a hammering. We were driven back, and had to leave the horses to shift for themselves. My small shelter was laid flat. I crouched down in my oilskin and helmet, trying to save my neck and face at the expense of my hands. I got whack after whack on the knuckles and back from huge and sharp hailstones. I could just see all the horses in camp were stampeding – no wonder, poor brutes. I would have stampeded myself if I had thought it would do any good. I fought my way backwards to shelter. It was the fiercest of the many bad storms I have been in. After 20 minutes the hail gave place to steady rain, and we all turned out to collect the horses. Luckily there were two hours of daylight left, and the swollen river three miles from camp stopped the stampede. We recovered all but one of our horses, now reduced to 73.'

Boer Convoy at a Drift.

It had often puzzled us how, in spite of storms and floods, the Boer convoys often eluded our forces. Here is an account which helps to understand:–

'We went down to the river to see the Boers who had sur-rendered crossing the drift. There were fifty waggons and more families, and a lot of cattle.

'The drift was about four feet deep with a very strong current. It was wonderful to see how they managed what would have seemed to us impossible. Sixteen oxen all carried off their legs: A Boer, naked and barefooted, swimming or standing on the stony bottom, tugging at the leading span of oxen, while others standing well up in their saddles in the river, yelled, shouted, and flogged the oxen. Sometimes a lot of oxen seemed hopelessly mixed up, but the Boers saw at once what was wrong, and put it right quickly. At times the waggons looked as if they must topple over, but someone always did the right thing at the critical moment and saved mishap.

'The Boer women and children sat with all their belongings in the waggons, and showed no signs of anxiety. Occasionally a chair, table, chicken, or other article was washed down the stream in the flood, but the Kaffirs were on them at once, and swimming like powerful fish, brought them back to the owners, who received them stolidly, without a 'thank-you' or a look of satisfaction.

'As soon as each waggon was across it was outspanned, and the "vrou" lit a fire and had something waiting for her man.

'Once or twice, one of the lighter carts did upset, and was overturned and carried, horses and all, down the stream; but the occupants jumped out and swam, and, with the help of others, the conveyance was dragged ashore, upside down or sideways, no matter! On the opposite bank the cart was righted, the owner jumped in and drove on, thinking it a grand joke. Now we see how they often gave us the slip at a drift.'

My Last Night March.

On the night of January 11th, 1902, I did my last night march.

'I do not know anything more trying than constant night marching. One goes on and on, struggling to keep awake when the road is easy, and struggling to keep touch when it is difficult. Twenty-five miles is about as much as you will do at a walk, if it is necessary to trot you are bound to have stragglers, and a straggler in the dark is probably a man lost. At dawn one wakes up, and it is possible to get a gallop out of the horses, but when the sun gets up, and it gets hot, then men and horses begin to tire. You have shot your bolt, and though the raid may not have been a success, it is not wise to go on. Certainly it is a mistake on exhausted horses to chase Boers on fresh ones. You will catch no Boers, and when the time comes they will give you a nasty time getting back.'

On this occasion, after long and well-timed marches, three columns had converged in the Ermelo district and captured 42 Boers. But not content with this, some of our troops chased 50 Boers a long way. They did no good, and lost men and horses.

And so, at Kromkrans, we camped my last night on active service. It was said that Botha was coming. We had good trenches ready, but Botha left Cirum and Kromkrans severely alone.

Leave Home.

And now I come near the close of this stage of my story. Having been granted leave home on medical grounds, in due course I found myself speeding South from Pretoria in the Princess Christian ambulance train, with all the joys of homecoming before me. How very much better than travelling North in a Boer ambulance train as a prisoner of war! What comfort after the veldt, and what a feeling of relief from all worries!

And yet there were qualms over leaving that splendid body of men to finish the job. They seemed to be a part of my life. With them, under leaders like Campbell and Benson, what valuable experience I had gained as a soldier!

My idea at the time was to get well quickly and come back to finish the job. I did not know how much I needed a rest. In the end it took me one year to recover completely.

The After-Effects of War.

I would end with a word as to the after-effects of war. There is bound to be a reaction. Courage and faith may well be needed to see one through tunnels of gloom. How many millions since those days have returned from the wars, and what millions have welcomed those who returned! Such homecomings are landmarks no one forgets, though each story may vary.

In this particular case, in due course, I got home and was happy indeed. (Few can have had a kindlier welcome.) And yet I was restless.

'Don't talk to me about war,' I wrote at the time. 'There is nothing inside my head but war, and yet my mind is a blank if you leave out the subject of war.' That was my mood at the time.

Then, after six months, I found myself back at the Cape, at De Aar. Army reform was then in the air. There were minor changes in drill and in dress, but we who were keen were longing for real reforms. It was not till later that Haldane came on the scene and told John Bull that he himself was to blame and not the British soldier. Here is a comment written from De Aar:–

Army Reform.

The Regimental Officers and men are being maligned by some at home. They have done far better than the Germans would have done under new conditions. As Napier wrote long ago, 'In the beginning of each war, England has to seek in blood the knowledge necessary to secure success' – a risky practice. Nearly cost us this war. Only good luck saved us. It might cost us more some day. The cry on all sides is 'Wake up!' What will be the response?'

At De Aar, in spite of its desolate dusty surroundings, time and change were doing our war-weary ones more good than they knew. It was certainly a bit of a change for young Murats to find themselves learning to 'stand at ease' and 'right about turn' and 'slow march' by numbers, and mastering the new drill, but no doubt this 'stand easy' and going slow, with a cheery crowd of brother-officers, all happy to be re-united after the war, was part of the cure. But it was not till the Battalion landed in Malta in December that the health and spirits of all completely returned. Here we were welcomed by the Governor, Field Marshal Lord Grenfell, our distinguished Colonel Commandant. Under him no Rifleman could serve and not do his best, and soon all ranks improved all round. A happy Battalion, no longer war-worn or war-weary.

As for myself, with a pat on the back of a ' brevet,' and the passing of pain in my arm, the call of the soldier's profession was clear as the Rifleman's bugle.

How is this for a sample of keenness returned.

December 6th. – 'I am getting all my keenness on soldiering back, and feel at times frightfully keen. We are starting a bicycle club for the men, so with that, and my company, and lectures to the whole Battalion, and polo, I am fully occupied. It is splendid getting one's keenness back. Experience without keenness is nothing. Ever since Bakenlaagte I have been more or less mooning about and taking a distant view of things. I hope in May to get leave, and I want to come home by Metz, when the Kaiser is to be there. I suppose the German trouble in Morocco is only a demonstration. I am sure it will come, but not yet.'

To Sum Up.

Here then let me sum up.

In these talks I have dealt with a young fellow of under 30. Five years before, he had seen war coming and worked all he knew to be ready. Then came disasters. He had shuddered to see the Union Jack hauled down, an unthinkable thing in those days.

Given another chance, after experience under two grand leaders, and with picked men, he emerges one of the many of Haldane's 'new generation of professional soldiers.' He visits Metz, Woerth, Spicheren, with Yate,* an expert on these German battles.

He hears the haunting drum-beat of tens of thousands as they assemble for massed manoeuvres. He sees them goose-stepping on the parade ground, and making impossible charges in the field, he even gets right up to the Kaiser himself at 'pow-wow' and hears the 'All Highest's' views on Boer warfare – all this, twelve years before the great clash when our gallant 'Old Contemptibles' shielded their country from ruin.

His whole idea was – 'Be prepared!'

How was it, then, that when war came, we find him – all thoughts of soldiering discarded and gone – engrossed and intent, not on training men for war, but wholeheartedly bent on trying to lead the men of to-morrow, in Baden-Powell's way, to 'Be Prepared,' whatever might come, through Service and Faith, to play their part in flying the Union Jack the right way up?

But that is another story.

---

* Captain Yate, Yorkshire Light Infantry, P.S.C., was shot by Germans when captured in 1914. He knew too much.

MEMOIRS
OF A
RIFLEMAN SCOUT

PART II

PART II

MALTA, 1903, TO OUTBREAK OF WAR, 1914.

CONTENTS

An account of service as a Rifleman with Scouts and Mounted Infantry in India, and of the early days of the Boy Scout Movement in Scotland.

10. MALTA.

Malta, 1903.

When I look back on Malta days, I see how much we enjoyed the relief of peace after three years of war. The 1st/60th Rifles, with leaders like Davidson, Dalby, and others, were a splendid Battalion, and under Lord Grenfell the whole garrison, Army and Navy, were one happy family. To me the Navy was a new and special attraction. In a cruise on H.M.S. 'Implacable,' as the guest of an old South African friend, Captain Prothero, with Commander Mark Kerr and other friends in both Ward Room and Gun Room, I had the run of the ship and was able to see and enjoy and learn a good deal.

There were also expeditions to Sicily to shoot duck and snipe, and then came our turn for leave home during the hot weather. At the same time we were all keen soldiers. We worked hard and we played hard. As for myself, having seen the Union Jack hauled down at Dundee in Natal, I was probably keener than most to make certain that no such thing should ever happen again, whatever the Kaiser's intentions might be.

Visit of King Edward VII.

In April, King Edward's visit was a big event and I see an entry 'Tunics, Tunics, Tunics! Glad I am not in the Guards!' But it was not all tunics. We had a great polo match, Army v. Navy. Twenty minutes before play, all was ready – expectant crowds, bunting, marquees, seats. Then suddenly a great storm arose, blowing clouds of dust right into the stand. It was then we saw what the Navy could do. In no time, at the double, they shifted everything across to the other side. The match was a ding-dong affair. We played our best as never before. When time was up we were 4 goals all. Then out came General Lane and told us the King had been thrilled by our prowess and wished to present a Cup to the winners. The goals were widened and we played extra time. The Navy won. Three cheers for the Navy! It was only later we heard that King Edward, overcome by State functions and the heat, had dosed through our doings and only been wakened in time to encourage us on!

Lecture to the Garrison.

It was in Malta that I made my debut as a lecturer. I look back on it now as a step which gave me the courage of my convictions on soldiering. At the time I was nervous, but I meant it to be a success. For a whole month I worked hard at it. At the back of my small mind, in every occupation, soldiering, polo, society, this lecture on 'Mounted Infantry' was there all the time.

It all went well. To others, no doubt, it seemed a simple thing for one who had spent five years on the job to speak on the subject. They would not have thought so had they stood in my shoes on the Mellieha cliffs rehearsing that talk to the waves!

The Bicycle Club.

Then there was our successful Bicycle Club. Bicycles in Malta were scarce and bad, and only hired out on exorbitant terms. It seemed good for the Troops to get further afield. With £500 from the Canteen we bought 50 good cycles from Singers, and sent two Riflemen home to be trained at Coventry.

10/3/1903. – 'Today we had a competition in riding and care of machines, lasting from 7 a.m., to 6 p.m., with 100 men competing. The best 20 can buy their bicycles on lenient terms; the rest, if they pass, pay a monthly subscription and have the use of the Club Bicycles. But cycles are fragile and expensive things, so we make our Members qualify, not only in riding, but also in character.'

In the end, the Club was a great success. Out of 500 men in the Battalion there were over 100 members. Some of the men got to know the whole Island, and Club runs were popular.

Polo and Football.

The Marsa at Malta is the common sports ground, where you will see football, hockey, and polo, all going on at the same time. When 'the Rifles' were playing 'the Gunners' at football, you would see Col. Bewicke-Copley standing conspicuously among all the big garrison gunners, in full Regimental colours, green and red blazer, polo-cap, and scarf, shouting for 'the Rifles!' or later umpiring in a polo match close at hand. He gave a good lead in such matters.

Leave Home.

1903. – One advantage of Malta was the leave we got home during the hot weather. This time, no longer war-worn and restless, I enjoyed my three summer months at home to the full.

In those early days of motoring, my father had an Arrol-Johnston car, one of the first motors in Stirlingshire. It was made of wood and had no wind-screen. To start it took strength and knack, hauling the starting rope up to your chin. In it we went all over Scotland. When we reached 20 m.p.h. on the straight Kippen road, we shouted with joy!

The First Motor-bike.

At Coventry I also bought a Humber motor-bike with which I hoped to lead our Bicycle Club in Malta. As a matter of fact, often it had to be pushed and the push-bikes got home first. It was both noisy and new, and scared every native and mule on the Island.

In addition to all my comings and goings at home, I visited Metz and the German battlefields, both coming and going, for in those days my thoughts were always on possible war.

Malta Fever.

On return to Malta in August, fever was rampant. The trouble had not yet been traced to goats' milk. At one time we had over 40 per cent down with fever. It was seldom fatal, but it was sad to go round the wards and see strong men reduced to such wrecks. My own prescription was a good gallop a day, and plenty of work.

We did all we could to keep the men active and interested, but I must confess there were times when heat and sandflies, not to mention the bells and yells and smells, would get on one's nerves.

18/10/1903. – 'I keep fit but there are days when one feels inclined to murder that bell-ringer, in full view, not 200 yards from my window, or the noisy, yelling Maltese on the Grannery down below.'

It was said that so far as soldiering went Malta was a backwater, but I always found myself well employed and certainly improving in the 'Art of War.' However, with the promise of a Mounted Infantry opening in India, and a chance of exchange with my old friend Major 'Tom' Mott, by New Year's Day, 1904, I had joined the 2nd Battalion 60th Rifles at Rawal Pindi in India.

Rawal Pindi.

29/12/1903. – In 1893, I had joined the lst/60th at Rawal Pindi as a very shy subaltern, and now I found myself joining the 2nd Battalion, still rather shy, as a brevet-major. Later, comparing notes with my old friend Tom Mott, also a brevet-major, I found that he too for a time had felt a bit home-sick.

But they did not give me time to get home-sick. In exchange for the splendid Company I had handed over to my friend, I now found myself leader of another fine Company of veteran Riflemen, one of the best shooting Coys. in India. Moreover, at my very first meeting, Colonel Markham gave me the unwelcome duty of tackling the Officers' Mess which was in a bad way. This was quite out of my line, but I had to 'keep smiling.'

Steady Drill.

I found myself still more lacking, on making my debut next morning at steady Battalion drill. In the end I improved, but I never grew fond of Battalion drill! Still less did I care for the steady Brigade drills on the barrack square, in which our Brigadier was a specialist. The whole garrison seemed a bit old-fashioned in such matters.

Lecture on Skirmishing.

Soon after my arrival General Wodehouse asked me to lecture to the Garrison. That gave me my chance and I chose 'Skirmishing' as my subject. Again I took much trouble and time and thought, and all went well. The General rode over to thank me again next day and said my lecture would do good. He sent it to the Simla U.S. Magazine of that date.

In a large Garrison such as Pindi much goes on – races, polo, and Society – this last not much in my line. Still, as President of the Officers' Mess, my duties plunged me into the vortex.

Social Duties.

On one occasion, I was invited to dine with General Sir Bindon Blood and General Walter Kitchener (K. of K's. brother) was also there. I remembered him well in South Africa. He was very deaf. It was told of him that once he was standing on an exposed height when a belt of pom-pom shells landed near him and his Staff. He put his hand to his ear and asked his A.D.C. – 'Did I hear a shot?'

On this occasion even a game of bridge proved difficult.

Curiously enough, in that very same house, ten years before, deafness had also been my undoing. On Xmas Day, 1893, General Sir Wm. Elles, then in command, had given a large dinner party to which I was kindly bidden. As there were very few ladies, lots were drawn, and the honour fell to me, the youngest man there, to take Lady Elles in to dinner. She too was sadly deaf, but ever so kind. We got on well, having mutual cousins.

I had just told her that our padre that morning had preached a good sermon, but unfortunately I added the comment, 'Our padre wears brown boots!' By bad luck, there was a pause in the conversation at this point and I found myself shouting this frivolous remark to all the table!

No one was more amused than Freddy Roberts who had joined the 60th just before me and was sitting on my left. Later, he was killed and posthumously awarded the V.C. at Colenso.

Polo and Hoti Mardan.

In addition to other activities, the Polo Club was one of my responsibilities. With Francis Grenfell (later V.C. and killed at Ypres) and others, we had hopes of doing well. We went to train with the Guides at Hoti Mardan.

13/3/1904. – 'I am enjoying a perfect holiday after a strenuous spell. Our polo team is staying with the famous Guides Regiment. You have no idea what a beautiful place it is, gardens and grounds reminding one of Lake Como, honeysuckle and roses creeping from tree to tree, all at their best just now. Col. Younghusband and all Officers so good to us.

'Two perfect grass polo-grounds and many good players to help in our training.

'The paper this morning had seven columns on K. of K.'s new army reforms. I knew he would not be silent much longer. All this time he has been looking round and saying little. Now he is going to get busy. It won't be popular, but that won't hurt . . . as for the Germans they can't go on smouldering for ever.'

Training in the Muree Hills.

By May we had moved up to Gharial in the Murree Hills. Here musketry and field-training kept us busy. In training I did all I could to interest the men. With the help of models (1 yard = 1 mile), and pictures and maps, I started with talks on the Battle-honours of the Regiment.

Our system was to give each man, and each squad, individual attention, and to bring on leaders. By July we had good results – 'A fine lot of men, I like them all so much and find them more intelligent and interested now, and a better tone.'

As for my own training, I had ambitious schemes – Hindustani and Promotion Exams., Veterinary and Riding Courses, all to be fitted in with other Regimental duties.

The Plans of Mice and Men.

In October, returning with the Battalion from the Hills to Rawal Pindi, as fit as could be, with my name at the top of the list for a Mounted Infantry School, and qualified now in Hindustani, all seemed to be going well. Then came an unexpected honour. I got orders to go to Simla as one of a Board of three, appointed to report on the whole question of Mounted Infantry.

But alas, suddenly, my arm went wrong again and gave me much pain. I got up to Simla, but there, after three days, I had to give in.

Green, the surgeon, was a very good man; he removed an inch of bone and some splinters which gave me great relief. He said he hoped the cure would be permanent, but that the arm was not to be used for six months (as a matter of fact it was not till after the war, in 1919, when Sir Harold Styles operated in Edinburgh, that the arm finally ceased from troubling).

Simla.

8/12/1904. – At Simla, the season was over, but those who were left, Colonel Birdwood, his sister, Mrs. Stewart, and others, were most kind. Having been so fit, the arm made good progress. I was able to have long talks with the rest of the Board, and on 8th December moved from the hospital to the Rectory where the Rev. Mr. Warlow was my kind host, till I sailed from Bombay, on six months sick leave, in s.s. 'Sudan,' arriving home in January, 1905.

11. SCOUTS IN INDIA.

Sick Leave Home.

January–October, 1905. – This quite unexpected leave home was a welcome change during which, along with the joys of homecoming and visits to friends, I was able to pass two promotion examinations and visit the Longmoor School of Mounted Infantry.

In July I paid two more visits to Germany. At Metz I found the garrison 'still saluting hard.' By November I was back in Bareilly with a draft of 300 Riflemen, just in time for the big manoeuvres in honour of the Prince of Wales (King George V).

The Pindi Manoeuvres.

If you read glowing accounts of lessons learned, of the interest taken by all ranks, of experiments with the latest weapons, it may sound all right; but my share as a 'Mud-Major' has been to walk, walk, walk, night and day, in clouds of dust behind 10,000 men. Hot days, cold nights, short rations, one blanket. I do not complain of all that; but why? why? from start to finish, even at the great climax of the battle, was not one of us given any idea of what was going on? Under Havelock, or Sir John Moore (or 'Monty' to-day) men were encouraged to think, and it pays. But the men at Pindi were splendid, even extra cheery through it all, bless them!

The Review at the end must have been a fine sight, some 50,000 men, all in full dress, the Native Troops especially colourful. After the Review the Prince of Wales rode round, and, as our Colonel in Chief, gave us a special call. The Officers were all presented. Col. Kays, on our behalf, thanked H.R.H. for the photograph he had sent us. 'I am afraid it was not a very good one.' said the Prince. Now it certainly was not a complimentary likeness, but Col. Kays was a diplomat. 'I can assure you, Sir,' he said, 'We were all very glad to have it.' The Prince would have stayed a bit longer, but the great K. of K. politely but firmly speeded him on.

We were glad to a man to get back those 600 miles to Bareilly. To me it had seemed a bit of a Barnum's Show.

Scout Training.

1906. – The year 1906 stands out in my mind as a year of success in the training of Scouts. On arrival at Bareilly I found General Martin and Col. Kays anxious to improve the Troops in Scouting. Thus I was given a spare-time job far more to my liking than running the Officers' Mess!

In the end we brought out a system which was later adopted by Sir Ian Hamilton and Sir Wm. Pitcairn-Campbell at home, and by Sir A. Gaselee in India.

I am puzzled how to convey in these notes some idea of the wide field covered.

After preliminary lectures and training down in the plains, we moved to Rhanikhet in the hills, where, mixing with the Gurkhas we had full scope for six months.

My best plan will be to give a few extracts from my log, and then more details from the Report, which the reader can skip as he wills.

15/1/1906. Bareilly. – 'General Martin is keen about Scout training when we go up to the hills, and I have just finished a long lecture which the Colonel wants me to give to the Battalion. My pony St. Thomas jumped like a bird, leading the whole way round but just caught at the finish. I go to Dehra Doon for X-ray as cold and rain have troubled my arm. My ambition is still – The best M.I. School in India.'

4/3/1906, Dehra Doon. – 'Here for ten days X-ray and electro-cution! The Princess (Queen Mary) is here for a rest, I arrived just before her and drove through streets lined with extra-smart Gurkhas. You should see them salute! Like the Guides, the 2nd Gurkhas were with the 60th at Delhi, 1854, a fact we never forget. A lovely place and all so good to me.'

11/4/1906, Rhanikhet. – 'Just back from unveiling Nicholson Monument in Delhi. A five days plunge into heat, mosquitos and flies. I can't understand how some men prefer that Turkish bath down below. The unveiling was memorable. It set the sword quivering. I thought of his famous forced-march. He seemed to be calling "Come on!"'

10/6/1906, Kharma. – 'Here, 7,000, feet up, for a short rest after training the first sixty Scouts. I felt like a sucked orange. Wonderful views – To the North, hills and snows so clear. To the South the Turkish Bath! and here such beautiful woods, trees covered with ferns and orchids and moss-birds, butterflies, flowers., All has gone well so far, each step a new success for which very thankful. Now for a new lot with more confidence. Sixty more picked Riflemen. Scouting is a peg on which to hang other things – fitness, alertness, character.'

Gurkhas and Riflemen.

24/7/1906, Rhanikhet. – 'Second party got in yesterday after three days of desperate climbs, 3,000 feet, dense jungle, lost, and almost done, but tails right up on return. They felt they had done a 'big thing.' Colonel Rose, O.C. 3rd Gurkhas, has honoured us by asking for his Scouts to work with ours as a new experiment. You should have seen our first day. Sixty of our men, sixty 'Johnny Gurkhas' (all exactly alike and each with his own unpronounceable name). The first step was to mix them and allot patrols. We showed them the way to fall in at a given signal. Then ten minutes was given for them to have a look at each other, then we dispersed. At the 'fall in' sign, what a scene! What laughter! Then came a spell to tackle the names. That, too, was amusing. But, now each Patrol is a team with its own esprit-de-corps. They vie to be first to fall in, the quickest and quietest being best.'

15/8/1906, Company Training. – 'Just back from lecturing my Company one hour by the clock. At the start I gave them leave to fall out at half time, but none of them did. Now we are off to practise the talk. Get them keen – the rest comes.'

Challenge to My Company.

7/9/1906. – It wasn't quite fair. For weeks I had been training. My training course was across a deep nullah, some 600 feet down, and up to a hut on the opposite side. I had practised leaping down-hill like a Gurkha, hands above head, and placing my feet at best points. I used to give a small hill-boy a start, and reward him if I failed to catch him.

One morning, for our early run, I took the whole Company down to the starting point on the Tonga road. The road ran round by a hair-pin bend to the hut on the opposite side.

As umpires I sent two Sergeants (not built for speed) round by the road to the winning-post hut. Another less agile old soldier acted as starter. I took up a position well, in rear of them all. When I gave out that I would give a rupee to each man who got there before me, there was great enthusiasm, for the distance across seemed nothing.

What a hoorosh it was at the start! but I was through the whole lot like a flash and, knowing the route, arrived at the hut in 11 minutes 5 seconds. We waited some 3 or 4 minutes for the next to appear. Later, I told them how it had been done and 'Khud-racing' took on as a sport.

I will now give the gist of the Report of our Scout Training, and also the story of our Khud-race with the Gurkhas which was quite a historic event at the time.

REPORT ON SCOUT TRAINING.
Rhanikhet, April-October, 1906.

With every assistance and advantage, after six months constant work, we had established a new system and carried out the training of 120 picked Riflemen. They were trained in two parties of 60. Then came a joint course of signalling and work with the Gurkhas; but throughout the whole time small parties of our men went camping with Gurkhas, on their own, learning to shift for themselves, to try their hand at shooting game, skinning and cooking what they shot, baking bread, making rope-soles for night work, finding their way in difficult country, and seeing 'Johnny Gurkha' at work in soldiering and as a shikari in the jungle.

While the Gurkha excelled in eye for ground and tracking, in scoutcraft, cunning and language, our men were more expert in reporting, sketching, maps, compass, writing, etc. They soon got together, made friends, and did good work.

The Training.

The previous training of our men had been thorough. Our first object was to get them interested and keen. Every duty of a Scout was gone into separately with individual attention. Lectures with blackboard and models, each Scout taking notes. Next day questions were asked and answered with the help of their notes, if required, and any misunderstandings put right. There were prizes for the best notebooks. The Subject of the lecture was carried out practically on the ground. As a rule it was intelligently done.

Other Duties.

Though the first duty of a Scout is to get useful information and report it quickly and well, there were other uses for Scouts, for instance, to act as a picked mobile force.

For all these duties they had to be fit, e.g.: on one occasion, 50 Scouts raced 4 miles downhill from Rhanikhet, down 2,650 feet, to seize and defend the Durand Bridge.

We also practised covering retreats in Hill-warfare, tying up wounded men and carrying them down the steep spurs followed by yelling Afridis in costume. We were helped by Chas. Bruce, Col. Beynon, and Digby Shuttleworth who had all seen the real thing.

The Country.

The country in places was open and rocky; in others it was wooded, sometimes with pines and no undergrowth, sometimes dense jungle. The hills were steep, a climb of 1000 feet was nothing.

Night Work.

A great deal of time was devoted to nightwork, which, when made interesting, was very popular with the Scouts. We had our private signs and signals, for instance, at night to crouch down was an essential preliminary to the pass-word. White arm-bands proved useful at night, and also helped to semaphore by day. By day, a helio or flashing glass, or a blank shot, were used to let a man know when he was exposing himself. We had many ideas and grew wily.

The Monsoon.

During the Monsoon much time had to be spent indoors, with lectures, map-reading, writing reports, war-games, signs, signals, and words to help in contact with Gurkhas. But what went down best, and later spread through the Battalion, was practice in marching songs; this with the help of the bandmaster and a few good leaders.

The Value of Company Scouts,.

After training the Scouts, my turn came to put my own Company through Company Training. Each Coy. had now 4 Battalion Scouts and 8 Company Scouts, who had been through the training and earned their Scout badges.

It was then I saw the value of having 12 trained men. They were given the job of passing on all that they knew. Not only were they useful assistant instructors and leaders, but they also spread their excellent spirit. They banished all slackness and promoted good-will.

To me that was the greatest achievement of all. Imbue right ideas. Get character first and the rest will follow.

THE GURKHA KHUD-RACE.
The 60th Rifles Challenge the Gurkhas.
(See K.R.R. Regimental Chronicle, 1906, p.50.).

On 3rd April, 1906, the thirteenth annual Gurkha Brigade Khud-race took place at Rhanikhet. It was won by Dharmjit Pun in 24 minutes, 45 seconds. The whole of our Battalion turned out to see the famous event, and were duly thrilled.

The course was up a steep 1,100 feet, then 600 yards along a rising spur, another 275 feet, then down 1375 feet. It was astonishing to see how the hill-men with bare feet bounded down in leaps from stone to stone. Very soon our Riflemen were timing themselves over the course. Inter-Company races started and our times proved better than had been expected.

In those days we had a champion athlete, big 'Tim Widdrinton.' He had successfully challenged the Sergeants to an eight-a-side contest – a 20 mile race in full marching order. The Officers won and Tim's time was the best – 3 hours 42 minutes.

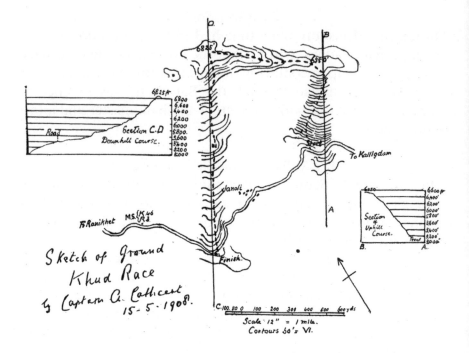

Sketch of Ground
Khud Race
by Captain A. Cathcart
15-5-1908.

Scale 12" = 1 mile.
Contours 50's VI.

Encouraged by this success he sent a challenge to all the Gurkhas in India. We would take them on over their own course, a Company team-race, 100 a side. Our friends and neighbours, the 3rd Gurkhas, were deputed to take up the gauntlet. Their rivals, the 5th Gurkhas – and Chas. Bruce – spread rumours of our wonderful feats, and chaffed them so much that, in fear of disgrace, they trained all they knew. We also trained hard.

On 27th October, four teams of 50 men ran. In the whole Gurkha turn-out of 100 men there was only 4½ minutes between their first and last man. Santbir Thapa won in 25 minutes – their last man took 29 minutes 15 seconds.

And what of our men? Our winner, Rifleman Osborne, took 28 minutes 27 seconds and close to him Rifleman Ingram but it cannot be said we finished all in one pack. 'And what about you?' I hear someone ask. Well, I led to the top, and, with many others, proved that our time going uphill compared well with that of the Gurkhas, but it is in coming downhill that the Gurkhas excel. I finished sixth in 29-40s, 25 seconds behind the last Gurkha.

To us it was no surprise that the Gurkhas had proved far ahead

The author after his release from Boer captivity.

Sergeant George Ross, commended for the DCM, who served with Crum in the action involving Kitchener's train during the South African War.

The 'cockpit' at Bakenlaagte.

Sergeant George Rowat, DCM, MVO, on 'Tommy': 'the very best Rifleman I ever knew'.

Corporal Jarvis, Rifleman Deasy, Rifleman Goodwin and Rifleman Leonard:
all served throughout the South African War.

Frederick Maurice Crum at polo, Malta 1902–3.

The 1/60th Rifles Bicycle Club in Malta, established by Crum in 1903.

British and Gurkha scouts training together at Rhaniket, 1906.

British and Native scouts in the Plains, 1908.

Mounted Infantry School, Fatehgarh, 1908.

Scouts at Auchenbowie, 1911.

Scouts at Windsor on
St George's Day, 1909.

Auchenbowie Scouts, 1909.

Dear Sir,

I have now spent one month lecturing, visiting, and investigating the

BOY SCOUT MOVEMENT IN GLASGOW.

I see, very clearly that if this movement were better understood, it would receive far greater support, and would at once go forward.

At present only the advance guard of the Boy Scout spirit has reached Glasgow. A small and capable body of men are working hard, giving up their spare time for some 2000 boys. Give them more support and encouragement, help them to find new workers, and you will see a wonderful change for the better.

All over the Empire, thousands of boys, of all classes and creeds, are learning as Scouts to love their Country and put their duty before themselves. This spirit is spreading to others beyond the boys themselves. In every direction those who have seen the good results become enthusiastic supporters.

The movement is not in any way opposed to the Boys' Brigade. It appeals to boys in a different kind of way. There is more than room for both these movements in Glasgow, and our earnest wish is to co-operate with all.

I have sent a full report to the Committee, with suggestions. The chief of these are:—

A CENTRAL OFFICE. A PERMANENT SECRETARY.
PATRONS FOR ALL TROOPS IN THE POORER PARTS OF THE CITY.
A COMMITTEE OF LADIES.
MORE GENTLEMEN TO HELP AS SECRETARIES AND TREASURERS.
CIRCULATION OF LITERATURE TO EXPLAIN THE MOVEMENT.

With an unbounded faith in the cause we have at heart, I feel convinced that any citizen of Glasgow who comes forward to help this movement now, will be astonished, as have been hundreds of others, at the good results obtainable. Personal interest is what we need, I earnestly, and with confidence, invite a full and business-like enquiry.

Information as to the movement may be had from the Hon. Secretary, Mr. K. B. WRIGHT, 8 Alfred Terrace, Glasgow.

I am, yours faithfully,

F. M. CRUM,

Stirling, 19th March, 1912.   Scottish Head-Quarters Commissioner.

Glasgow Boy Scout
propaganda leaflet, 1912.

Scout fire brigade display

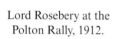

Lord Rosebery at the Polton Rally, 1912.

The visit of King George V to Stirling on 11 July 1914.

on their own hillside. On Cumberland Fells they had beaten Cumberland men. They had also defeated Swiss Guides on the Alps. We enjoyed the whole contest. We suggested to them we should run it again, all of us in ammunition boots; they said – Yes, if you too will run it again in bare feet! At least we had proved that Col. Sir T. H. Holdich was wrong when he said we should be as southdown sheep racing with ibex. Moreover, this started a great advance in the prowess of British Troops in hill-climbing.

The Staff College.

After this happy and successful summer my luck seemed to change. Up till then my mind had been full of plans for Veterinary and Riding Courses to fit myself for a M.I. School, but in the meanwhile a new Staff College had been established in India, and with it there came a new decree.

The only road to my goal now lay through this Staff College. Here then was I, with only six months left, and with only moderate brains, completely ignorant of Algebra and Euclid and other forgotten and detested subjects. Could I hope to get even the half-marks required. It seemed a tough proposition. However, as Col. Kays encouraged me, and kindly arranged leave for me to go home to a 'crammer,' I set my teeth and decided to ride at this very grim fence.

The examination was to be in London, but later there came another frustration when the venue was shifted to India, Aden being the nearest point. It was a hectic business; a few entries may give some idea.

10/11/1906, Austrian Lloyd s.s. 'Imperator,' Red Sea. – 'The feeding is good but I can't tackle pastry for breakfast. The Austrian Consul helps me with sums. An industrious German works all day in the Saloon, so do I – but not all day. At Aden he emerged for a view of the "Barren Rocks." "Some day," he told us, "The German flag will fly over Aden".'

22/11/1906, London. – 'Went over the course with the Crammer. What a lot to work up and how little I know. If I could borrow the brains of my twin, even so, a tough proposition!'

12/12/1906, Auchenbowie. – '6½ hours work. Old dominie

129

Mackenzie in Stirling makes algebra a bit clearer than the good 'Friar Tuck' did at Eton, but, may be, I give more attention.'

Cramming at Home.

6/1/1907, Headly Bordon. – 'On General Sir Wm. Pitcairn Campbell's Staff for a month to qualify. Arrived in dark. Looked out with interest next morning. Sun out, lovely village, ivy-covered Church, green fields look well after India. Fed the birds, but puppy clears the board and wags his tail.'

13/1/1907 – 'Head "on strike" again. It is trying to look at the clock and do nothing, surrounded by books shouting at me to read them. Even with work, a close thing; however, self-pity won't help. I will stop. The clock may tick on. Even if not intended to go on with soldiering at all, well, I am content.'

21/1/1907, Bordon. – 'Simla wires that examination must be held in India, not London. This means Aden, 12th March. Long talk with Gen. Campbell who gave me certificate. No better friend to me ever than 'Johnnie Campbell.' The Kaiser is shouting 'Deutchland Uber Alles!' He will ride down all that gets in his all-highest way! Seeing many old friends in London. I find I work better away from the crammers, but how I do hate it all!'

3/3/1907, m.m. 'Ville de Ciotat' from Marseilles to Aden.'A huge strange trunk, in my cabin, studded with brass nails and labelled – 'Major E. P. Eastwick.' His hats and coats on both bunks and on every available peg. I was in the act of rearranging boundaries when owner appears and dispels my surprise at his trunk and his cheek.

'Say, my name's Eastwick, E. P. Eastwick, what's yours?' Later we became great friends and, along with a young Dutch Count, bound for Borneo, we formed a happy trio. We had our own small jokes, mostly at the expense of 'M. le Colonel' bound for Cochin-China, covered with medals, who parades on deck with spurs and is said to sleep in uniform!

'His obsession is Prussians – so is mine. We become good friends and my French improves. Have worked pretty hard all the way.'

Examination at Aden.

12/3/1907, Aden. – 'On arrival, someone lets out I am the most unpopular man in Aden. For nine days, one Colonel and two Majors have been detailed to see I don't crib in the examination. However, I find them friendly. Examination starts well; Moltke himself could not have done better in tactics! In Law, Military History, Geography, Topography, Administration and even Euclid – not too bad, but by now my poor head is buzzing. Finally comes French in which the old Colonel's good wishes uphold me. That ended my trials. It had been a big strain and I was glad of a day off – catching sharks. A big farewell dinner and all parted friends. I do not know how the examination has gone; having done all I could, I won't worry.'

So much for that horrible examination. After three weeks suspense, I heard I had failed; but a happy month at home in Scotland soon put me right.

Jubbulpore – My First Indian Hot Weather.

On 13th June I sailed from Marseilles again, and having sampled the Red Sea at its worst rejoined the Battalion at Jubbulpore.

It might have been thought that with so much travel one would grow more accustomed to change. But in my case I found that while each parting from home grew more of a wrench, the process of settling down on return seemed more of an effort. Certainly from the moors of Scotland in May, to the plains of India in July, is a bit of a trial. I think the cure lies in one's work; once the interest grows, then surroundings come second.

5/7/1907, Jubbulpore. 'I never felt more limp and useless. This week is said to be the worst so far. After morning duties, we lie doggo through the heat of the day in the darkened bungalow. Pouring with sweat, I read the same page four times and am none the wiser. Myriads of strange insects buzz round the lamp. At 4 p.m. I turn out and face the oven outside. The men look washed-out, but on the whole are well.

'My duties include the Canteen and Institutes. There has been a problem of "glorious beer." The Brewery has a contract, many complaints! Am becoming an expert in beer; hope to get prices down, quality up, and Troops kept smiling again. There are also accounts, and you would smile to see me auditing accounts like a qualified Chartered Accountant. There are times when one feels stupid, useless, unenterprising, with a kind of nausea for soldiering in India, but I never miss Muffler's exercises though dripping at every pore; that, and something to do, will see me through.'

Thoughts on Soldiering.

15/8/1907. – 'I like the Sunday Evening Services: they remind me of the telegraph poles as you speed along in a train. At times the wires seem to be running down and down, then comes a pole to steady the wires. Look next time you are in a train and think of it that way. Tonight I regret to report the padre made little impression, as I sat dripping in thinnest clothes, at 6.30 p.m., the natives pulling the punkahs overhead; but I begin to get more acclimatised, more interest in life. I suppose we all want to be of some use in life. Take this soldiering profession. It is up to us to work hard and turn out efficient soldiers and good men. Often at home when I have found them begging in the streets, I have asked myself – would it not be better service to work in the streets? The great thing is to get keenness and character first, but the difficulty is that in peace it is all so imaginary. When war comes it grows more real. We have to see the real thing and make the need clear.'

18/8/1907. – 'Rain, and very much cooler. I begin to see light through this tunnel. That Staff College red herring upset things. As polo is barred I have bought a good steeplechase Arab, "Cinque Ports," and entered for October races. It will wake me up to do something more active than books and beer and golf. What does Bacon say about books and the cavalry spirit? "And generally all warlike people are a little idle; and love danger rather than travaille; neither must they be too much broken of it, if they shall be preserved with vigour."'

'We have our men out early, running and skirmishing in lightest attire. Today a lecture to 200 Riflemen – thrilling accounts of Japs in recent fighting, plenty of "Banzai!" and dash and patriotism. It made them keen when we practised. General Kitson (mostly known as "Kitty") caught me stripped at my Muller's exercises. He wants me to act as his Staff Officer. I protest that the duties of 2nd in Command, and of putting my Company through musketry, and of writing a book on "Mounted Infantry" leave no time – but must do what I can.'

Geoffrey Cookson.

25/8/1907. – 'Sad days for the 60th Rifles. We have lost our beloved "Cooky." The whole Battalion is sad and subdued today. He had worked very hard as Adjutant all through the hot weather, and was much run-down. He was just due for leave home. Last Tuesday I was on my way to see some of my men in hospital when he asked for a lift.

'"Maurice," he said, "I have got the plague!" I thought he was joking. We lost him next morning. No pain, everything possible was done, good nurses and doctor. There is no one we could miss more. The doctors advise getting the Troops out, and interested in sports, football, hockey, gardens, etc. So far the plague had been confined to natives.'

Col. Kays goes home.

15/10/1907. – 'Just back from the Railway Station. Everyone there to see the Colonel off. Band and Buglers playing "Georgia," sound doubled in station. As the train, by arrangement, draws very slowly out, the Buglers sound the Regimental Call; the Band plays "Auld Lang Syne!" fog signals and an ovation of cheering. A good Colonel to copy. He leaves a splendid Battalion.'

In Command of Battalion.

'On 15th October the official cold weather begins in India. All Officers are back from leave and a general stir of drills, manoeuvres and inspections takes place. In addition to this the "Jubbulpore Week" with its polo, races, and dances is due, to say nothing of training for the "Kitchener Test." It was at this time that providence detailed me to take over command of the Battalion for three weeks.'

Talana Day.

20/10/1907. – 'So far all has gone well. Two Generals' Inspections. It is an ordeal, your first morning, to ride up to the "Orderly Room" and make your debut as C.O. To be received with all the ceremony due. To find yourself "in the Chair" dispensing justice, then dealing with all the correspondence and business affairs. Then interviews. 50 old soldiers off home, 50 young Riflemen just arrived, and so on.'

30/10/1907. – 'Practice for "Kitchener Test" goes well. An early start. Took whole Battalion out three miles. Breakfast out and started an inter-Company Competition in skirmishing. Each Coy. now has distinctive flags and colours. Spectators watch and comment on each other's doings. A prize to the winners and all home by 11 a.m. The Sergeant-Major pleased with the novelty and asks for more.

'The "Jubbulpore Week" has come and gone. "Cinque Ports" did well. We have started building a Band Stand and Gardens in Barracks.'

2/11/1907. – 'Very little "crime" and all goes well. Practice night work for "Kitchener Test." After a lecture to Officers and N.C.O's., we rehearsed the Scheme in daylight 3.30 p.m. to 7.30 p.m. Then at night, a realistic event with bombs, flashes, etc. Men played up well.'

11/11/07. – 'Second lecture for "Kitchener Test." Got whole Battalion, Band and Buglers into Regimental Theatre. Talk on details of marching, famous forced marches, etc. Band and Buglers play "Georgia." Scouts lead chorus. A splendid show. Encouraged by enthusiasm of my batman!

'Handing over command to my great friend Wm. Barnett, glad of a rest and week-end visit to the "Marble-Rocks" with him and his "Laura" both just out from home.'

The Wearing of 'Shorts.'

20/11/1907, Jubbulpore. – 'The inspection by General Sir Archibald Hunter was a triumph. We had always wanted to wear "shorts" in the plains, as we did in the hills, but General Kitson was horrified at the very idea. "What would Lord Kitchener say?" However he had agreed to submit the matter to Sir Archibald Hunter at the coming inspection. The Battalion paraded in shorts and never looked better. Sir Archie Hunter thought it a grand idea. That settled the question of shorts in India.'

Gardens and Bandstand.

10/12/1907. – 'The garden and band stand* make good progress – soil, manure, flowers shrubs, pots and tubs – hustling the leisurely natives – Riflemen in relays on paths, a hundred men at a time. The gardens are in the shape of our Regimental Maltese Cross.

'The grass lawns spring up in ten days with the Lipo system. Some 20 native women sit on their hunkers and chatter and chop "doup grass." Then, mixing it with cow-dung, they smear it over the dry barrack square with their hands. The "Behistis" then water it well every day and you have a green lawn in no time! By the end of the year it was good to see the gardens doing well with roses, phlox, corryopsis, daisies, ferns and shrubs (where before had been bare waste ground) and crowds all round enjoying the Band.'

The 'Kitchener Test.'

12/12/1907. – 'We have just finished our "Kitchener Test." Three very hard nights and days. I never saw men work better. You should have seen them marching and heard them singing on return to Barracks. The General told them he had never seen a keener lot of men. And everyone said the same.

'On return from leave with my cousin Stewart at "Ooty," my time with the 2nd/60th came to an end, after a final experiment of training Scouts of British and Native Troops in the Plains.'

REPORT ON SCOUT TRAINING IN THE PLAINS.
BRITISH AND NATIVE TROOPS.

Experiment with British and Native Scouts, February, 1908.

Under General Kitson at Jubbulpore much had been done to promote good relations by bringing the Buglers, Signallers, Bands, and Gymnastic Staffs of all the regiments together.

In February, 1908, we went a step further and carried out an experiment of training our Scouts with Native Infantry Scouts in

* In February, 1945, I received a photograph of the Bandstand and Gardens looking splendid, together with word from the local Scoutmaster that they were caring for Geoffrey Cookson's grave.

the Plains, on the same lines as we had worked with Gurkhas in the Hills. On this course we had 48 picked Riflemen, 28 of the 33rd Punjabis, and 16 of the 1st Brahmins, each with one Officer.

The first step, before bringing them together, was to explain each other's customs and prejudices, and to dwell on their many good points. Our Riflemen were told of the native regimental records of courage, loyalty and discipline. The prejudices of Sikhs, Pathans, Punjabis and Brahmins were explained. The British troops were also reminded that these native scouts were picked men who knew a good man, when they met one.

Preliminary Training.

During the preliminary training in Barracks they came together and were allotted in patrols of five. Two Riflemen, two natives, and one Rifleman as leader. Two days were spent in learning the system. Each step was explained in two languages. It was then demonstrated by trained men, and carried out well. During the intervals the Punjabis were keener on football, the Brahmins would crowd round the new rifle, or exchange lessons in language. In each patrol the men were set to learn each other's names and a few useful words such as 'left' and 'right', etc. This helped to break the ice. It was important that our men should learn not to shout 'Boy!' to high-caste Brahmins, independent Pathans, and lordly Sikhs.

The first few days in Barracks did good; all quickly made friends, but it was when these patrols found themselves isolated and working separated over 40 miles of unknown country that we saw the full value of this Scout training.

Native Prejudices.

No doubt there were often mistakes. The Sikh may have loathed the Rifleman's 'Woodbines.' The Brahmin may have been offended at some well-meant offer of sharing rations. Trouble about water or shadows may have puzzled our men. They would chaffingly reply by marking out their own water bottles and canteens and declaring them sacred. Such incidents seemed rather to increase than mar their good-humour and friendship.

The Language Difficulty.

It is well known that the British Soldier has an 'Esperanto' of his own which gets him what he wants in any land. In addition to this, both sides knew their mutual job and it was surprising how well they got on. But in the matter of taking pains to learn, our men were outclassed.

The Sepoy would walk about repeating such sentences as – 'Get away out of it!' and seize every opportunity of practising it on the villagers. It was also a fault of our men that they would leave the trouble of finding the way to the Sepoy, not bothering to learn how to distinguish the many village tracks or find the way for themselves.

Certainly our men returned not only greatly improved as Scouts, but also with a much enhanced opinion of both Brahmins and Punjabis. Especially did they appreciate the Sepoy, when acting as a kind of Shikari, after a long day's trudge, and after finding his way with ease to some remote, unknown village, the Sepoy would summon the villagers to bring 'charpoys' (beds), eggs, milk, and 'chupatties' for the 'Sahib.' Then, while the Rifleman rested, his comrade would insist on keeping watch himself!

Results.

After our preliminary training, we had moved to a camp 25 miles by train and 10 miles out into jungle country. Then after three days training we finally carried out a rather ambitious scheme. With our 90 men we watched more than 30 miles of country, for 48 hours, and challenged a Patrol of 6th Cavalry to get through our line.

Extracts from Diary, Jubbulpore.

2/2/1908. – 'Start new experiment, "Kitty" very keen and helpful. Talk to Scouts on Native ways, mutual respect, Indian unrest, good-will, etc.'

5/2/1908. – 'First mixed parade a success. What a joy to be back with our Scouts. Being old hands, they act as Instructors.'

8/2/1908. – 'My Regimental Birthday. Offered M.I. at Fatehgarh, February 27th. Accepted.'

12/2/1908. – 'A lot to do arranging rations, trains, carts, doctor, scheme, etc. Sad at idea of leaving splendid Battalion, and yet happy and contented.'

A Happy Camp.

17/2/1908. – 'Full moon. Moved a party of 95 to Mujhan. Such a happy camp: football, bathing, camp fire. All seem to have their own jokes.'

18/2/1908. – 'Three separate parties. Reconnaissance. British Soldiers are unknown in these parts. In each village the Sepoy looks after his Rifleman pal and all have a good time.'

19/2/1908. – 'A Tactical Scheme over a wide front. I put a price on my own head and rode miles – was cunningly caught by a wily, exultant havildar.'

21/2/1908. – 'Great Treasure Hunt begins 6.30 a.m. to last 48hrs. Umpires rode many miles day and night. Scheme went well. One Patrol claimed to have held up Lieut. Abbay and his ten Sowars.'

23/2/1908. – 'Sunday, 4.40 p.m. Train back to "Jub." all in great spirits.'

24/2/1908. – 'Settled up and final good-byes. G.O.C. most kind and good wishes. 8.30 p.m. slipped off, avoiding all fuss.'

12. – M.I. SCHOOL AT FATEHGARH.

The Mounted Infantry School.

At Fatehgarh, a small cantonment on the Ganges, some 80 miles N.W. of Cawnpore, there was one of the only three M.I. Schools in India. It was commanded by Major H. O. Parr, a first-rate Indian Army Officer who had still six months left in command, after which I was to take over. This suited me well as it would give me time to look round and especially to learn all I could from him as a Leader of Native Troops.

On arrival in February, I found the last British Course in progress, 5 Officers and 180 'Jocks' of the Gordon Highlanders, practising 'Haute école' and learning to groom and feed some 200 ponies. The Staff included the keen Sergeant-Major Hilliar (R.B.), a Farrier Sergeant, a Q.M./Sergeant, and some native cavalry assistants and syces. All was running smoothly and well.

Cantonment Magistrate.

To me it seemed splendid. Now at last I could give my whole mind to the job on which for so long I had set my heart. But it came as a bit of a shock when I heard that my duties also included those labelled P.M.C., S.S.O. and C.M. Mess President, Institutes, and Station Staff Officer – these were all right, but what did Cantonment Magistrate entail. I had only a vague idea – was it not some Indian Civil Service appointment calling for brains, languages, gifts of administration, and leading to K.C.I.E.s and K.C.S.I.s?

In the end I found that there were 4 villages and 1,000 acres. As Magistrate it was up to me to administer justice and deal with the squabbles of 3,000 natives. There were home farms and fruit farms. There were questions of sanitation, and milk and water supplies.

There were rates at R. 8000 a year to collect. To help me in all this there was a Staff of 40 Babus, Police, Collectors and others. It seemed a tall order.

However, for six weeks, in the hands of an excellent Babu, I did what I could and kept smiling. Then Heaven came to my rescue, sending the excellent Hobbs, an Indian Army Captain, who jumped at the job. With his Regiment at Hong Kong, he arrived with only 6 Sepoys, a wife, and little Geoffrey to look after. Just the man for the job, so all was well. With Parr I soon picked up a great deal that was new or had been forgotten. A few notes from my log may give some idea:–

Dispensing Justice.

Fatehgarh, 12/4/1908. – 'After "Stables" I ride up to the Office. Crowds of natives rise and salaam to the ground. Two men rush to raise the curtain and admit the Cantonment Magistrate. The Babu salaams and explains the business on hand. Two women are brought in and have a lot to say; one is accused of stealing the other's nose-ring. All the witnesses too have a lot to say. A Native Pleader appears in barrister's gown. (Why no wig?) The Babu interprets. I clear the Court. He tells me all are not speaking the truth; the whole truth, and nothing but the truth – which I quite believe! He produces a large book, not unlike our own Military Law (a book I always disliked). I take his advice which seems good, and hope for the best.

'Next day, glad to be quit of the job, again I ride up to the Office. All the natives are waiting, but not for me. Not one of them stirs, for Hobbs is now on the throne.

'My bungalow is lovely. It has a grass lawn sloping down some 200 yards to the Ganges. There are roses and hollyhocks, but the grass begins to get brown, and two bullocks, working all day at the creaking well, can hardly compete with the thirst of the garden. We have built a diving board and have lovely swims in the early mornings.'

16/4/1908. – 'The official hot weather has begun and some 200 Sepoys start a new course. We shall see what Parr can make of them in four months. A farewell dinner to the Gay Gordons. The ladies kindly helped the Mess President and all went well. I do a bit of practice in grooming and shoeing myself. After six weeks' solid work we had a grand day pig-sticking.'

19/4/1908. – 'Native course is interesting. Instead of Hilliar we have a splendid Jamadar, Dost Mahomed of the 18th Bengal Lancers. He has served as Orderly to both 'Bobs' and 'K. of K.'

'We have stopped our bathing in the Ganges. A mugger (crocodile) seized the Commissioner's gardener next door.

'The visiting Padre asks me to take Services when he is away. Dost Mahomed encourages me. He tells me he also reads the Koran to his men, but the big Pathan Fateh Khan, though a fine horseman, does not attend.'

30/4/1908. – 'A little progress each day. I wish I could talk the language better. Each day the Moonshi says I improve but Dost Mahomed is sad because I cannot converse as Officers do. The men are so keen and pleased even with a look of approval, but to teach, one needs more than a look.'

Here is an example of what these men will do for their Officers:

A plucky Havildar

'In one of our lines of tethered ponies – all of them are greys – one of them, "No. 22" is a noted "badmash" (rascal). He is always tethered securely and wears a leather muzzle to prevent him biting. We had recently shifted our lines from under the trees to inside the old Fort, and, by some mistake, "No. 22" was not tethered tight enough and wore no muzzle. As I walked down the line of greys with Dost Mahomed and a Havildar, suddenly there was a squeal and I saw "No. 22" with ears back, making straight for me. But as I drew back, the Havildar had thrown himself between us and he himself was seized by the arm-pit. In great pain he called out, while still being savaged, "Sahib, I am glad the badmash did not get you."'

Pig-sticking.

At this season our chief recreation was pig-sticking. The Ganges by now was in flood and looked more like a vast lake than a river. We used to cross in large native barges to the open country beyond – horses, syces, beaters and all – and many a good gallop we had.

In the course of one of these I found myself swimming a branch

141

of the sacred river. When I was in full pursuit, suddenly the pig jinked in the scrub, and vanished just below me. The next thing I knew was that my gallant old war-horse, trained to the cavalry charge, had leaped into space, and I found myself plunged into a branch of the Ganges, some 15 feet below a steep bank. As we swam together towards a sand bank some distance on, I held on to the stirrup with one hand, holding the spear in the other. We were doing well when the safety stirrup and leather became detached from the saddle. I reached dry land alone, stirrup in hand, but no horse and no spear. The pig looked on from the opposite bank! When the rest came up all ended well.

In May I had the bad luck to fall on my bad shoulder. The Doctor was one of our party and got me home with difficulty, but I was able to carry on till June when my six weeks' leave to the Hills was due.

Leave to the Hills.

'It is good to be back to the cool of the Hills, like a trip to Heaven, after the plains. Health, brain, spirits all improve, and yet the work "down below" had been a great interest. Visits to Almora Gurkhas, where Howard-Bury has 50 of our Scouts in camp. Never saw a fitter, cheerier lot of men. They have built a large hut without nails, using bark for cords. They were felling a tree; with each blow of the axe, the axeman was encouraged by snatches of song –

> 'The old way of fighting (Wump!)
> was shoulder to shoulder (Wump!)' etc.

At night there were sing-songs in the woods and moonlight – a great time they were having.'

16/7/1908, Fatehgarh. – "What is wrong, Jamadar Sahib?' I asked, as Dost Mahomed came up to me looking ill-at-ease. He shows me a telegram:– 'Do you want to go to Teheran in command of the Body-Guard there?' 'Well,' I say, 'of course you must do what you want. It is an honour.' But still he looks puzzled and sad. 'Sahib,' he says, 'If they say "go," I will go, and if they say, "stay," I will stay. I do not know what is wanted.' It is a case of

"Jo hookum" (whatever the order). His code is to do as he is bidden.'

20/7/1908, Fatehgarh. – 'School going well. Parr away on leave. Busy with jumping, field days and sports, and writing my book on *'Mounted Riflemen.' With French and Haig at the head of affairs it seems to be 'tabu' to say that the sword and lance can no longer face the Rifleman. Two welcome visitors, Bernard Paget and Wm. Barnett, so interested and helping with Sports. Arm X-rayed again and still tied up to ride. Ugly rumours that all M.I. Schools are to be abolished.'

10/9/1908. – 'Orders received to report on Fatehgarh as a possible Cavalry School! A lot of fever now and syces go down like nine-pins, or walk about like corpses with blankets over their heads.'

Closing of Fatehgarh School.

17/9/1908. – 'Rejoice with me! The thermometer is down to 80°. A lovely fresh feeling. Quite a change in the air. The cold weather is on its way. But, sigh with me! Alas, after long suspense, our School is doomed. A wire from Simla says so. There seems to be some fate against my plans; each time some new frustration, and yet, I never felt more confidence than now.'

24/9/1908, Dehra Doon. – 'Here once more for X-rays. It seems my trouble is not due to the boar, but to the Boers! Also I am here in a last forlorn hope of saving M.I. School. The great Lord Kitchener is here and with him Colonel Birdwood and two of K.'s A.D.Cs., also good friends.'

---

* 'The Question of Mounted Infantry' by 'Rifleman.' Hugh Rees, Ltd., 47 Pall Mall, London, S.W.

'Tell Major Crum what a valuable book it is . . . He has written so well and convincingly.' Lord Roberts, Xmas, 1909.

'The time will come when the views held by "Rifleman"' will again prevail, but at present the advocates of shock tactics, and subordinates, find it politic to keep such progressive views very much to themselves.' Gen. Sir Ian Hamilton. 5/11/1909.

'I think it is splendid . . . French appears to be the great stumbling block.' Sir A. Conan Doyle.

'Do not be discouraged . . . the cause must triumph in the end.' Gen. Sir E. Hutton 12/12/1909

Colonel Birdwood.

The Gurkhas all drawn up, full dress and glittering medals. Long talk with Birdwood ('Birdie' to all the Army in those days; to-day, Field Marshal Lord Birdwood) kindness itself as always but no information! That is what he is there for – to keep us nuisances out of the great Chief's way. This he does wonderfully well. So interested and full of sympathy about the School, the arm, about the 60th, calling me "Maurice" all the time. Then on to the next man, Subaltern or General, or Gurkha veteran, so nice to each in turn and all sincere and genuine.

8/10/1908, Fatehgarh. – 'Winding up the School, what next? General Nixon, Inspector of Cavalry, invites me to attend the Cavalry manoeuvres. Twenty more pages of my book on "Mounted Riflemen".'

20/10/1908 (Talana Day). – 'Offered M.I. School at Poona. Colonel Rowlandson, whom I am to follow, sends a generous welcome.'

6/11/1908, Fatehgarh. – 'My last day. Was it symbolic? This morning my buck-jumping whaler kicked me clean out of the saddle, up in the air and down on "os coccyx." Painful, but otherwise splendidly fit and keen to take over at Poona. The new Battalion, Xth Gurkhas, now in possession, gave me a kind send-off at their first Mess dinner. My name has been sent in for Brevet Lieut.-Colonel.'

But once again, when prospects seemed so bright, Fate intervened! Arrived at Poona, suddenly I felt I could not carry on. I did not know it at the time but it was a case of overwork, which in the end took not 'six months sick leave' but six times that to set me right.

13. – THREE YEARS ON THE SHELF

A Long Illness.

At this stage of my story I have felt inclined to skip two or three years and pass on to the pioneer days of the Boy Scout Movement in Scotland; and yet to do this would be to omit part of my training for days yet to come.

For a whole year the command of that Mounted Infantry School was kept open for me with extensions of leave, three months at a time. The suspense, and the wish to get well in time, only upset me more. At the end of the year the Doctors were quite decided – it would take at least one year more and, even then, India was out of the question.

Peace of Mind.

If, from the first, they had said – 'You will not be fit for two years, you must banish all thoughts of M.I.' – it might have come quicker. I do not know. What I needed in those days was 'peace of mind.'

If some Prophet could have shown me then that *all* mounted men, whether Lancers, Dragoons, Hussars, or the poor old M.I., would soon be replaced by others who rode jeeps and tanks and armoured cars, to say nothing of those who were dropped from the skies – if only I had known that the Kaiser (to say nothing of Hitler) would in the end be utterly routed, that my role in the next war would be with Snipers and Scouts (nothing whatever to do with M.I.), and, above all, had I been sure that at the end of it all, the Union Jack would be flying more bravely than ever – had I known all this, then 'peace of mind,' my great need at the time, might well have come sooner.

As it was, in the end, it took three years before the cure was complete. It may be that trials of body and mind and spirit are part of God's plan to bring us in sight of that 'peace of mind' which follows on doing His will.

Certainly Faith is the secret of courage and hope!

A few extracts from my log may help to keep up the trend of this part of my story:–

15/1/1909, London. – 'I do not sleep, all thinking means headaches. My arm and back give trouble. Friends say I look well. I try to feel well, but my face seems a mask behind which every thought seems to lead to depression. I try to shake it off and go about and do things – motoring lessons in London traffic to wake myself up. I have got my book printed and circulated privately; but all these efforts only make me worse.'

March, 1909. – 'Nursing home for rest-cure, two months, but worries about extensions of leave.'

24/5/1909, North Berwick. – 'Slept from 10.30 p.m. to 5.30 a.m., the best for a very long time, feeling better each day. Tracking on sands, not up to golf yet. Baden-Powell's new book, "Scouting for Boys," seems a great idea. Would like to help. Parr wires me not to resign. Poona kept open . . . . As to the Kaiser, we can't help coming to blows within four years.'

3/6/1909. – 'Bathing and fishing at Bass Rock, but the idea of India hangs over me like a cloud. Speeches by Haldane and 'Bobs' on universal service.'

But these ups and downs were to last a long time yet and every small effort was followed by troubles of head and back and sleep.

Meanwhile, as an onlooker, there were sights at home which troubled me. At the Golf Club in Stirling, for instance, that ugly rush of ragged, gambling, boy caddies, or the neighbouring pit-boys, or the slums and poverty in London and Glasgow. How was it that no one seemed to notice or care for these things? I was not yet in touch with good work being done.

Then followed months of massage and osteopaths helping me out of my troubles. These seemed to be slowly passing in ever-diminishing cycles. All the time I was learning more of conditions at home, and finding myself more able to help.

The Church Army – January, 1910.

In January, 1910, I made friends with Prebendary Carlile and saw much of the Church Army and Salvation Army work in London. I had to go slow, for the sights I saw and the work being done were no part of a rest-cure. In the good Carlile I found a true friend and one who understood, for he too had had a break-down from overwork.

A Night with Carlile on the Embankment.

20/1/1910, London. – 'At 9 p.m. we met at the "bottom rung of the ladder," a tumble-down tent with a hundred or more men chopping wood. We sampled their supper and after a word here and there, started off for the Embankment. Here we found long queues of men assembled by Church Army workers. The problem was to sort out the men willing to work, from the "artful dodgers." The system was, after an interview, to give tickets to admit suitable men to the "All-night Shelter."'

With a Church Army man I pottered round making contacts. He sees a man with a collar. This, he says, is a hopeful sign. We talk with him under the railway arch. Once a Hussar, he now wishes he had never left the Army. Things had gone wrong till at last he found himself offering to carry bags at the Railway Stations. People had looked at him as if to say – 'That's no man to be carrying bags.' He look down at himself and says, 'Now I have come to this, when I am not ashamed even to fight for carrying a bag.' Whatever his story, willing to work or not, here is a typical case. We give him a word of encouragement and a ticket.

By 11 p.m. we assemble at the 'All-night Shelter' close to the Abbey. Here men are allowed to sit up all night, but not to lie down, for they would then come under boarding-house rules. This seems hard, but at least it is shelter and the nights are stormy and cold.

Here we find 130 men, among them our Hussar. They sit on forms with backs, each man his bowl of soup and chunk of bread, a distressing collection. Many look sad and down; some seem to make friends and talk. Some look young, hopeful and able to work if given a chance. Others look listless and old for their years. Here is a man so well-dressed that they had hesitated to offer him a ticket and there is a boy of 16 just up from the country. There are men of all sorts, some like beasts with matted hair, some cropped like convicts. Their dress also varies. You see a fellow in a tattered black coat and pot-hat next to one in dungarees.

For half-an-hour they sit and eat. Then old Carlile says a word. 'Gentlemen, –' he starts. A few interrupt and some laugh, but at once they are stopped by the others. As the fine old veteran explains the system of work at Trade-union rates, with hope of promotion, some sit sullen, one is pointedly reading a paper, another is snoring, but mostly they seem to listen. A few look more hopeful.

Did Carlile preach to them? No! When we, just two or three, had started off on our mission together, as we left, he had said a short prayer which impressed me, just a simple request, as though made to a friend, and so sincere, that we might be able to help some poor fellows that night.

Meanwhile the question for me began to arise – Should I go on with soldiering or take up some social work? I felt quite in the dark and yet quite sure that when the time came guidance would come. For all that year I kept in touch with three different worlds – With my Regiment, with the Boy Scouts, and with Social work.

Baden-Powell.

On November, 3rd, 1910, I had my first talk with Baden-Powell. He showed me a letter just received from Scotland. A certain Scoutmaster had written complaining that Scotland had no patriotism! It seemed that this warrior, at the head of his boys, with blaring bugles and beat of drums, had marched his commando past some Church while the service was on. 'What did you do?' I asked 'B.P.' 'I told him not to be a silly ass,' said the Chief, and he added, 'I just look ten years ahead. That's what we have got to do.'

Leaving the Scouts, I used to pay visits to our Home Battalions and Depot, where there were many old friends to cheer me up, or there were Point-to-Point Races, or Regimental, or Veterans' Dinners. Next day, perhaps, I might find myself doing some small job for the Church Army, and always after each effort, I see in my log some comment on good or bad behaviour of head, or back, or sleep.

By August, 1911, I find more cheerful entries:–

11/8/1911, Auchenbowie. – 'Climbed Ben Ledi with. J.G.S. and A.McN. and none the worse. Good progress with Scouts.'

25/8/1911, Boat of Garten. – 'Climbed Cairngorm twice in three days, felt grand. Offered Cadet appointment in London, but the question now is – 'Soldiering or Scouts?' As in the past I shall be guided.'

Religious Influences.

I have said nothing so far of the influences which helped me most throughout these troubles.

In these notes I have left out all mention of father and mother and family life. Of course it is in the home that our course in life is first guided.

Nor do I forget those evening services in India, with padres like Warlow at Murree or Palmer at Jubbulpore, which, as I have said, were as telegraph-poles upholding the wires.

It will also be understood that I did not visit Prebendary Carlile and diffidently abstain from all talk of religion and prayer.

During one of our tête-à-tête talks in his vestry he spoke of his own breakdown from overwork. At that time, he said, his doctors had even told him to put his Bible aside for a bit. 'I know your trouble,' he said, 'God at one time put me on my back that I might look up and see Him better. You too are a Soldier of Christ.' With him it seemed quite natural just plain common sense to speak like that. He was a great leader.

But it was at St. Andrews I always seemed to find help.

9/10/1910, St. Andrews. – 'First Sunday of New University term. Professor Menzies in College Chapel. Text, 'I am the way.' 'In what direction would Christ have us to march? Ambition? No. Meekness? Unselfishness? Yes.' A glorious day, sun and sea breezes. Walked on pier with the Hannays. Students all in red gowns.

'In the evening Dr. Playfair speaking of Bethel. Jacob's plans in life altered. Consecration. When he spoke of 'a life surrendered in some real service to Christ' and of 'one whom God will draw near to and not leave till His purpose is accomplished,' I knew that, in spite of my back and my doubts and all else, God was there to help me.'

8/10/1911, (one year later). St Andrews College Chapel. – 'Professor Menzies Text. 'Christ is the way,' 'Who will go? Send me.' Army or Scouts? I had no notion what the answer would be. In four days time it was due. A great feeling of confidence.

For some time before this I had made up my small mind to leave the decision to October 12, 1911 – my 39th Birthday.'

29/9/1911, Stirling. – 'On the way back from the wedding at Coodham. Tête-à-tête in the train from Kilmarnock to Glasgow with Archbishop Cosmo Lang. "Well," he started, "what is your work?" "I do not know, Sir," I answered, "but I will be able to tell you on 12th October, that is my birthday." We talked the whole way up to Glasgow. As we parted he said – "I will not advise you. You will do what is best. God bless you".'

12/10/11, St Andrews. (39th Birthday) – 'Army or Scouts? Wrote out and weighed all pros and cons. Fog all day, no golf with Faichnie. Finished writing after tea. Put it to the vote. Scouts win. I feel it is right and am thankful. 7.15 p.m. Rubicon crossed. Peace of mind. All is well.'

13/10/11. – 'After two days of fog the sun is out. Played golf extra well – for me! A feeling of great content. Splendid speech by B.P. – "Wake up, England!" Scotland too I presume.'

15/10/1911, 'St Andrews College Chapel. – Professor Menzies to Students at start of new Term: "Blessed is the man who knows that God is with him in the work He has given him to do."'

16/10/1911, St. Andrews. – 'Letter to War Office resigning Commission. Golf with Faichnie. Playing and feeling better in body, mind, and spirit. Out of a long long tunnel and into the Light!'

14. – THE EARLY DAYS OF SCOUTING IN SCOTLAND

In 1909, being still far from well, my first contact with the Boy Scout Movement in Scotland was that of one looking on with approval, yet not fully convinced; for it took me some time to get drawn right into the stream.

At St Andrews in May of that year, I found myself reading B.P.'s great book – 'Scouting for Boys.' I read it again. Bits of it I read over and over again.

In long walks on the sands I would test myself reading footprints and tracks of horses and birds, and in telling the times and dates by the tides. I did not know much about boys, but it seemed to me strange that boys should be able to master tracks and do so many things which my grown-up Scouts in India could not do.

B.P.'s Methods.

It had not yet dawned on me that part of B.P.'s great scheme was to throw out ideas, to attract both leaders and boys and leave it to them to work things out for themselves; to trust them and to expect great things of them all.

Some three years later, when I found myself on these same sands, helping the boys with their tracking, enjoying their friendship, and that of their famous Scout Pipe Band, I had learned a lot more about Scouting – its wide range of interests, its appeal as a game, and, above all, the Code which, under good leaders, it seemed so sure to inspire.

Troubled Times.

Those early days were troubled times for poor old John Bull. At home there was great discontent. There were strikes, unemployment, slums and poverty. Women were claiming their rights by desperate means. Ireland was fighting for separation. While abroad the danger of war on a terrible scale was clear to all with ears to hear and eyes to see and at the same time, eminent men in all walks of life, including the King himself, uttered warnings that our national character called for attention.

It was then that B.P. came on the scene. He had seen our great need more clearly than most. We must tackle the young. We must cease to neglect their spare-time and their character training. Boys who were well-to-do, boys who had never been given a chance, all must be trained in a practical way in brotherhood, service and duty. This was the vision he put into practice. The start was up a steep hill. His very success meant added difficulties. By ceaseless work, always cheerful, always 'looking 10 years ahead,' he gave us that wonderful lead which has built Scouting into all that it stands for today.

Clearly the need in those days was to get a right spirit into the land. With all its attractions for boys, could Scouting help to do this? At the time it seemed a wonderful dream, but was it only a dream?

Today we may smile when we look at old pictures of Scouts with their shirt-sleeves down, their sloppy hats and their un-Gilwellian turn-out, but when we remember that it was these, and such as these, who faced fierce criticism and ridicule, and built up the spirit which won; that but for these there would have been no King's Scouts marching past the King at Windsor on St. George's Day, no cheering, happy, world-wide Jamborees; when we remember all this, we smile again. We give the full salute, and pray that we in turn may help to carry on the torch.

Get the Spirit right – that is the answer to the Atom Bomb!

The Bannockburn and Auchenbowie Scouts.

It was in June, 1909, that I saw my first Scouts. At Bannockburn, 2½ miles from Auchenbowie, Sergeant Penny, a keen Territorial, had a troop of 25 boys. He arrived resplendent in kilt and sporran, tunic and sash, glengarry and medals, and gave a display of drill and semaphore. The boys were keen and smart. Penny was a miner, extra patriotic, and very proud of his boys, but I was a bit surprised when, as a car passed us, he gave a smart salute. 'Who was that?' I asked. 'I don't know,' he answered, 'but I tell the boys to salute all motor-cars because it is probably an Officer.' That made me wonder! However, by July we had started a Troop at Auchenbowie. Mr. Robert Miller of The Boards was the moving spirit. We engraved the Scout Promise and Law, on the cement stable floor. In due course with hats and shorts and staves complete, two patrols were enrolled by Mr. J. W. Campbell, the Stirling President, who gave them a talk on their code and promise, parents and friends looking on. For the rest of that Summer these two Troops together had games in the woods with stalking, woodcraft and cooking. There were also monthly Sunday Services with neighbouring Companies of the Boys' Brigade.

A Scout is a Brother to all other Scouts.

In September a new patrol was added. At the Bore Row, a mile distant, there was a small mining community. Would they mix? Was it only in theory Scouts were brothers? How did it work? Not too well at first. Complaints about language, etc. But in the Bore Row I had an ally, an old collier, crippled by an accident in the pits. We both had time on our hands and long talks. Eventually things settled down and better reports came in.

'Shorts.'

Another problem was 'shorts.' In those days boys used to wear too many clothes. They wore knickerbockers and long drawers, and Heaven knows how many vests, so that when it came to wearing shorts mothers were apt to protest in a way they would not do in these days of coupons and more sensible dress.

'An Inspection'.

In September our boys went to Stirling for a local 'Inspection' – a great event for this country troop. They were formed up in line and duly inspected in the King's Park. A few faults were found by a benevolent Commissioner, stockings were not all of one pattern, hats and haversacks wrong, then they marched past in fours, and that was that!

Was it then, after all, as some people said, 'a purely Military

Movement?' Others found fault – 'It was not a Religious Movement.' To me our whole aim seemed the practice of true Religion.

Visit to Glasgow.

In October we sent the boys to Glasgow where nearly 6,000 Scouts
assembled to greet the Chief. I was rather surprised to find that for
some of these country boys the great event was, not seeing the hero
of Mafeking, but passing through a railway tunnel for the first
time!

As for myself, I was just looking on. I would sit in the woods
with the boys, one or two at a time, and talk about trees and tracks,
or themselves, and what not, but each time I tried to do more I
had to do less.

Room for Improvement.

1910. – By the summer of 1910, I found myself able for more, but
the more I came into touch, the more I found how much there was
to be put right. Childish local squabbles and jealousies. Recruits of
three months' service not taught the Scout Promise and Law.
There seemed to be no leadership, no sense of duty, no initiative,
no wide outlook, no local 'esprit-de-corps.'

In September, when 400 Scouts were to be 'inspected' in Stirling
by the Duke of Montrose, and there seemed to be no one to make
arrangements, I offered help. It went off all right, but it was not a
Scouting Display.

This minor effort cost me my sleep. Clearly I was not yet fit.
However, we followed it up with an important meeting in Stirling.
Some 30 keen men were there, and after supper each had his say.
All were agreed that things were not as they should be. We resolved
to get together and see what could be done. This was a turning
point.

Soon after this I went to London for another Medical Board the
doctors were emphatic, another whole year at least before I would
be fit to soldier at home. While in London I had a long talk with
B.P. and also visited various Troops and Rallies of Scouts in
London. To keep in touch with the Army, I also met many old
friends, while, as to 'Social Reform,' through the Church Army I
learned much of conditions unknown to me before.

The Major's Trousers.

One day about this time, as I was catching a train from Waterloo, an old friend, Reggie Kentish, hailed me loudly from his carriage in an out-going train. 'Did you get your trousers?' he shouted, and gesticulating, threw me the 'Evening News.' The story was this. While living in rooms in London, I had not noticed the loss of some of my kit, it so happened that in the same flat was living a friend who had lost a valuable set of sleeve-links, given him by King Edward VII. The links and the thief (Bedford, the Boots of the establishment) had been traced by the laundry marks on my best Jaeger drawers. In due course, to oblige my friend I found myself in a London Law Court, being duly sworn and asked to identify my possessions, among them the missing trousers! The idea of an old Army Major chasing post-haste from Scotland to recover his pants had tickled the reporter. It was all there in big head-lines.

Poor Bedford, on his release I guided his erring feet to the foot of the Church Army ladder, but unfortunately he shied off at the very first rung. As an effort in Social Reform it was not a big success, any more than my man who had run off with the Church Army chopper, but it taught me yet more of a world of which I knew so little.

Move in to Stirling.

On 11th November, 1910, the Rev. John Arnott persuaded me to help Scouting in Stirling as the Local Secretary. Finding it too much to do this from Auchenbowie, even with a small car, I moved into rooms at 13 Pitt Terrace, on 13th January, 1911, for two or three months – so I thought at the time! But in the end I lived there for 21 years, and now, looking back, I can say that '13' brought me no bad luck. In a way, this move led to the happiest years of my life.

A New Start in Stirling.

Up till now my time at Auchenbowie had been an apprenticeship for days to come. Each little trial of petty squabbles, or failure in duty and honour and 'playing-the-game,' had been good practice in patience. Each set-back in health, sleep and back and head, was always off-set by hopes and signs of progress which followed, and all the time, with growing Faith came a steady increase in confidence. So also the work in Stirling which followed, helped to fit me for work which followed in Scotland.

In this account of our doings in Stirling much must be left out. My first step was to visit all the Troops and get to know the leaders.

Leadership.

It must be remembered that it was the enthusiasm of the boys themselves at the start which led in early days to shortcomings in supervision organisation and leadership. There was much to be put right. Our next need was to improve the Scout Hall. By the end of February we had got this done. We held a successful Rally in the Hall, newly fitted with heating, lighting, cooking, water, gym and other amenities. Provost 'Davie' Bayne (a great character) encouraged the boys who gave a varied display. 'A new spirit,' said someone, 'seemed to be in the boys.'

Publicity.

Then we had to awaken more interest and explain what Scouting stood for. Very few grown-ups seemed to know or care what it was all about. This brought me in touch with Padres, Schools, Town Council Officials, Employers, leading Citizens and the Press, all quite a new world to me. On them we inflicted many appeals and much literature. By the end of April the need for help from reliable men became evident.

Helpers.

It was then that Messrs. Hunter, Tom Wilson, J. D. Steel and two or three more, got together and came to our rescue; and from that time to the end of their days did so much to forward our cause.

There were two other sources of help. From the Castle, two young Officers, Lieuts. Bertie Couper of Craigforth and Archie Stirling of Garden, personally helped with the training. They thought it no shame to sally forth past the sentry, and down through the lively Top of the Town, in shorts and Scout hat.

We also had help from Col. Oliver of the Ordnance, indeed one difficulty was that though we did all we could to rope in civilians as Scoutmasters, none would come forward.

'Rovers.'

Our other most encouraging source of help was from a Senior Troop of keen young men, with Jenner and Drummond as Leaders. These lads were pioneers. They, too, with a smile, faced much chaff as to hats and shorts. They were what we call 'Rovers' today and proved a very great help in their day.

Outstanding Events.

There were many mile-stones on our way. In May 400 boys, B.B. and Scouts, marched to the Wallace Monument, where ex-Provost Thomson and Dr. Menzies Fergusson gave them patriotic addresses.

In July the Scouts were thanked by the Provost and by the two flying men, Beaumont and Vedrines, for helping with the huge crowds which collected to see the great flying contest from London, round Stirling and back.

They were also thanked by the Chief Constable for good work at two fires. Some of the boys went to the Windsor Rally. There were Sports and Outings to Airthrey, Auchenbowie, and up North Third Glen. Picked Scouts gave displays to help in forming new Troops. All these doings and others were well reported in the Press at the time.

Of course it was not always plain sailing. There were many difficulties and, as in all pioneer work, there were ups and downs. I will spare you the downs and close with this 'up.'

17/1/1911. – 'Much encouragement today and signs of progress in many directions. Old Dominie MacKenzie, who helped me with algebra in 1907, says he hears good accounts of the Scouts on every side.'

H.Q. Commissioner for Scotland, 1912.

In October, 1911, having decided to leave the Army, and having climbed Ben Ledi, Ben Lomond, and the Cairngorms with no ill-effects, I now felt it right to do what I could to help Lawrence who was then working single-handed at Scottish Scout H.Q. in Edinburgh. While Lawrence was tied to his office in Edinburgh, at the same time he was being bombarded with calls for visits from all over Scotland.

At this early stage organisation was incomplete and much was left to our discretion. The urgent need was to make our aims and needs known and to enlist new supporters and leaders. We decided to ask Lord Rosebery, the greatest orator of his day, to make a National appeal, and meanwhile we drew up leaflets calling for help and personal interest.

The Chief Scout himself was sending out stirring calls and warnings as to the growth of unemployment, and discontent, and youth neglect:–

'The prime cause is that the mass of boys, though good material, never get a fair start in life. We have it in our power to help the boys of the country if only we can get the agents to come forward and help. Time is precious, hundreds of boys are slipping away daily to form the mass of wasted human material which is at once a disgrace and a danger, instead of being an additional strength to our country, simply through want of a guiding hand to direct them at the critical point of their lives.'

Publicity.

In pushing the Chief's appeals we would add some call from Scottish H.Q. Was the hard work which the Chief had been doing, almost single-handed for the last four years, fully realised? Not even he, for all his cheerfulness, could stand the strain for ever.

In Scotland the work was being decentralised. Each County had its own Commissioner and District Commissioners, and now the great need was more men of the right sort to come forward in Scotland. The field was unlimited. The need was evident. The good results, under right conditions, were little short of marvellous.

'If this appeal from our Chief should catch the eye of any patriotic man who feels the slightest prompting of conscience to help, let him write to the Secretary, 1 South Charlotte Street, Edinburgh. We will receive him with open arms.'

Glasgow, 13th February–14th March, 1912.

I began my tours in Scotland with a four-week stay in Glasgow, where, upheld by the enthusiasm of Leaders and boys, I was able to do more than expected. K. B. Wright, the Hon. Secretary, was my bear-leader and guided me round each district in turn. In 'Boss' Young, the County Commissioner, and his Leaders I had many good friends. There were meetings and visits to Troops and schools, and notes to be made and reports to write, but the chief feature was a series of talks with a lantern. It was more of a talk than a lecture.

Lantern Talks.

As a rule I dealt with three kinds of Scouts:–

(1) *Scouts in the Army*, as I had known them in India and Africa, with photos and talks of stalking, tracking and camouflage, and yarns of good work done.
(2) *Peace Scouts*, leaders like David Livingstone, Gordon and Sir John Moore, all with a Glasgow connection, and many others whose names were unknown.
(3) *The Boy Scout*, the man of tomorrow, pictures drawn by the Chief, photos of camping and games and all his many activities, his code, the flag and the way to fly that flag mast-high.

They would listen well for an hour or more, an occasional question or joke would help to keep things lively.

Visits to Troops.

I have always felt a bit lost in large cities, so I was glad of 'K.B.' and his leading strings as we went round so many Troops of all kinds.

On one occasion he handed me over to a splendid Patrol Leader. of some 14 summers (and winters), mostly spent in the slums, except for his scouting ventures. He called at my den and at once took charge. He caught some bus and paid the fare as a matter of course. I do not know where we got to, we got out and walked, it was somewhere near the docks. He told me there was no Scout-master. The boys had run their own show for some time and had been at our meeting overnight.

As we drew near his Scout Den, there came sounds of music and dancing. He made some secret sign at the door and we were admitted cautiously. The dance went on, biggish lads, pretty tough, with their girls, ditto! I was led through the 'ballroom,' then up to a loft where a dozen Scouts received me with full Scout honours. We saluted the flag and later broke off and spent a cheery half-hour.

They later explained that when the Troop started, hooligans had plagued them, so they made a bargain – For the use of the hall of their Den the dancing fans would protect them, and, ever since, all had gone well!

On the way home my 'Leader' escorted me to some underground railway station. As we passed a Pub, a loafer was standing under a lamp. He clicked his heels loudly (he must have been in the Guards at one time), drew himself up and gave us a full salute. I returned the salute in a friendly and less formal way.

'Ach!' said my escort, 'Dinna heid him! If youse dinna heid him, he'll no heid you.'

At the Station we sat and talked as we waited for my train to come in, and so we parted. After 37 years and two World Wars, I wonder what became of my guide. I am sure he did well.

This busy four weeks in Glasgow closed with a big final rally, a general meeting of Leaders and a Church Parade Service.

From Local Press –

One Press cutting and a sample Leaflet will help to give some idea of this and other such visits:–

Major Crum sends the following message –

'To *Scoutmasters* – Get as many boys out into the country as you possibly can. Make these outings interesting – that needs imagination. Read and reread 'Scouting for Boys.' Look at the 'Gazette' and the 'Scout.' Consult the boys themselves. Think of some story you know. Think of some free ground in the country where you can do no damage. Then think – could you adapt some scheme to the ground? Suppose it all as real, picture it in your mind and on paper; think it out for weeks beforehand.

You will improve and your Scouts will be keen. There is no limit to Scouting once you learn to think. Give your Leaders responsibility – don't do too much yourselves. Above all realise your own responsibility in guiding this splendid enthusiasm of your boys. Keep in with the Parents – tell the boys to do good turns at home. Be a good Scout yourself and lead the way in all the laws of Scouts.

'*To the Leaders* I say – Stick to the Scouts. If you are getting fed up, you can find new interests and keenness by teaching a tenderfoot all that you know. By teaching you learn yourself, and you learn to take a lead, which will help you all your life – but more than that, you will be helping your country. A good leader is worth his weight in gold.

'*To the Scouts* I say – Copy the smartest and best Scout in your Troop, and try to help your Leader to have the best patrol.

'And to all ranks I say – Go on and prosper. Good luck to your enthusiasm.'

More Visits to Towns and Counties.

After Glasgow came many more such visits spread out through 1912. Visits to Paisley, to Greenock, where Ryrie Orr had set local enthusiasm alight, to Dunbartonshire, Stirlingshire, Rothesay and Dunoon: to Perth where Herbert Pullar was the moving spirit; In May, two weeks in Edinburgh and Leith and last but not least, three weeks in Dundee.

Overwork.

With each visit I paid, correspondence grew, so that, what with visits to Scottish H.Q. and writing 'Scottish Notes' to the 'H.Q. Gazette,' to say nothing of still being Local Secretary in Stirling, I was finding that, even with Miss Hooper's help in typing, I had too much to do.

When things reached a limit I used to take time off, a day alone on the moors perhaps, or catching a trout, or perhaps a day's outing with a dozen Scouts or more. In August I went right away from it all, but even so, looking back, I sometimes wonder how, with a throat needing constant massage, and with sleep and back giving frequent warnings, I was yet enabled to get through so much.

Faith in the cause seemed to lift me along. Another great help was of course the boys themselves.

Stirling Activities, 1912.

In Stirling, Major Aytoun, Captain Couper, Sergt.-Major Keen and many others were doing great work. To us Stirling had now become an experimental training ground. We had good men to train the boys in boxing, wrestling, ju-jitsu and gymnastics. Mr. Forsyth took a great interest in their singing. A keen Sergeant helped with football. There were helpers in Ambulance, Astronomy, Miniature rifle shooting, Model flying, and in April some 360 boys gave a fine display.

Under ex-Provost Duff, a Fire-Brigade of Senior Scouts was started. They had a special mobile engine which later gave displays at many a Rally and today, 37 years later, is still in service at the Buchanan Camp.

At Xmas, Scoutmaster Logan and his Scouts gave their first entertainment for the children at the Whinwell Home. This also has kept going all these years.

In Summer, week-end camps were started by D. T. James with trek-carts to the Trossachs and to Loch Lomond, while in Menstrie Glen I got my first experience of camps with boys.

Lord Rosebery's Speech.

I have left to the last the chief event of 1912 – Lord Rosebery's speech at the Polton Rally. To this Rally we sent 30 Scouts under Logan, Ogilvie and Kerr, with 3 trek-carts, camping gear and Fire Engine all complete. They went by train, returning by road and camping en route.

The Fire Brigade.

Arriving at Princes Street Station, Edinburgh, the train being late, there was barely time to catch the connection at Waverley Station. Then was seen what these old soldiers and their Scouts could do! As their train drew in, they were toeing the line. Detraining, and forming up smartly, with Fire Engine leading, and bell ringing loudly they 'doubled' the whole way down Princes Street, and duly arrived at Polton just in time for the display.

As for the speech –

On the previous day I had met Lord Rosebery at the New Club. He took me to a small room looking out on the Castle. There we sat at a small table, tête-à-tête for an hour.

'Now,' he began, 'I am going to pick you to the bone. I have got to speak for ten minutes tomorrow about Boy Scouts and I want to know more.'

He soon had me pouring out all that I wanted him to proclaim from the house-tops. Occasionally he would make a note, just one word, 'Schools,' 'Ladies,' 'Parents,' 'Militarism,' 'Friendship.' Occasionally he would have a far-away look. I would pull up or pause, and at once he seemed alert and intent again, and there came a flicker of a smile which seemed to say – 'Yes, carry on.'

As we parted – 'Yes,' he said, 'I will speak at your Rally. Arrange two separate talks, one for the Scouts, then, at the "Votes of thanks," an appeal for public support.' And would I also arrange for him to come straight to the ground with no distractions?

We shook hands. He returned alone to that room, to ponder his notes, I think.

I wish we could broadcast that speech today, or better, with television catch the twinkle in Lord Rosebery's eye. The speech went out far and wide in the Press, and we added our quota in thousands of leaflets; but what is cold print compared to the orator's magic of voice and of eye?

'If,' said Lord Rosebery, 'I was to form the highest ideal for my Country it would be this – that it be a nation of which the mankind was exclusively composed of men who have been trained in Boy Scout theory. Such a nation would be the greatest moral force the world has ever known . . . . What you are is this – a high fellowship, embodied to preserve and observe great principles, self-help and help to others, patriotism and loyalty, honour, faith and duty. You wish to form character, by far the most important education we can impart . . . . It is because I have this movement so much at heart that I venture to urge, with all the power that God has given me, that you should co-operate in it.'

1913.

In 1913 things were beginning to move. In Glasgow Sir Wm. Smith with his Boys' Brigade, and Robert Young with his Scouts, spoke of growing numbers and an increase in public support. In Aberdeen, my first point of call that year, I certainly found no signs of 'National Decline.'

I suppose that, after seeing over a million men on strike, what with unemployment, the Irish and Suffragette troubles, and the threat of war on an unheard-of scale drawing nearer and nearer, John Bull was at last about to awake from his slumbers. It was surely high time,

Was not Lord Rosebery right when he urged that in all our training and education Character must come first? To us it seemed that our Chief was a Heaven-sent Leader, who, looking ahead and looking wide, had found a practical way towards God's will – service and true manliness.

As for my own visits all over Scotland, I will give just one more sample from a letter written from Aberdeen on my opening tour of 1913.

Letter from Aberdeen, 1913.

Palace Hotel,
Aberdeen, 1/2/1913

'My Dear M.

'I arrived safely in Stirling and, after two very cold, snowy, busy but satisfactory days, arrived here in Aberdeen at 2 p.m. just in time to get into uniform for a 'Café Chantant' in aid of Scouts. Guided from the Hotel by a friendly Scout, I was ushered into a room full of various magnates. Practice has improved me at sizing up such gatherings. There were City Fathers, Gentlemen from the County, the Lord Provost – a fine fellow – and many others.

When ready, we solemnly marched to a platform, the Lord Provost and 'yours very humbly' in the position of honour. A fine hall, galleries swarming with jolly Scouts; and young people. A guard of honour, pipes, drums, bugles and down below the hall was full of little tables and tea, not to mention the ladies, and all Aberdonian Society.

So much for the 'theatre of war.'

The Provost spoke kindly of the Scottish Scout Commissioner, and most encouragingly of the cause. Good Scout cheers from the gallery, your humble servant then stood up and after thanking all for their kind reception pulled up his socks and gave tongue as follows:–

'My Lord Provost, ladies and gentlemen. – I have only been to two 'Café Chantants' before, one was in Belgrade, the other in Paris. At neither was there a chairman or any opening address, so I have no precedent to go on. There are two things however about this particular 'Café Chantant' which I do know. First, it has been entirely organised by our very kind friends the ladies, headed, we Scouts are proud to say, by the Lady Provost. (Cheers).

Secondly, that it is in aid of our great cause. I think therefore that I should say a word to the ladies, and then a word as to Scouting, but it is a very big subject, and, as I see you have 41 items on your programme, I must be brief. However I hope to tell you more of our aims and methods and needs at my talk in this hall on Tuesday. I hope to be able to interest both grown-ups and boys, and I make a special appeal to you to send along any likely Scoutmasters.

We are always sincerely glad to get the ladies on our side. In Glasgow 90 ladies have now formed a ladies' Scout Council, with a president, two Secretaries, and other office-bearers.

They have helped to raise an interest, distributing literature and telling all their friends about the Scouts. They have helped us to find Scoutmasters, Instructors and others, by making it the fashion.

They have found patrons for poorer troops and have helped them to get out into the country. They have also helped to raise funds, so that out of 75 Troops not one has been unable to camp for want of £ s. d.

But perhaps most important of all, they have helped to raise the tone of the movement through and through. Ask Miss May Buchanan in Glasgow all about it. Can you wonder that with this experience alone, I cry with all my heart – 'Votes for women!'

As for the Scout Movement, it is indeed a huge subject. I have not time to dwell on Scouting and Education or tell you of successes in Leeds and Manchester where there has been co-operation. Nor will I dwell on openings for Social Reform. I will not speak of the bogey bogus cry of 'Militarism,' though a very few words would convince you. Nor will I speak of Religion. I will only say here that in my opinion every single person who helps this great cause is doing more for the nation than perhaps he yet knows.

Even by one helpful look or encouraging word he is helping to foster a great and growing Brotherhood of over 170,000 boys, scattered all over the Empire, and yet banded together as one, by their promise, given on their honour as Scouts, to be friends to all the world and brothers to every other Scout, no matter his class or creed or even the colour of his face. (Cheers.)

If you help the Scout to follow this trail, to live up to his simple, manly code; if by a look or word, or better still by example, you let him know that you value his 'one good turn a day,' you are sowing the seed, so needed today, of personal service, seed which, wherever you sow it, among future soldiers or civilians, ministers or laymen, is bound, God helping us, to bring forth fruit ten-thousand fold. (Cheers.)

One word more. Two years ago I travelled to Aberdeen. I remember on that occasion there were two men in my carriage. One of them sat on my right in the window seat. He was deaf and dumb. His friend who sat opposite him, occasionally talked on his fingers like this. (Illustration to boys in gallery.)

Occasionally, I continued, they scribbled notes to each other and (to the boys) I am sorry to say I was un-Scoutlike enough to peep over at one message. It was this – 'What are the people of Aberdeen like?' The answer came – 'They are very canny!' At the same time he opened and closed his fist like this – (demonstration, loud laughter.)

Ladies and gentlemen, all over the world I have heard it hinted that North of the Tweed, we keep the 9th Scout Law of Thrift, and that you in Aberdeen lead the way in Thrift, but my experience is that in any good cause, no one is more open-handed than the Scot – so then I know we can count on you all today.

Boys! It is now up to you. You have done very well. Keep it up. Come and hear more about Scouting on Tuesday.'

The Battle of Bannockburn – Scouts and B.B.

One of our aims in Stirling always was to promote specially good feeling between Scouts and Boys' Brigade. All our leaders were good friends and got together in various ways. Our famous 'Battle of Bannockburn' was a good example of this.

The event was carefully thought out and arranged, with plenty of umpires. Some 400 boys took part and this was followed up on Sunday with the joint Church Service. For the battle each boy was armed with 3 rag-balls made by himself. (These to be soft, no stones or 'spuds' inside!) He also wore the distinguishing badge of his side. The rule was that any boy could pick up lost balls, but if he was hit, it was up to him, on his honour, to hand over his badge and retire from the fray.

The B.B. and Scouts of Stirling assembled in the King's Park under Captain Harry Drummond (B.B.). The Scouts and B.B. from Plean, Bannockburn, and St Ninians, rallied at Cauldhame under Ian Bolton.

Zero hour was 3.30 p.m. At 3.50 p.m. the opposing Scouts got touch on the Bannock and after thrilling stalks, reinforcements came up on both sides. Exciting scraps and wily manoeuvres followed. At one time all seemed lost for Stirling. Then Captain Cunnison, like the Camp-followers of old, appearing on the scene with the 1st B.B., decided the day.

Badges were counted. North 66. South 56. Soon friend and foe were mixed and eagerly comparing notes. All enjoyed a great day.

22/4/1913. – Extract from B.B. Notes. – 'The best day I ever had in the B.B. was the verdict of an old-boy Officer of many years' experience.' And the Scouts too said it was 'great.'

Another effort about this time was to raise more interest in flying. In December, 1912, I had met Miss Bacon, a great enthusiast who was lecturing all over the Country, warning us that as a nation we were being left behind by the Germans and others. She was a pioneer, the first lady to fly in a balloon, the first in a dirigible, the first in an aeroplane, and finally the first to venture in a hydroplane.

Her first trip in an aeroplane, she told me, was in a 'kite' not built for two, so she had to sit on the fuselage. When this seat grew hot she called out to the pilot, but he only called back some joke about 'fried Bacon!' She was a real sport and lent us a model 'Zeppelin' which flew with success round the Albert Hall in Stirling on the occasion of the Chief Scout's visit.

Later we formed a Model Aero Club and had competitions in the King's Park.

The Chief Scout's Visit – April 5th–9th, 1913.

An outstanding event of the year was the Chief Scout's visit to Glasgow, to the Counties of Renfrew, Ayr, Lanark, and Stirling, ending with Edinburgh. Anyone knows that success in such ventures hangs on good team work, and careful preparation, with attention to detail. At all the key points we had good leaders and all went well.

Early in March, with Lord Provost McInnes Shaw presiding, the Western leaders assembled and hatched all plans as to route, timing, hospitality, halls, displays and meetings. We were out to make the most of this chance and command success. One difficulty was that the Chief, who had recently been abroad to recover from over-work, was not yet really well. There were uncertainties and changes of programme.

In Stirling the Chief was due on 8th April. Colonel Edwin Bolton and Captain Couper had only recently taken over Commissioner duties, so that, as local Secretary, even with the help of Captain Watt from St. Andrews, I found myself busy indeed. However, owing to good team work, when the time came, all I had to do was to drive round with the Chief and enjoy his amazing triumphal progress.

It is *before* such events that our grit is tested. You hear from London that the programme won't do; it must be cut down. Who will have to be left out? Will they keep smiling? You go to Glasgow and plans are happily readjusted. Then, motoring back, you call at a village on the route, only to find that none of the instructions sent out have reached the Scoutmaster!

Arriving in Stirling, you visit the Troops and find excellent work being done, but here and there, some fly in the ointment.

Some petty hitch or squabble. Some Instructor let down. Here is the champion 'tiny-weight' boxer refusing to box! or here a young piper hands in his pipes in a huff. It is here Scout training comes in. Wherever you go, keenness is in the air. Our job is to guide that enthusiasm. You know that all will go well.

Correspondence.

On such occasions correspondence grows. From 9 a.m. to 8 p.m. I worked in my room with only intervals to go to the post, or on to the Printers (my old friend ex-Scoutmaster Judge Wingate). On the way, as a rule, there was always something to cheer one up – some Scout or friend with a smile.

The Scouts' best salute.

On one occasion, I had just been amused by a far-away salute from a slater-boy, high up on a roof, when, passing on, I saw two painters in white coming along the Terrace towards me. As they drew near I noticed the boy handing to his gaffer one of his paint-pots. This seemed unusual, then I saw why. The boy was a newly-joined Scout and intended to give me the Scout Salute, which he did. I stopped and we all three laughed and had a few words. I told him the Scout's best Salute was his smile.

The Chief Scout's Tour in Scotland.

In the Scout H.Q. Gazette of May, 1913, a special Scottish number tells of these days:

'At Glasgow the Chief Scout began his tour by opening an excellent Exhibition of Scout Work which opened the eyes of all to the scope and usefulness of the Movement. Then came a great Rally of over 2,000 Scouts and a meeting arranged by the Ladies' Council.

At Greenock 700 Renfrewshire boys assembled at a Service . . . . Again the same vast crowds but with this difference – it was the Sabbath – respectful greetings took the place of cheers.

In Ayrshire as in Renfrewshire, flags at every window and possies of Scouts at many a village. At Kilmarnock a patriotic wave of enthusiasm seemed to have gripped the whole community.

The streets were packed. Some 800 boys from Ayrshire, Bute and Arran gave a display in Kilmarnock.

In Lanarkshire again the route was crowded. At each village and town, there were Scouts and flags, and inhabitants were cheering. At Airdrie an eloquent Provost welcomed 'the Leader who has won all hearts by his desire that all the boys of our beloved land should grow up noble, true and gallant men.'

In Stirlingshire at every School en route there were hundreds of children. At each the Chief alighted and had a kindly word or look for all, teachers and bairns. In Stirling, there was another royal welcome. Not one 'Son of the Rock' but felt proud of the Stirlingshire Scouts and of the Chief Scout that day.

In Edinburgh there was an outstanding exhibition. 'Then a great gathering of ladies and gentlemen from all over Scotland, when Lord Dunglass eloquently and sincerely thanked the Chief for all he was doing for the nation. Then the Chief replies. It is perhaps as enthusiastic and inspiring a speech as he ever made. To start off he deprecates any idea of its being a one-man show and he warmly thanks all his fellow-workers.

After a tribute to Sir Wm. Smith as founder of the Boys' Brigade, he speaks of training in courage, reliance, resource, and of results all over the Empire.

'In our country,' he says, 'there are two many idlers, rich and poor.' With Scouts, usefulness, service and sympathy were aimed at, nor was there any barrier of class or creed – all must be brothers. It was a National and it was an International movement. Let all who realised and approved its aims, come forward and help financially, or better still, by personal service.

The fluent straightforwardness of the speech, the strong manly voice with which it was delivered, and the great heart from which it came, combined to carry all before them.

And what of the boys? From Clackmannan, Kinross and Fife and the Lothians, Scouts had poured in to reinforce their Edinburgh brothers.

What did the Chief say to set them cheering so wildly? I do not know. On paper it wouldn't sound much. It was what he was as he spoke. He seemed with such ease to generate the great force of enthusiasm with which he sought, under God's blessing, to speed the good of mankind.

Two points I would add as one behind the scenes. After five years of unceasing work, he was far from well. Of this, in public, he betrayed not a sign. He would not spare himself.

The other point is his modesty. Over and over again as we got back into the car, I could see his head was troubling, and yet with a sort of boyish happiness he would protest how unworthy he was of it all.

At Cumbernauld the children had given their cheers. Their lady teacher had curtsied almost as though to Royalty. It was then as we moved on into Stirlingshire, that he passed a remark which I never forgot, and he said it more to himself than to me. 'We must be better fellows ourselves to give a good lead.'

Camping in 1913.

My early efforts at camping with boys in 1912 had made a great impression on me. How much the boys had enjoyed it all! How much good it had done them in health and manners and outlook. They grew more friendly amongst themselves and with their leaders. A wonderful change for the better, all round. And yet, in arranging a camp, there are so many points to be seen to, that a badly run camp may well do (and often has done) more harm than good.

From all sides came requests for advice, but who was I to advise, with so little experience? So then, with Lawrence and James and four others we decided to run a trial camp.

In Stirling, seven Troops were camping on their own, while five others were unable to arrange any camp. We decided to run a camp for those left out. Again we found that planning and team work spelt success. With 60 boys we camped for ten days in July at Achnacloich on Loch Etive, where Mr. Nelson and all the neighbours made us welcome. We climbed Ben Cruachan (3689 ft.). With boats and bathing and exploring we had a wonderful time and all went well.

Ladies' Camping.

A printed account appeared in due course, giving details which would help others. Indeed, we had grown so confident that we also

171

helped to arrange a Ladies' Camp the following year. This venture almost cost me the favour of my excellent landladies, Miss Stronach and Miss McLean, who were very much shocked! It is strange to look back on those early days when today we find the Girl Guides well up to (if not in advance of) the Scouts in camp training.

Since those days I have written many books on various forms of camp, but these are now out-of-date. Take for instance the menus and prices. Though the prices of sugar, bread, and butter are down, due to subsidies, we find tea, milk, oatmeal and potatoes double the price, while nearly all else is on points or rationed. Could anyone now feed his ravenous boys as we did then on 10/- a week?

And so, having gradually handed over local duties in Stirling, and with Sir Henry Dundas now at S.H.Q., I was free to go further afield.

Thus ended a year of great progress in Scottish Scouting.

1914 – The Gordon Lecture.

My opening move in 1914 was a lecture on General Gordon given on his own special day, 25th January. In re-reading a letter written that day, it set me thinking so hard that I venture to reproduce it here:

LETTER TO E.G.E.C. STIRLING, 25/1/1914. 4.30 p.m.

'I spent the last 48 hours fighting a throat in preparation for a lecture on Chinese Gordon, which is due in two hours from now. With the help of the doctor and landladies, and various inhalers and blisters, I think it will go all right, but it is a stormy night. I seem now to have exhausted my Summer store of warmth and to be no longer climate-proof.

Grangemouth and Dollar visits went well, but it is as though a none-to-good engine was missing fire, so I am glad that my time with you draws near, and thankful so much has gone well this winter.

P.S., MONDAY, 26th JANUARY:

The meeting went well. I sallied forth in a cab; muffled up and munching cocaine in a deluge of rain.

On arrival at the Lesser Albert Hall, surprised and pleased to find it packed, and sorry some turned away. Is it not strange on a stormy night, that, while never a boy or young man is seen inside a Church on Sunday evening, an old crow croaking inefficiently about Gordon, with a few pictures of him and his fights, can fill a Hall?

I would like all Padres to note this fact and make use of it. I only wished I could have done Gordon more justice, but after weeks of reading up his life, I saw it was hopeless to aspire too high, and so was content to be simple.

Now, as to talking Religion, a Boys' Brigade Officer volunteered that if I wanted someone to say a prayer, or ask or pronounce a blessing, Mr. —————————— was "the very man." The room was half full of R.C.s and Episcopal boys and even boys of no Church. What I wanted to do was to stamp the idea of an example of "duty, not self," into each boy in that Hall. You and I and Mr. —————————— may have realised that this step depends on prayer and help from above. That comes when you have climbed a certain distance, but I think in beginning to climb it is not wise to distract the beginner's attention.

In speaking of Gordon, I did not dwell on his being a man of Faith who carried his Bible wherever he went. That to my mind would have scared some away from our hero. On the contrary, I rather dwelt on his escapades as a boy. The nearest I got was to say he remembered his Gravesend boys (his 'Kings' as he called them) whenever he looked at the pins on the map, and wished them good luck in his thoughts and his prayers, wherever they were all over the world.

In speaking to boys I used to feel shy of treading on sacred ground. I still feel unworthy, unless clearly guided, to do so. But may it not be that to put, say, the example of Gordon's life, in a way so real as to attract and inspire, is a step the average boy can see, and later will follow?

I have puzzled and puzzled over these things. Why does the average man hold back from the Church? Why does religious talk so often repel? Oh! for the gift to see what is best and then to act with simple commonsense and courage. My constant prayer was for help to speak to these boys aright. When the time came, I never felt more at ease and less inclined to preach, or to speak in a way unnatural to myself. May it not be that those we would lead are finding it hard to keep touch?'

The Scottish Constitution.

In 1914 our good progress continued. Counties like Fife, Forfar, Argyll, Stirling and the Stewartry had many bright spots, but there was still much to be done in the way of organising.

At Scottish Headquarters, the Scottish Council, under Sir Henry Dundas, was giving a lead and getting more co-operation. There were legal affairs and the question of a 'Scottish Constitution' in which I took no great personal interest. To me the cry of more Scottish 'Home Rule' seemed a bit overdone, though in London there also seemed to be those who needed reminding that Scotland to Scotsmen is more than a province of England.

National Flags

But even in Scotland all did not see eye to eye. Take for instance our flags. We were all agreed Scotland must have her own National Scout flag, not the green and yellow Scout flag. But what was the National flag? There were two opposing schools. One led by Messrs. Thomson and Bell, claimed the right of all Scotsmen to fly the Lion Rampant.

On the other hand, that high authority, Mr. John A. Stewart of the St. Andrews Society, wrote indignantly of 'atrocious perversions of Royal Flags.'

In the end, with the consent of the Lyon King at Arms, we came to compromise. As a County Flag we encouraged the Red Lion on a plain yellow ground, while the more numerous St. Andrews Troop flags went far towards meeting the wishes of others undoubtedly experts in heraldry.

But for us it was chiefly a matter of 'esprit-de-corps.' In this our Flags have helped greatly, one must never forget the thrill that they give at big International gatherings. They seem to be shouting 'Scotland for ever!' and the Scouts who uphold them, you can see, to a man, mean to be worthy.

'The Union Jack.'

As for the Union Jack, that, of course, is the flag you will find in every Scout Camp, in every Scout Hall. At the start of the day they unfurl it with honour. At the close, it is given a final salute.

Lady Scoutmasters.

In early days it was said that Scoutmasters were all either 'cranks, crocks or criminals.' I don't know about that, but in Stirling at one time it might have been said that they were all either ladies or soldiers, and, moreover, that the ladies' chief help came from soldiers.

It would not be fair in these Notes to leave out mention of the good pioneer work done by ladies. Miss Blackburn for instance. Here was a lady who devoted her life to the good of her boys. She liked her own way, and she went her own way. First as Church Lads' Brigade, and later on as Scouts, she helped hundreds of boys to make good.

Then we had Miss Lorraine and Miss Colville who donned Scout hats and with two Troops of kilties did valuable service. Later came Mrs. Robson in charge of the R.C. Troop, which at one time under Father Rattrie and Sergt.-Major Keen, had 60 Scouts in two Troops (Seniors and Juniors).

Old Soldiers.

Their first Scout-master was a fine old warrior, Sergt.-Major Ryan, whose son Tommy Ryan was our first King's Scout.

The last time I saw this old veteran he was dying. As he lay in his room in Bow Street, at the top of the town, the whole of his body, except his right arm was paralysed. Still keen on the good of his boys, he gave a last old-soldier salute.

Among other ex-soldiers I must also mention two pioneers now also passed on, Logan and Greenhorn. The Troops they started in 1909 are still going strong.

Miss Nairn.

In later days came Miss Nairn and the Cubs. She too put the whole of her heart and soul and body and mind (with her special gift for such work), into the cause. She also brought on many splendid Akelas. She won the M.B.E. and also the love of hundreds of boys, who, later as men, before she too passed on, got together and proved how greatly they valued her labour of love.

A Good Summer of progress.

In the summer of 1914, Scouting seemed to be reaching a zenith of progress; then, all of a sudden, came War. Wherever I went – it might be on visits to Troops in the county, Drymen or Inversnaid, Strathblane or Banton; or it might be to towns like Falkirk or Alva; or further afield to the Perth County Flag Competition, or a week-end raid on Dumfries for a Rally – always things seemed to be shaping well, and always I had with me two or three Scouts, not only as cheery companions, but also as excellent 'samples.'

Visits to Conferences.

There were also Conferences which we used to attend with parties of our local leaders, making new friends and drawing fresh inspiration. Each of these visits would mean more letters to write, and at times an over-active mind which would cost me my sleep.

At Manchester in particular, I remember a wonderful uplift with 'Uncle' Elwes, Roland Phillips, Everett, and the Chief at his best summing up at the end. I see in my log – 'Never slept a wink all night, but happy over the spirit which showed itself.'

But these setbacks were not lasting. A few hours sun-bathing on the moors, enjoying the wonderful views, or carving a stick, or calling up an inquisitive curlew; or a week-end at St. Andrews, would soon set me right and fit me to tackle our four chief coming events – Bannockburn Day, the King's Visit, and two important camps.

A few extracts from letters and log may give some idea of those days:

Stirling, 1/6/1919. –

'One of those perfect days one never forgets. Rain had laid the dust and cleared the views of Ben Lomond, Ben Ledi and Co. Hawthorns, chestnuts, laburnum, brooms, beeches, all at their best and the little car in good form. Took two good Scouts to County Flag Competition, all went well. A forward step in the great game of putting new spirit into the boys. Fifteen Troops keen as mustard. Each boy out for his Troop and not for himself. Out to win the emblem of his County, no money prizes.'

8/6/1914. – 'A very hard day arranging Trek Camp, Bannock-burn Sex-Centenary Day, the King's Visit, and Achnacloich Camp – 9 a.m. to 10 p.m. Must take time off at St. Andrews. Thirty letters, and circulars – stamp bill goes up.'

9/6/1914. – 'It is wonderful how a person like me should be able to do so much from this strategic centre of Scotland, this wonderful summer. At it all day yesterday – writing and posting, posting and writing, circulars, letters, orders for Bannockburn, for the King's visit, for the Trek Camp and Achnacloich, and a weekend camp at Auchenbowie. For Bannockburn Day we are inviting all the Scottish County Flags and 3 picked Scouts with each to be guests in brother Scouts' homes.

The Trek Cart Camp takes shape. Last night, a relief to leave writing for shirt sleeves in the King's Park, testing and packing carts; pitching, striking and loading tents, kits, gear, etc. The older hands show up the progress, now they are efficient and help young hands, so keen and ready to do whatever is wanted, and all in great spirits.'

Bannockburn Day Sex-Centenery.

28/6/1914. – 'Celebrations went off with éclat, 450 Scouts, 16 County Flags and 2 Scout Pipe Bands. Visiting Scouts were kindly looked after by parents and friends. All went top-hole and couldn't have been better. Never saw such crowds in Stirling. After the show, a "Banquet." Interesting speeches, Professor Rait and others. Sat next to Lord Provost Stevenson of Glasgow, a noted pacifist! Had been warned to reply for "Imperial Forces". Whatever I said, he forgave and shook hands as I sat down. Many congratulations from all on the good turnout of B.B. and Scouts who were indeed a credit. Church Parade Service this afternoon at Bruce's Statue. Tomorrow off at 6.30 a.m. with 3 trek carts on ten days tour. With Lawrence and James we hope to bring out a booklet to forward such ventures.'

Trek Camp 29th June–8th July.

'Twenty-seven Scouts, four S.M's, 84 miles via Balloch, Rhu, Rosneath, Innellan, Sandbank, Loch Eck, Strachur, Kilmorich, Rest-and-be-Thankful, Arrochar, Tarbet, Luss, Balloch and back to Stirling. Full instructions out by 6th June with all details – a special word about boots and blisters!'

Visit of Their Majesties King George V. and Queen Mary.

Stirling, 11/7/1914. – 'I write this in bed at 6 p.m., after helping to welcome their Majesties from 11 a.m. to 3 p.m. We had some 600 B.B. and Scouts drawn up on the Castle Esplanade. There were also Girl Guides, V.A.D.s and Veterans. As we stood there ready, ten big cars drove up. Unexpectedly King George made a personal inspection of all the boys. I was sent for and had the honour of going round with H.M. When introduced, the King held out his gloved hand, which, after saluting, I took, feeling not oversure how far and how long it was right to grasp such an honour!

As we walked down the line he asked many questions as to tartans and pipers and flags, and seemed pleased and really interested. I got in a word about leaders and public support. I just spoke naturally and with respect. His manner reminded me of naval officers I had met in Malta. He seemed to put one at one's ease, indeed I quite forgot my foot! Did I tell you that on return from our trek two days ago, as we detrained our carts, the ramp of the truck, weighing half-a-ton, came down on my big toe?'

Achnacloich Camp.

Stirling, 20/7/1914. – 'I went to the Station and saw Kenneth Campbell and the Rev. Mr. Miller off to Achnacloich where I hear the camp is going well under James Lawrence, Jimmy Crichton and D. T. James. This is the third party I have seen off to the Camp, as foot still troubles, but hope to be fit to join them with Bernard Paget before the end of the Camp. Am hoping to join you soon and get a rest from Scouting. I cannot yet realise our wonderful progress during last year.'

War!

Then came the bomb-shell of War declared. That again is another story. Here is a last entry:–

Stirling, 4/8/1914. – 'You will be bewildered at the extraordinary pace at which events are moving. 1 have wired reporting myself to the War Office in London. I am packed up and ready whatever may come. A long telegram from the Chief Scout full of ideas for using Scouts. Have passed them on to Edinburgh, Glasgow, Aberdeen, Perth and Dundee, etc., and got busy here in Stirling, passing word to all concerned. Boys so keen to know what they can do to help. At 8 p.m. was able to wire to the Chief: 'Satisfactory steps have now been taken in Scotland.' As the plot thickens, these well-trained Scouts will prove more and more useful. I feel sad. How little do we know of what it all means? God grant we shall play the man and do our duty.'

MEMOIRS
OF A
RIFLEMAN SCOUT

PART III

PART III.

FIRST WORLD WAR TO VICTORY CAMP 1914–1919.

CONTENTS

15. 'BE PREPARED.'

I had been so completely absorbed in Scout doings all the Summer that, when the *Scotsman* of 3rd August, 1914, arrived and found me resting at Stirling, that large type heading – 'ULTIMATUM' – came as a bombshell.

Though for all these years instinct had told me that war with the Germans must come some day, yet when it did come it dazed me completely. It seemed so vast an upheaval, and we were so little prepared. No one yet knew what it meant when millions of men were engaged with new weapons of war. For the moment, nothing but prayer seemed to help.

Then came the trying days of waiting for orders. For a bit I was busy with Scouts. It was holiday time. The boys were ever-so eager, and worked with a will as messengers, hospital orderlies, clerks and in a hundred and one ways.

I remember at 10 a.m. on 8th August we were called on to help with coast watching. The Scout movement was organised and ready. By 10 p.m. we were able to wire that 24 Coast-Guard Stations in Scotland had been provided, each with a party of one Scoutmaster and one Patrol of Scouts, with tents, blankets and rations complete.

Something to do.

What a relief it was to feel something of use had been done. Everyone had that feeling – 'What can we do? For any sake give us something to do.' But as a Nation we were quite unorganised for War. Those who were ready and able and anxious to help could not be placed – there was no one to place them – while thousands, anxious to help, only added to the confusion because they were neither trained nor prepared.

185

With our Boy Scout house set in order, I was itching for Army work, but day after day no answer came from the War Office. They were snowed under with letters and telegrams. I went to the local 'War Office' in Edinburgh and asked for a temporary appointment. When it did come, it came like a whirlwind which all but finished me off at the start of my three more years of war.

Hamilton Barracks.

At Hamilton Depot, with its limited Staff and accommodation, thousands of would-be soldiers were trying to get inside the Barracks; thousands inside, after waiting and waiting in vain, were doing their utmost to get out. An excellent peace-time Staff were doing their best to compete with the situation under impossible conditions. A climax of chaos was reached when rival Liberal and Conservative agencies started a keen competition with each other as to which would secure the most men, and proceeded to fire into the already overcrowded barracks, all and sundry, many of them halt, maimed, and even blind, often without any papers at all.

It was impossible to provide food, clothing or shelter; and the poor fellows, arriving uplifted with patriotism, love of liberty, 'usquebah,' and seeing things from no red-tape point-of-view; would storm with indignation. Why, they asked, were they not sent by special trains, then and there as they stood, direct to Belgium, to sweep away the Kaiser, his legions, and every other form of tyranny,

Extracts from Log.

10/8/1914. – 'Sent to Hamilton Barracks to help organise recruiting as fast as possible in Southern half of Scotland. Work quite new to me.'

15/8/1914. – 'Have spent long days and travelled hundreds of miles, Berwick, Glencorse, Edinburgh, Hamilton, in own car at own expense. The complicated forms for "Special Reserve", "General Service." "National Reserve," etc., etc., are confusing. The great 'K. of K.' has made stirring appeals for more men, but there is no organisation for receiving them. We were just getting right when political agencies started a blizzard of confusion. We need simplified forms. Red-tape means delay, but with no forms, quite hopeless. Everywhere changing orders, doubts, confusion and chaos.'

17/8/1914. – 'Motored the Chief Recruiting Officer from Haddington to Hamilton to let him see for himself the conditions there. On arrival we were surrounded by a mob which included some of the riff-raff of Glasgow. Did what we could. Extra Police from Glasgow. Got help from Provost with feeding, shelter, etc., then motored back to Edinburgh, very dark night.'

19/8/1914. – 'After Edinburgh and Berwick, back to Hamilton, 5 p.m. Chaos. Chaos. Chaos. Chief difficulties –

(1) Orders to keep men till clothed but no clothes available.
(2) 1600 men in barracks meant for 600.
(3) Feeding, washing, sanitation.
(4) Utter confusion of papers.
(5) Want of N.C.O.s and trained men.
(6) Constant inflow of scum of Glasgow with coloured political tickets – these all mixed up with decent recruits and old soldiers.'

20/8/1914. – 'Another hectic day of unravelling chaos. Many are filthy, verminous, and quite unsuitable. After days and nights of discomfort and short rations; no wonder discontent. Wherever I show myself they come up and mob me with questions and grievances. We are short of staff and to get any order is difficult. Names from 600 papers are called out and all who answer are disposed of as fast as possible. All day this goes on, an exhausting business. But they also have to be fed and housed. Hundreds sleep on the grass out of doors. It reminds me of Thames Embankment days. The Town is ashamed, and no wonder. All very helpful once they understand. Urgent wires from 'K. of K.' ref. complaints from politicians that we won't take their men, etc., etc. Again late to bed with breaking back, no proper meals.'

21/8/1914. – 'Another desperate day of sorting out the rabble chucked at us with tickets. How sorry one feels for all the good men among them. Gradually we fix them up. At the close, some 80 special cases are left. We take those who have waited 5 days first, then 4 days, and so on. All have to pass the Doctor and fill up papers, etc. The Doctor ploughs 50%. What to do with those rejected? Send them away? Yes but they clamour for 5 days pay.

Who is to pay? In the end. I advance 1/6 on my own, and sign railway warrants, sending them back whence they came, with details on cards to explain.'

25/8/1914 – 'Today things are calmer. In Glasgow McLeod and others have done all they could to remedy errors. The Staff have done wonderful work. Today I saw vast crowds of likely young fellows heading for some big football match, later come roars of cheering. What does it mean to them that the Hun has this day entered Brussels? We shall not win this war on a voluntary basis.'

30/8/1914. – 'My three weeks have been strenuous but am thankful to have been in a position to help in 101 ways, in arresting the flood of chaos, which, unless cut off at the source, and dammed up at each new danger point, must surely have caused a complete breakdown. It is now just routine work. The next pressure will be with training.'

5/9/1914, Hamilton. – 'Things still in a pretty muddle, but the zenith of chaos is over. There will be a big to-do when family allowances, accounts, etc. have to be settled. Now they talk of raising Battalions of Footballers, Clerks, Tramwaymen, Boys' Brigade, etc. If we can shunt the recruiting on to their own blessed shoulders, they will get on better with less red-tape and worry. It is a desperate thing to find oneself a shuttlecock with W.O. Red-Tape on one side, and uncontrolled civilian enthusiasm on the other, playing their game of hit and scream. Give me the Boy Scout motto "Be Prepared." I never found it so hard to keep smiling, but, so far, I have, thank God. It is well to record such events as a warning.'

Good Work by Boy Scouts.

As order began to appear on the scene, I remember how much I was struck by the spirit of those dour determined men, who, in detachments, poured in from all the surrounding pits and ironworks. They knew nothing of drill or military ways, but you could see their one idea was to serve at this crisis.

At all hours of the day small parties fetched up at the Depot. At the head of each lot you would see a Boy Scout acting as guide, philosopher and friend, in sole charge of railway-warrants, certificates and enlistment papers, which he would hand over on arrival with a cheery smile and smart salute.

The men seemed to look on a Scout in uniform as one who knew, there was tolerance and good humour. Enough for the Scout to call out – 'You'll be late for the Kaiser!' and his commando would promptly conform. And the boys, so self-reliant, intelligent and alert, at the same time were modest, just bent on their job. Thanks to their Scoutmasters and the Chief, when the time came, they were able to do, without fuss, this good job of work.

Splendid Men.

For some time there was no one, in those early days, to train the men. Poor fellows, I often wondered how they 'stuck it,' for when at last their papers were all in order, what next? There was no uniform, no proper sleeping or washing accommodation and the cooking facilities were quite inadequate. On the overcrowded parade ground you would see the squads doggedly marching backwards and forwards, up and down, up and down the Barrack Square: with no proper instructors available.

Glorious fellows! The pity was that those who had laughed at Lord Roberts in 1912–13 did not have to join these stalwart Scots, or share in the strain thrown so unfairly on Regular Officers. Suffice it to say these men became heroes of famous Scottish Divisions.

August and September.

Meanwhile the war was taking its course and in every club and office hung some large map with pins and flags which marked the German advance on Paris and explained the heavy feeling of greatest anxiety at home. Mercifully the weather was ideal, so the want of shelter and accommodation was not felt as it might have been.

October.

As for myself, invitations came in from many directions to do this or that – from General Hutton to help to form a new battalion of Riflemen; from the Duke of Montrose to help in forming a new battalion of Argylls; from brigades and divisions to help on the Staff; indeed, so many offers came pouring in at this stage that the

Staff-Captain thought fit to 'pull my leg' with a wire purporting to come from General French himself offering me the choice of any appointment desired!

But I had got my own measure and definite object in view. I knew myself physically to be unfit, as yet, to command, let alone to raise a new battalion; moreover, after three years' work with Boy Scouts, I had so completely forgotten my old trade that I must first do an apprenticeship under some good brother officer who, knowing my physical limitations, would make allowances.

Aldershot – October, 1915

Accordingly, I was happy indeed when, on my birthday, October 12th, I joined the 8th King's Royal Rifles, under my old friend, Col. H. R. Green, and so became one of Lord Kitchener's 'First Hundred Thousand.' The story of this splendid battalion in its early days is well told in the Regimental Chronicle of 1915, nor should anyone who wishes to get the atmosphere of enthusiasm of those Service Battalions miss reading Ian Hay's wonderful book, *The First Hundred Thousand*.

To these I will add a few outstanding recollections.

'Kitchener's Men.'

Coming back to soldiering was to me the greatest trial. Men seemed so clumsy after boys; I seemed out of touch with them. The barriers, too, of rank had become hateful. The punishment of small military offences on the part of civilians – brimful of keenness and ignorant of military ways – often gave me a real disgust for the Army, and yet looking back I do not know that the thing was overdone. The result, anyway, was good. The men seemed all the more proud of being treated as Regulars. They loved their officers, quickly grew into the smartest of riflemen, and inherited as if by magic the spirit and best traditions of the 60th Rifles. I hear them still – returning from work singing, 'Here we are! Here we are! Here we are again!' Great fellows! How often I left my work and looked out from my window at Malplaquet and wished them God's blessing.

The Officers.

The few Regular Officers we had with us looked at first upon this whole crowd as a rabble. Their one secret wish was to overcome the fate which had left them behind – for their hearts were with their brothers in France. But they stuck it and saw the thing through. As for the Colonel, the wise old 'Verdant,' he just looked steadily ahead, alert in every direction; no skipper on his bridge in a difficult sea, with storms ahead, could have paced his bridge more cheery and confident.

Another impression I have is – what a noble collection of fine young fellows this 41st Brigade of Riflemen had: Rugby Internationals and Varsity Blues from Oxford and Cambridge, young schoolmasters, lawyers, planters – the pick of the flower of the nation. At times, accustomed to quiet, I used to find it tiring to sit down to tea in a large Mess with a hundred young athletes in the prime of life, for you need to feel young to share such company. What appetites! I did my bit in the war if only in this that I ran that Mess and encouraged the astonished caterer not to give in. I have never ceased to admire these young sons of Anak, whose hearts proved as sound as their limbs.

In another respect I was more fortunate than most. No regiment ever had a better Mess Sergeant than Sergeant Leather, and no officer was ever looked after better or more unselfishly than I was by Rifleman Matthews, and I owe it to these good fellows that I was able to stick it as long as I did.

For a time my prospects of getting to France at all looked shaky. I never felt well, and got chills easily and soon tired. 'If you go,' they said, 'you won't last a fortnight.' But I intended to go. It was not till I got to the 'health resort' of Ypres that I really began to feel well. There can be no doubt that it was thanks to these two good Riflemen and the open air life that the forecast of two weeks in France was extended to two years.

16. THE NEW ARMY TESTED.

Nine Months in the Ypres Salient.

I now propose to tell my story with the help of extracts from letters written at the time.

May to August 1915. – How impatient the battalion had been to get off to France! For weeks and weeks they had been asking: 'When shall we go?' and the wise Verdant had chaffed them, answering that it would not be long before they would be asking: 'when shall we get back?'

The first Division of K.'s Army to land in France.

At last, on 19th May, 1915, we were off, and I find this last letter written from Camp at Aldershot:

'I write this sitting in an easy chair in the sun, surrounded by officers sitting and talking. It is 3 p.m.; at 3.15 teas; at 4.15 p.m. my train leaves, and so it is really good-bye. The men and young officers, in great spirits at being off, all so heavily loaded, for we are separated from our transport.

'And now, what shall I say – we are off, well off, I feel. A fine battalion, a grand lot of officers, and all well arranged. Regimental bills, etc., all paid, and no hurry or fuss getting off. The future all unknown; best not to worry about that, but trust for health and strength to do each little bit as it comes along. It will make me happier if I feel you do not worry and are not anxious. Good-bye.'

We were now to begin a long nine months in the salient of Ypres, a time during which we lost over 1,200 men. I will try to convey the feeling of those months by means of letters. To me the whole experience of this extraordinary trench-warfare fighting was so novel and difficult, and so different from my galloping Mounted

Infantry experience of war in South Africa that I found it of intense interest.

I do not pretend to be brave, but I can honestly say that my interest and keenness overcame every unpleasant sensation. There were turns of duty when pounded ('crumped' we used to call it) from three sides by Hun 5.9 guns, 'whiz-bangs,' and 'minnies,' or trench mortars; poorly supported by our own artillery, which was short of experience and still shorter of ammunition, we would lose from 20 to 30 men a day with nothing to show for it. There were other days when things were quiet enough.

Arrival in France.

Let these letters take up the story:

21/5/15, Merckeghem. – 'After three nights on the move we are now established in billets in a beautiful village within hearing of the guns. I am with the Colonel and 'William John' Davis, the Adjutant, at the Schoolhouse, M. Hechinger and his family – nice people. Shared a smallish bed with W.J.D., but we were both so tired that we knew nothing of each other's presence from turning in at 2 a.m. to getting up at 7 a.m. Madame H. brought us coffee, and was much amused because I told her she was an angel and would go to heaven. It is wonderful to see all our carts, etc., transported and in good order. It all seems so simple, this moving of a thousand men and transport and horses and wagons and mules, etc., when you have done it, but there had been a good deal of work in the doing of it. Every one is very much interested in the New Army. Did I tell you we were considered the best of the New Army?'

23/5/15, Merckeghem. – 'A beautiful village standing high, rather as Longworth does, and distant views. But for the shape of houses and look of natives, one might be in some Berkshire country in June, trees, flowers, green fields, swallows, lanes, cottage gardens, all so beautiful. It is still difficult to realise that one is doing anything more than a pleasure trip with the battalion. Yesterday a route-march through the country, the brigade looking A1. One sadly realises that it cannot long remain so complete and well turned out, but it *starts* well and in good spirits.

All yesterday and last night guns booming some 20-30 miles

away. The Schoolmaster tells me he has seldom heard it so continuously. I am sitting under a willow tree, on my Argyll tartan rug, with Laton Frewen, in a green meadow just opposite the school, with a cow and a horse grazing and sniffing round us, the grey mare nibbling at Frewen's legs, as friendly as all the rest of the natives. We have our home papers of 21st, and nothing to worry us for the rest of the morning.

I like the people here, population 700, all R.C., and apparently pious, for they all turned out in their Sunday-best and went to the large church not 100 yards from where I sit. The Padre, the Schoolmaster, and the Mayor (a local farmer) all most helpful.

Yesterday I amused myself with the schoolboys, turning them on to play the Scout game of jumping over a string which was circled round with a weight at the end – one sou to the winner and great enthusiasm. Then the schoolmaster clapped his hands twice; they fell in and marched into school. It is jolly to see the way our men make friends everywhere. For the Colonel, Adjutant, Quartermaster and Company-Officers there are more worries and duties, but as Second-in-Command I have more leisure and save myself for future use.

12.45 p.m. – Interrupted by grey mare; jumped on her bare back, and nearly got kicked off.

On return from horse exercise this letter then deals with matters of messing and parcels and comforts and necessaries. It is the same with all letters written on service. You will find it in Bismarck's letters of 1870 . . . letters asking his Frau for socks or sausages, or thanking his lady for sending socks or sausages. I will omit all such references, and merely say that while of little interest to readers in later years, the arrival of parcels is one of the most important of all the events on Service. May all those who send out parcels to the troops receive their reward in proportion to the pleasure they have given. I will not attempt to say more.'

27th May, 1915, Nr. Cassel. – 'We *get nearer the guns* and see more of the troops from the front. These old hands look at us with a critical eye as we pass, the whole Brigade of Riflemen, dirty, dusty, and hot, but in good and soldierly order. The tendency is to think we are mere amateurs, but the most critical has to change his mind as we pass along. We do make our mistakes, of course.

The officers are late packing up their Mess after an early breakfast. The wheel of the Mess cart came off. Some men fall out from swilling too much water. The Brigade Staff order the Padre to hold his service in two places at the same time, and so on, but, on the whole, we get on wondrous well.'

31st May, 1915. – 'First experiences of trenches (near Kemmel). I will try to tell you something of my doings and experiences, for you will like to hear something first hand, from a pen you know, of the life, the trenches and feelings, both of the old war-horse going into battle, and of the new Kitchener soldier, bobbing or laughing, according to his kind, at the sound of the first bullets and shells passing well overhead, or occasionally unpleasantly close.

On the whole, I am satisfied both with myself and with what I have seen of the men and young officers. To tell you the real truth, I was not quite sure of myself, for a man's nerve does not improve as he gets older, but, so far, I have felt much as in South Africa. It is like getting up to ride in a steeple-chase, once the flag is down one settles down to ride.

As for the men, it was an interesting study, this first 48 hours in the trenches. With each day's march we had been getting nearer the Hun. Lectures from distinguished Generals and experienced Regimental Officers, practice in putting on respirators, talks en route to men of the Old Army and Territorials, all had given them a feeling that we were getting near the real thing.

All the previous day we had bivouacked in a beautiful green meadow, surrounded by tall poplars, the men keen and as fit as could be, awaiting orders lying about in groups watching for the first time occasional aeroplanes passing along above our lines, with puffs of shrapnel bursting all round them, a beautiful sight in the sun against the clouds and blue sky.'

The New Army.

'At 8 p.m. guides were sent to show us the way, and off we went. I stood and watched my half battalion go past in fours as it marched out, fit, bronzed, soldierly, well-turned-out, and equipped. I then came along in rear. As we marched through the town of Wytschaitte, full of troops who crowded round to see the first arrivals of the New Army, I think our men had the feeling a new hand has when he makes his *début*; a little self-conscious and not quite sure what to do; how to take the chaff of the older hands, whether to sing, or chaff back, or what to do? 'Have you come out here to fight or to sleep – with all those blankets?' 'Come up here and I'll show you what I came out for.' This, and such like, I noticed as I came along in rear of my half battalion. Soon after leaving the town an 'intense bombardment' (of Ypres) could be seen and heard some five miles to our left; it made them think, I expect, at least, it did me for it looked a fair sample of Hell. After marching three miles we came to our rendezvous, halted and waited for dark. I called up the officers and N.C.O's and spoke to them on the roadside at the head of the column. I expect they all remember it, not that I said anything special, but it seemed another milestone in our lives; the flag was down.

We fell in silently and marched to within the danger zone. A little further on eight young officers met our eight platoon commanders and led them off into the dark each to his own particular stance; and here I must leave them, for I myself was attached to the Colonel and Adjutant of the Sherwood Foresters, Territorials, and spent some hours learning the system and seeing all the arrangements for issuing rations and stores, a confusing business for a beginner.

Our Headquarters are in a doctor's house; a shell through the top storey has smashed his best bedrooms and a vine-house below, but the garden outside is still lovely with roses, rhododendrons and azaleas, and the nightingales have been singing all night. Up again at 5 a.m. seeing how the Adjutant ran his show, then out to the trenches.'

First sight of Trenches.

'It is really a very strange experience, something quite new to me. You leave Headquarters, where all is comparatively peaceful, say good-bye to comfortable rooms and baths and gardens, and start down a long winding communication trench. You see distant trenches in various directions, German or British? At first one has no idea; bullets come pinging over the top, occasionally one is advised to stoop to avoid some dangerous point. After a walk of over a mile one comes to some 'dug-out.' (You have seen them in the *Daily Mirror*), then one is lost in a maze of trenches, numbered and lettered and known to the particular moles who live in them. You see men resting and hear them snoring in holes which no tramp would say 'thank you' for – even on a wet day. These men have been up all night, improving the parapets and entanglements, perhaps, often under fire, or perhaps on sentry. They are as happy and sound asleep as in any four-poster bed. Or you see them cooking in their billies over smokeless braziers, or watching the German trenches through periscopes. You squash past them; there is little room to pass, 'Gangway there,' says some good fellow, and they all make room somehow. You dodge round traverses and under traverses, at some points the Hun is only 30 yards off, at others 300, and all day long you hardly ever see a sign of Fritz, in spite of a continual pinging and smack and whack of bullets passing mostly harmlessly overhead or into sandbags. With experience men grow more artful and the danger is reduced. But I can't go on with the endless impressions, the novelty of it all, and the interest – it is hopeless to try. One impression stands out – I marvel at the men who have stuck it right through the winter; it is marvellous, and they are heroes.'

10th June, Dickebush. – 'For the last four days we have been in the trenches. I find it hard work for all ranks, myself included – endless reports, telephone messages and organising of rations, water, trench store parties, etc., all a bit tricky to arrange at first. You would be surprised what a lot there is in it all and what a difference it makes if there is a good system and good men in charge. We finish our turn to-day, and then have four days comparative rest in reserve. We have lost a few men – I am afraid we must count on that each day, especially with new hands.

I write this from a bivouac under willows in a meadow, 8 p.m., getting dusk.

Last night it was a very dirty farm with a most insanitary farmyard, manure, pigs, roosters, refuse, flies, rats, etc. You never know your luck – Chateau or pigsty – we take it as it comes and are quite happy and comfortable.'

12th June, 1915 (12 Noon). – In Support. – 'We are back in

support to our 7th Battalion, which is taking its turn in the trenches; it has been a nomadic life, so far, not giving one time to get to know one place properly before we move off; still it is shaking us down to being more handy in moving, taking over billets, trenches, etc. It is sad how someone drops out each day, mostly slightly wounded, but sometimes killed, more often by stray bullets at night which catch relieving or carrying parties bringing up stores.

The men and young officers are splendid. Yesterday they had a real taste of mud, and one could realise what winter work in the trenches must have been. Thunder showers had filled the trenches and turned the clay to thick coffee-coloured mud, daubing the men from head to foot a real khaki (mud) colour, clogging rifles, and doubling the labour of carrying water, coke, ammunition and rations up to the trenches. With us at Battalion Headquarters it is more a work of organising parties, collating reports and returns of requirements, and sending out telephone messages and orders. It is hard work, too, often keeping one up all night, and so tied down that one has little time to visit the trenches.

By day one lies low, out of sight of aeroplanes. . . . At night along the hundreds of miles on both sides, the wagons come up to various bases, with stores, rations and water, with mails and trench materials and what not. Here parties are organised and carry each load (which has been carefully weighed and labelled) down the long communication trenches, or, if good going, across the open; each party to its own trench, with guides who know the way through the maze of trenches, all in silence and without lights. Stray shots go singing over the carriers' heads, or ricocheting off the ground with a buzzing, disconcerting sound, or strike with a loud whack some point which feels over near. . . . Occasionally some poor fellow gets hit, and arrangements have to be made for seeing to him and his load . . . The stretcher-bearers and doctor take up the duties they have been preparing for these many months. All the time, especially to young troops, what sounds like a great battle of musketry is raging along the front line . . . constant flares go up, mostly they come from German trenches, and light up the ground. We have now sampled various kinds of shelling, 'whiz-bangs;' 5-in. mortars, 'crumps,' hand and rifle grenades – all beastly, each in its own way, but not always as bad as they seem.'

In Reserve at Second Battle of Ypres.

19th June. – 'But for the censor, I could sit down and write you a long account of the battle we saw from a distance. I see the papers call it a success; well, it was not a reverse, so I will not contradict them, but what I do feel is that, as far as our two brigades were concerned, we would have been better employed where we now are, learning to throw bombs; for beyond losing stray men from chance shells and being brought up where troops were already overcrowded, we did nothing. At one time we were in a really warm corner, in the open, close to our own long-range guns and coming in for all the Hun counter-battery shells; the wonder was that we only had some half-dozen wounded. Personally, when I hear a shell whizzing over, I have enough experience to know, roughly, if it is coming my way or not, or to know whether the 'bang' comes from our guns being discharged, or from a German 'crump,' but to a beginner, the noise and confusion and ignorance of what is going on are trying.

We had three warm times, and each time the men did well, too casual in many cases, having to be ordered away from their cooking or washing operations. It may even be amusing to a young soldier, but the man who has been under a real pounding takes it in a very different way. Our men, if allowed, rush out and dig up the shell splinters or fuses as souvenirs. The nerve-tried veteran prefers the shade of a dug-out. Some poor chaps I have seen, who have had too long a spell, are quite undone, and needing a change which apparently they cannot be spared to get. Time in its course will certainly make our young men more respectful; I trust they may not get an overdose, like some have had. On our way up, we met German prisoners being escorted to the rear, glad, no doubt, for the time to be out of the inferno, but it would be foolish to estimate the German morale by such as these; we are up against a great and patriotic nation, organised in arms and all that leads to success in arms; we have got to realise that no one else is going to pull the chestnuts out of the fire for us.'

Conscription.

'We have left it late, very late, but not too late if we really wake up, but I do not see how you can organise the nation without the power to say 'you must.' The papers have not been cheering of late. Poor Russia, the great 'steam-roller,' is still in the reversing gear, and we ourselves stuck up, instead of making the much-looked-for advance.

At such times perhaps one hears of mistakes of the Staff, and experiences first hand marchings, counter marchings, alarums and avoidable losses, with nothing to show for them. Then you see a man tried; does he walk about grumbling and crabbing the Staff? or saying he sees no end to this war?, etc., etc., all in a whining voice, with a long face; or does he buck up all the more and help to buck up all around him? You never know your man till you see him on Service; it is only then you know whether he is a real Scout and a real Christian, or only one who bucks up when the sun is shining!

I was sad to see Jock Wood, my old Eton, Sandhurst and South African friend, had gone. In my rooms at Stirling I have a Sandhurst group of old Etonians – Boden, Gough, Blundell, Southey, Egerton, Paley, Gosling and others, all gone; truly, this Kaiser has much to answer for.'

From ramparts in Ypres, 27th June. – '. . . The life of a battalion in support is not always as restful as might be supposed; indeed, many prefer to be in the firing line trenches, where they have their regular job and more or less regular hours of duty and sleep. It is a wonderful sight to see the men who have been on duty, curled up and snoring, in some little hollow excavated in the side of the trench, perhaps alone, perhaps sardined together, covered up in greatcoats, in spite of the heat, to keep off the flies – and dead to the world, in a sleep which many at home might envy. Or, you pass them cooking in a tin held over a brazier made of a biscuit tin pierced with holes and filled with charcoal. Or you see them shaving with a fragment of looking-glass, or washing with only a canteen of dirty water. It is a strange life.

The line in these parts is the German line recently captured and converted to face the other way, a scene of much hard fighting. You find signs of confusion still uncleared up – rifles, equipment, bayonets, kitbags of both sides, khaki or cowhide, German iron loopholes and coloured sandbags, and sad sights of still unburied men . . . For some time yet both sides will be content to 'consolidate their positions' . . . In shelling the Hun still throws a dozen to one of ours, so we are glad to read of all Lloyd George is doing.'

Ramparts at Ypres, Sunday, 4th July. – 'Another Sunday nearly past. I have just come out of the adjoining vault where our Padre – Green Wilkinson – had 'gathered two or three (or as many shock-headed riflemen as there was room for) together.' He is a fine chap, and does a lot of good among the men. Last night at 10 p.m. we were burying three good fellows on the ramparts who had been killed at 4.30 p.m. the same day by a shell which landed where they were making tea in a house; twelve were hit. The funeral over, I walked through the town with the Padre, who was bound for the Hospital.

Today has been a glorious summer day; I went up to the trenches with ten men, trenches blown away in places, so one has to 'watch it' crossing exposed places. On the way home the Hun started shelling, so I left the trenches and scouted my party round across country. They thought it more exciting than it really was, and thanked me for safe conduct on return. It you watch the habits of the German gunners it assists.

We carried home in triumph a heavy iron German loophole plate, which we are having copied (for we are behindhand in these matters). On return an A1 wash and tea, then at 6 p.m., as I said, a nice little service. I am so fond of our riflemen and only wish the duties of Second in Command brought one more into touch with them than it does, for to me the chief pleasure of soldiering always was the men themselves.'

A rest in reserve.

Poperinghe, 8th July, 1915. – 'I have come on in advance to fix up the billets for the battalion, which is to have a week's rest after its spell of duty in the 'Lucky Horse Shoe.' It looks very comfortable comparatively and all seems fixed up, so I can now sit down and write you a line with a clear conscience. Also, if you were to meet me you would want some explanation as to why I wear a bandage round my jaw, for a bit of shrapnel got in my way yesterday. I had been round the trenches with Laton Frewen and one of the scouts

(Rifleman Sims, an old Boy Scout), and on our way back they suddenly planted four shells near us. It was all very sudden, and I could hardly believe a splinter had hit me. We soon patched it up, and on arrival at Headquarters the doctor put two stiches in and bandaged it. This morning I was injected for tetanus.

Our brigade is very glad to get a rest; for ten days they have had a trying time, but have done jolly well, and improved enormously, building up the trenches and accounting for a good many Huns who thought fit to despise the markmanship and enterprise of the New Army.'

10th July. – 'Many thanks for parcels and for all you do. I feel like the young swallow I was watching this morning, always asking for more. There were five or six nests in the shed which we use as our temporary 'Orderly room,' and in each nest two or three young swallows bullying and shouting to their parents as they constantly flew in and out over the Colonel's head while he was dispensing justice to defaulters and disposing of other business.

There is a jolly little garden with roses, wisteria, clematis and asters in front of our dining-room, where we have a jolly party. The Mess is all in good order now, and I have it arranged so that anyone could take up the reins and carry on without difficulty. Leather is now our Mess Sergeant and does A1. We live on 1 franc a day for local produce – potatoes, green peas, French wines, eggs and milk occasionally, plus rations and various parcels.

The officers' batmen are a good lot, all pulling together, as the French schoolmaster said. He was struck by the friendly relations between the officers and their men. He had himself turned socialist after his army experiences.

Well, we are having a good rest here, and shall be ready to face the Kaiser if he does make his threatened push on Calais. The Germans have a way of spreading such rumours when it suits them. I expect our Generals know; anyway, it is no use worrying if the Huns do try a Hindenburg battle with phalanxes and 2,000 trains of ammunition. We will not retire as in Russia; there is nowhere to manoeuvre to; we shall have our backs to the wall. Let them come on with their clouds of gas; they will find us here with smoke-helmets on, waiting to receive them; Let them try; we will get it over all the sooner. We shall win, and what else matters?

Our men have just driven off (7 p.m.) in 25 grey-painted London motor omnibuses; they are off for a night's digging somewhere in Flanders. Your Boy Scouts starting out on a Whit Monday holiday could not be cheerier. 'Hullo, hullo, here we are again,' and all their old Aldershot favourite songs. They have had three day's rest, hot baths and clean clothes, and are full of spirits after their trying time in the trenches. I feel very proud of them. They have been put to a pretty severe test (34 casualties in one Company alone), and they have done right well. They will do well if put to still greater trials. Hooray for them all! We are getting up a concert for to-morrow night. And now, halt! Enough.'

15th July, 1915. – 'It does me good to see people waking up at home, and I feel sure the tide will turn soon, but, by Jove, old John Bull *had* grown self-satisfied. Almost one began to dislike him.

Busy winding up and arranging Mess, Institutes, maps of new trenches, kit, etc., for we move tomorrow to trenches where Kenneth Campbell is lying (Zouave Wood). We expect to be 'in' a week, then 'half in' for a week, then 'in' a week, then 'right out' in support.

So we shall be doing our bit and relieving hardpressed battalions, which is more satisfactory than doing nothing. Things have been lively of late at the front. Today we had sports, including pony-jumping – my pony did all right. Last night I dined with Nugent; he keeps well and is always a very good friend, but he seems tired, at times, and, like the rest of us, is not so young as in South African or Indian days.'

German attack on Hooge. 30th July, 1915.

Sat., 6th August, 1915. – 'On the night of 29-30th July, we had just finished a hard week in difficult trenches at Hooge. I had devoted the whole of my thoughts to the Snipers, and we had got a fine system going. That night we were relieved by our 7th Battalion. I handed them a full report with maps and plans and pictures showing all the German trenches and loopholes and details of their habits, dangerous points, etc., etc.

The whole of the previous day I had been watching Germans with a good telescope, and Corpl. Evans and I had even drawn a bead with telescopic rifle on three Germans 700 yards away from the very hill which they captured next morning by using liquid flame.

The whole battalion had done well and was tired out, and glad to be returning. We got off about 2 a.m., having completed the relief satisfactorily (this is by no means a simple operation). I walked back to our Rest Camp 6 miles off, with Bowen and his machine gunners; got into a farmhouse and slept like a log for an hour till about 4.30 when we heard a terrific bombardment, and got a message very soon that we were to go back at once and reinforce our 7th Battalion and the 8th Rifle Brigade, who had been attacked and were hard-pressed. Two of our Companies were in the ramparts of Ypres. I went off with two Companies, while the Colonel collected the other two.

Now, while an attack is going, the artillery make what is called a 'curtain of fire' to prevent any reinforcements coming up. This is exactly what the Germans were doing, raining shells of all kinds over the 6 miles interval between us and our 7th Battalion: However, our advance was lucky and well-timed. We went a round-about route, away from the usual lines, and I arrived about 7, and reported to Colonel Ronnie McLachlan with two companies intact. (It was here we lost our Dr. Hawkes, killed by a shell; his loss proved a very serious one before the end of the day.) I found McLachlan at what we will call the S. end of Kenneth's Wood (Kenneth Campbell, 9th Argylls, killed in Zouave Wood). Here very few shells were arriving, but at the far end, which was held by R.B., huge 'crumps' and explosions were taking place.

It was a difficult position for a Battalion Commander to be in. He knew two Companies a mile away had been attacked and over-come. Wounded and messengers kept pouring in. All his Company Officers seemed to be getting wounded, and he had to send younger ones to replace them, and as fast as sent they in turn seemed to get hit. The situation in the thick wood was obscure; it was important to know what was going on, so together we went to the further edge of the wood. The real attack had been 1,000 yards away, but even here casualties were constantly taking place; men lying wounded or dying everywhere . . . one officer dead . . . and wounded and sometimes very shaken men returning back to the Dressing Station. It was as trying a time as any Colonel could wish to have, There was nothing to do but find out what was going on, and report to the General (Nugent), who was not very far off. About 10 a.m. the order came for me to join our other two Companies, who were now with our 7th Battalion, in the woods which I knew so well, having been there all the previous week.

About 11 a.m., 30th, the order came for us to counter-attack; at 2 the guns would bombard; at 2.45 we were to attack. The actual scheme only reached us about 1.30 p.m., and I well remember the occasion. Our old-established firm – the Colonel, Adjutant, 4 Company Officers and myself – how often we seven had collected for 'pow-wows' over sham fights – Aldershot, Hindhead, Borden, etc.; and now we were in for a real attack, and one in which I for one honestly felt there was no fraction of a chance of success; 800 to 900 yards across the open, up a glacis held by trenches, with no covering guns, and under an unholy bombardment from every kind of German gun, fired from every side into our salient.

Barely time to say a word to their Companies, our four good Company Officers got to their stations. It certainly seemed a case of good-bye to this world, but I only felt a kind of regret that it was not a show more likely to succeed. I wrote you a line from my notebook, then looked through some notes I have on 'attack.' One after another I noted our omissions and errors. It made it harder because I knew our Brigadier had personally protested, and yet had received peremptory orders to counter-attack. Even if our men had taken the hill, how could they face the terrific 'crumping' which always follows and the inevitable counter-attack? . . . Our good men, 36 hours without food or water, or rest, and no training with bombs and rifle-grenades.

But I kept all such thoughts to myself. I will say this; we *did* 'keep smiling.' We went at it, Officers and all, as cheerfully and as gallantly as ever at Talana or Delhi, or any other historic Rifleman's charge. But the odds were too great. Our 45 minutes bombardment had done nothing to save us. At least four or five hours *scientific* bombardment was needed. The Germans had done splendidly. Without losing a minute they had brought machine guns up to the captured positions, so that when we advanced there must have been from six to ten machine guns. There was not a square inch of dead ground. The 7th Battalion led the attack; then came our four Companies, the Colonel keeping two of them, and me myself in reserve.

My chief job was to try and see what was going on. I crawled out to the edge of a wood and saw what I could, and kept telling the Colonel that I could only see men being shot down, and could see no sign of progress of the attack. The great difficulty, as always, was to know what was going on. Poor William John Davis was sent up to find out. I found him later, lying as he had fallen, shot dead in a path near the edge of the wood. The fire of the Maxims was terrific; nothing could live in the open or near the edge of the wood. Few got far beyond the wood, and the wood itself was an inferno, from East, from North and from South, every kind of gun showered down shells and explosions. Away to our left, from what we will call Kenneth's Wood, the Rifle Brigade met the same fate as ourselves.

At about 3.30 Colonel Green, seeing no sort of hope of success, decided not to send in his reserves and to report that the attack was stuck up. Again I believe the 'Superior Authority' from some spot miles away wished to attack again, but Oliver Nugent protested again, as also another Brigadier, and so further losses were for the time averted.

To succeed, a counter-attack must be *instantaneous*. You can't give an enemy twelve hours to defend himself and then attack him in a minority with tired troops. On the other hand, if you can't do it at once, you may have to attack, and then it is a case of clear-thinking, careful reconnaissance and planning, superior numbers, every man his objective, fit and worked up to enthusiasm; then, if well led, an attack succeeds, but . . . well, well, I will not join in the fashionable pursuit of Regimental Officers – slanging the Staff.

To go on . . . the attack failed. In our battalion we lost 11 officers, 176 n.c.o's and men. Our 7th Battalion and 7th Rifle Brigade lost more than we did, while poor old Ronnie McLachlan's battalion – 8th Rifle Brigade – lost all but 4 officers and most of its men. Darkness found us digging a new line as best we could in the confusion of woods, then new troops came in and helped.

By 1 a.m. we had sent two Companies home, and were just thinking of getting the other two off when we heard a terrific outburst of rifle fire. I ran out from the dug-out. The whole sky was lit up with flare lights, when a wall of flame, which I knew must be liquid flame again; then two red lights, then every gun on each side and Maxims and bombs. What a row! We thought the Germans had followed up their success and were attacking, and indeed there was little to stop them pushing through to Ypres.

I ran to where Capt. Moor's company was. It had no officers left. I got them together and lined them out beside a Maxim . . . catching hold of each single man and bellowing in his ear where to go and not to fire without orders from me. The Maxim we turned on to one place we knew to be safe.

We lay there and waited, a wonderful sight and noise; the Colonel and I, each with a rifle, expecting every moment to be engaged, hand to hand. A terrific night battle raged. At one time it looked as if they had worked right round us, and we were cut off. One man went fighting mad from the excitement and had to be held down. For an hour nearly the battle raged.

We lay under cover and watched and watched, ready to stick it and stand a charge, or charge ourselves. Then daylight began to appear, the firing died down; messengers came in from various parts that all was well. It had been a false alarm on both sides; the Germans even pouring liquid flame on our imagined charge at their trenches.

I think the thing that I felt most was the terrible plight of our wounded. It was impossible to rescue those beyond under fire from the Germans; any attempts were fatal. Usually it was the most gallant and foremost in the charge who suffered most. Then when they got back to the wood, no proper arrangements had been made. One doctor and six stretcher-bearers were all that were available for over 500 cases in our two battalions alone. It was impossible to get Ambulance wagons up so far, and only by night could they come within a mile. So there these poor fellows had to lie, starved, cold, no proper attendance, groaning and dying, full of pluck, splendid fellows. I went round at intervals all night, with water-bottle, flask, cigarettes, chocolate, and did what I could. They were grand, a word here and there seemed a help. I had learned in Natal what it meant to be left wounded and waiting on the field.

And now I must close and send this scribble as it is. Verdant and I walked back to Ypres, called on the Divisional General and gave him our account of it all. He is an old Rifleman and a good friend. A lift in the Divisional motor soon put us down, two dirty-looking tramps, in our new camp, then breakfast, then a thundering good sleep.'

'Sunday 1st August, found me recouped enough to take a distinguished General (General Congreve, V.C.,) and Colonel Boyd, D.C.M., D.S.O., round and show the ground I now knew so well; made very good friends and spent an interesting day.'

From Monday 2nd, if I ever take up the narrative, it would require a book by itself to carry me on to my return here yesterday, (Friday, 5th). How, just when we were hoping to reorganise and rest after our troubles we were sent back to take up an important part of the trenches; how we went out and stuck four very hot days, losing another 120 men in this fatal salient; how the men stuck it.

Of all the difficulties of carrying on with hardly any officers left; of how splendid the Colonel, Verdant Green, was, and of our 'find' of a new Adjutant, Maxe Cullinan, who turned out A1; of the new German trench mortar) 210 lbs. of strongest explosive; of the urgent messages to our gunners giving its locality; of wires cut by shells just when most needed; of men buried alive in debris, or shaken for life by the explosion; of wounded men having to wait all day in trenches before it was possible to attend to them; of night attacks and false alarms; of German aeroplanes hovering over us; of a hundred and one other things, I have no time or energy to write of. Many a man has broken down from the strain alone. To me it is granted so far to keep better than usual, and for this I am very thankful.

After Hooge.

Instead of getting the rest which the brigade was entitled to, our battalion was lent to another brigade to make up their casualties.

The 6th Division, under General Congreve, was now preparing to counter-attack, and evidently the Hun suspected that something was coming, for the days that followed between the Hooge affair and General Congreve's attack were as lively as any seen in the salient, and came very hard on our poor chaps, crowded as they were those early days of the war, in the advance and well registered trenches. Our Battalion Headquarters were on an exposed knoll just off a trench called 'Union Street.' The companies of the front line held trenches recently taken from the Hun, with many detachments isolated by day and very much exposed to view and shell fire. Two companies under Charley Seymour and Laton Frewen held a salient within the salient, and came in for a special dusting. I well remember the 'crumping' Headquarters came in for too. It went on day and night for four days.

There were three small dug-outs. In one were Sergeant Leather and the Orderlies and Office Staff. In another were the Signallers, whose telephone lines, when not smashed up (or 'gone dish' as they called it) kept sending message after message of fresh casualties.

In the centre dug-out verdant, Cullinan and myself crowded and huddled up with papers and maps and orders and log-books, squatted on the floor. There was hardly room to sit upright or lie full-length. This was the bridge of the ship in the storm.

'Wanted on the telephone, Sir.'

'I say . . . can't you stop our own . . . gunners murdering us?' 'Another six of my best men and Lieut. ———— gone up!'

This was a type of message received, for the Hun was firing from the Domines Canal, 6 miles off to our right rear, and hard it was to feel yourself shelled from behind as well as pounded from flank and front. There was nothing for it, but to 'stick it' – but I remember whole days when we talked in a low, strange, faraway voice, as if it were part of a dream. We took it in turns to go down to the lines and see what was doing. The Colonel, who had been put in command of an extra battalion, scattered away to our right, would sally forth with one of his gallant Riflemen Orderlies, and one never knew if one would see him again, for his venturesome spirit took him crawling right up to diagnose the situation and visit isolated parties of men who had been cut off for days and were sticking it out among the ruins of Hooge.

I remember the shambles of dead and the debris of discarded equipment and shattered timber and sandbags, and amid this scene of ruined trenches and noise our own wounded men patiently awaiting darkness before it was possible to get them back to the doctors.

Here was a poor fellow with his thigh broken, bleeding and dangling. It had taken him half the day to reach thus far, no very heartening sight to his comrades as he dragged himself painfully along. Poor fellow, I can see him, standing and leaning for a space against a dug-out. I offered him a drop from my flask, but he shook his head and thanked me saying he was a teetotaler.

That night I offered to relieve Blane, who had had no sleep for nights. It was the kind of night one remembers. The moon was shining, and for the time being there was a lull in the storm. Rations, stores, bombs were being brought up and any repairs possible were being made to wiring and parapets. The stretcher-bearers were doing noble work, and all were making the most of the short spell of quiet and darkness.

I visited every sentry along the line; not the usual official 'Officers' rounds' inspection, with its sentry challenge and shout of 'Halt!' followed by a still louder 'Pass and all's well.' I was alone and on my own, with a subaltern left in charge who knew of my movements; I stood for some time beside each man on his firing step and joined him in his watch, listening hard. (I have always maintained that listening is a high art and insufficiently taught.) We would listen, then whisper, then listen again, and so the time would pass as we searched for and interpreted sounds, in the space beyond. All seemed well.

On occasions such as these good Scouts should get right home and in touch with each other. Give this good fellow 'a pat on the back'; let him know he has played a man's part these anxious days; make him feel that his comrades depend on his promptness. You may even whisper a joke, or a word about home. It may go a long way in making a man, and will help to hold the Hun at bay better, perhaps, than the fiercest challenge. Undoubtedly during those strenuous days, all seemed to point to a coming attack, but, had it come, the Riflemen were there.

The Limit of Endurance.

On the fifth day, while the Colonel was away on one of his venturesome trips, using my discretion, I took upon myself to do a thing he never would have done. I wrote to the Brigadier, who knew me well, and told him straight that those glorious men were being tried too high, and that a week of such hell on the top of Hooge, and the ten days' 'tour' before that, was unwise and unfair if other troops were available. When Verdant got back, I told him what I had done, and he did not disapprove, for he knew it was true. It was not long before the Brigadier came up himself, and that night we were relieved.

Throughout these days my mind seemed specially clear. At Talana, Bakenlaagte, Hooge, and in any tight corner, I have found myself helped in this way. It may be psychology, anyway, it is a thing to be very thankful for.

And now with notes from two letters written at this time, let me close this period of fighting.

Railway Wood, 5th August, 1915. – 'I write this from Bernard Paget's dug-out, waiting to hear that 'the Relief has been completed.' We have had a very hard time; I have been living from hand to mouth and quite unable to think of anything but the show on hand. I have hardly slept for days and am very tired, but hope to get a rest now for a bit. I send this as I know you will be anxious. Goodnight and love. Your v. sleepy son,' F.M.C.

Watou, 9th August, 1915. – 'Ref. my account of Hooge, several wrong rumours got about, and one would like all to know the truth. No-men and no officers, no Riflemen ever did, or could, do more.'

'We have had three or four days of real rest here, and the men are far better, but this is our first time out of range of German guns since June, and the time is all too short. We are off again to new trenches tonight. It is a great strain, and no one could stand such a time indefinitely. Artillery and explosions play an altogether new part in war; the greatest bravery and tactical skill may be useless. This is becoming recognised, but one must see it first hand to realise it. We learn from the reports that the Hun has a horror of Hooge. It only remains for all to buck up and face facts. Shells and men we must have; a courageous spirit and always a deaf ear to all pessimism.'

17. IN THE SALIENT.

For the next few months the Battalion was kept busy with trench warfare. There were interruptions in the shape of attacks in September and December, and a short leave home, but during most of the time I was serving my apprenticeship as a sniper in the Salient, and here perhaps a few words on sniping may be of interest.

Sniping.

It was in Sanctuary Wood in July that I first made my debut as a sniping enthusiast for it was here that we started with the band of picked Riflemen whom we had trained as Scouts and Snipers at Aldershot.

A day spent in the company of a splendid fellow, Sergt. Forbes, 4th Gordons, started me off on right lines. He was an Aberdeen divinity student; a book has been written about him. I will only say here that this day spent with him was one of the best days I spent during the war.

From that time onward I was sniping mad. Sniping was then in its infancy. The Hun had got the start, and was 'top dog' nine times out of ten, while we depended for our superiority on the chance of there being in any Battalion some enthusiast sufficiently fortunate to win the support of his Battalion or Brigade Commander.

Its Early Days.

It was not till later that it began to rain telescopic rifles, so fast that Major Sclater's and Hesketh-Pritchards' Schools could not keep pace with instruction in how to use them. In those days we enthusiasts spent large fortunes privately on telescopes, periscopes,

212

elephant guns, etc. We were the pioneers who proved the need of some sound system and of official sympathy; and, as is always the case with pioneers, it was an uphill and expensive task.

In my case, with Verdant Green as a warm supporter and the various Brigadiers, who succeeded each other only too quickly, all in our favour, I was more fortunate than most.

Good Men.

What men they were! Some two dozen picked Riflemen. The names that occur to me are: Scott, Evans, Otterwell, Liddiard, Sherry, Hicks, Riches, and others; Corporals then, but later mostly commissioned officers, and today – where are they? Every one of them killed, wounded, or missing! Names mean nothing to you who read; only a Sniping Officer can understand.

In India my sporting days with 'Juttu' and other Shikaris, had taught me much . . . but little compared to the days I spent doing Shikari myself to this loyal band of marksmen. Having lost my skill with the rifle, I was always accompanied in prowling about by one of the best of the band.

There were those who spoke of this sniping as 'sport,' but to me it was not sport; it was part of the great crusade in which I was glad to find some useful opening.

The Doctrine of Hate.

There were also those who preached the doctrine of 'Hate,' but wiser men preferred to leave the 'Hymn of Hate' to the Hun. And yet, though it may seem strange reading and ill to reconcile with Christian teaching, there was a time when it became an urgent necessity to preach the duty of *Killing*.

What was the average British soldier but a good-natured civilian dressed in khaki? Nor was his trench-warfare existence by any means calculated to promote a fighting spirit. Crouching all day underground, he would only emerge at night to play the part of a beast of burden – no wonder if he little realised that in the Hun, so seldom seen, he was right up against a foe filled up to the brim with hate, and trained *to kill* by masters in the art of war.

The Development of Sniping.

As a science the art of sniping grew steadily, thanks to the efforts of a limited number of experts, who would not be denied. Gradually, from their constant watching, snipers grew into expert observers, and often the reports they sent in were of the greatest value. This led to their being specially trained and employed, and worked on a system, as observers. Later, their enterprise leading to successful work on patrol at night, they became instrumental in bringing about a scientific training in night work which eventually reduced the terrible wastage of men, sent out with every possible blunder of management, to reconnoitre and stalk the Hun in the dark.

Science and System Required.

With regard to actual sniping, some of the tales in a book called. *Sniper Jackson*, by Frederick Sleath give some idea. Wherever the Hun was scientifically tackled we beat him every time, and more than once we left trenches, which we had taken over with an evil reputation for casualties, without a single mishap from hostile snipers. It was sometimes enough to kill a single really trouble-some Hun sniper to secure complete moral superiority. In one sector, I remember, on our arrival, it was unsafe to show your little finger. When we came away, three weeks later, I saw one of our men coolly lathering his face in full view as he did his morning shave.

Letters from the Salient.

29th August, 1915. – 'Frewen is back from leave already, and the Colonel due to-morrow. Seymour and two or three N.C.O's go next, and then I hope to follow. I am sending you some papers to help in the training of snipers at home. One had so little idea oneself as to what was wanted that I hope this may help. I have got on all right in command of the Battalion, but as you know, on grounds of health, I prefer the post of Second-in-Command.

We got up a successful concert last night, and I said a word and gave out that two Riflemen had won the D.C.M. for doing well at Zouave Wood, which was a great encouragement. General Plumer,

214

who saw us the day before, was very encouraging. Also a message from the King, so it was not difficult to buck them up; not that they need it, but it is a mistake to forget the pat on the back. We have 350 new men to replace casualties, a good lot and keen to do their bit.

It is difficult to understand the Welsh miners, going on strike except that to talk, still more to teach patriotism and unselfishness, has been looked upon as a mild form of madness by the average Britisher for several self-satisfied generations. As for saying 'you must' to the 'free Briton' – of course that was rank 'militarism.' If only Baden-Powell had been able to start his movement of self-discipline and citizenship earlier! However, we win in the end, and that is the chief point; though what it has still to cost us in the pick of our manhood one hesitates to think of.

My letter to the Scouts in Stirling has drawn several jolly letters from boys doing their bit, recruiting, working at munitions, hospitals, coast watching, etc., and counting the days till they can shoulder a rifle.'

Letter to Scouts.

24th August, 1915. – 'My Dear Scouts, – We are all old soldiers now, having been engaged in two or three battles – besides all the trench fighting – one of them as big a battle as any in the South African War, and yet in this great conflict it will scarcely be noticed. In the small hours of the morning the Germans come up to our trenches, armed with 'liquid flame' carriers, which, to look at, resemble portable fire extinguishers. On the tap being turned on, and the nozzle pointed at you, it shoots a flame 60 yards and burns everything. It is, however, a dangerous weapon for both sides, for one of a number of prisoners we captured the other day had both his hands burned using the instrument.

Then, besides the fire, they use gas, as you know, which comes drifting along in clouds. Every man now has a smoke helmet in his pocket and has to BE PREPARED to put it on the moment the order is given. So far, luckily, the wind has been from the West and we have not been troubled. Then there are all sorts of ways of throwing shells and bombs at us, resulting in great explosions like a mining accident, or an earthquake, not to speak of lesser

215

explosions, sudden and sharp, which catch you before you have time to get into a 'rabbit burrow,' in other words, your 'dug-out.'

Well, we 'stick it' all and keep smiling, with our rifles and bayonets ready, while our guns answer back to the Germans, the missiles whizzing over our heads to any distance from 1 to 8 miles. Our men are splendid and, like good Scouts, they do not get down-hearted. Indeed their pluck quite astonishes even myself, who know them. The other day, on getting back to camp, tired out, having been fighting 48 hours without food or water or rest, we found we had lost a quarter of our strength – 10 officers and 250 men. After a few days' rest the order was given to start back again into the firing line. Well, of course, we should have liked a longer rest, but I never heard one word of grousing; no, the men marched straight back to the sound of the guns, singing all the way. So you see I was right when I told you Kitchener's army would do well.

The strain of the war is very trying, and often some poor fellow gets tired out or shaken so that he is no more use for a bit. I there-fore hope that all likely men at home are getting ready to come and do their share. We have got to win this war, and to do it means straining every nerve. The Germans are good soldiers, brave and patriotic men, and we shall need every available man we can get, so if you see any likely recruits just send them along. We are fighting not for the Belgians only, but for our own homes and families. How lucky it is that we are fighting away from home. You should just see this country; there is scarcely a house of any kind left in Flanders now with a roof or a window. Where are all these poor Belgians now? I hope if any Scout gets the chance he will do a good turn for these unfortunate people.

Well, I must stop and wish you all good-night, for I have had a long day; up at 4 a.m., planning, arranging, thinking, map-drawing, and sniping. All this afternoon with a good telescope I have had my eye glued on the German trenches; one hides one's head and the glass in a sandbag so as to look something like a sandbag and so be invisible. If you keep very still you may safely look over the parapet, but if you make a mistake, cause a flash in the sun with the periscope, or make any quick movement you may be sure that one of the Huns will let you have a bullet pretty close. But we give them back as much as we get, and so it goes on. War, my dear Scouts, as I used to tell you, is a terrible thing. If we had been prepared, probably there would have been no war, certainly it would have been over by now, and I should be back with you in Stirling. As it is, I am afraid the Kaiser will keep us busy in these parts for some time yet.

In the meantime, good-bye to you all, and good luck. I often see the *Stirling Sentinel*, and am so pleased when any badge news is chronicled. It would cheer me up to get a letter or a post card from some of you occasionally to learn how things are going, but I know that letter-writing is a bit of a nuisance to most boys.'

Leave Home.

7th to 12th September. – 'First leave home. What a rush, but how well worth while it seemed. So much to do in London, seeing War Office and gunmaker experts about ideas for sniping, bulletproof shields, armour-piercing bullets, elephant guns, masks, paint, periscopes – all these things at this stage in their infancy and left to the private enterprise and financing of pioneer enthusiasts.

Then there were friends to be seen and relations of brother officers. Every minute was mapped out in advance – then the 48 hours in Scotland, and Stirling friends revisited; then a few glorious quiet days at Longworth, my last with my mother, sitting in the garden, roses, nieces, perfect peace, far from all sound of guns – a perfect holiday.'

Train to Folkestone, 13th September. – 'What shall I say; it was all a lovely time. I felt inclined just to sit back and enjoy it without any fuss. The only time I hated was saying good-bye to you. But you have that jolly family around you – and no distance or events can really separate us. Good-bye and love.'

Transport Lines – Poperinghe, 14th September. – 'It is a bore being back, and seems less comfortable after beds, hot baths, etc., but the change does one a lot of good, and I enjoyed every minute of it.

Yes, those short spells of leave were a great blessing; the only pity was that whole Battalions could not go on leave. The turns seemed so slow coming round, and for the men it was the one thing they had to look forward to. One might have expected these short glimpses of home to make men discontented and to unsettle them, but it did not take long to settle down again.'

Potige, 19th September, 1915. – 'It is a cold, bracing, beautiful autumn morning. I have been up since 5 collecting reports and sending in summary by 9 a.m. Occasional strolls to high ground just outside dug-out to see an aeroplane being 'straffed,' or to observe the shelling, a crisp feeling in the air, leaves and beechnuts falling. Soon the trees will be bare and the winter upon us and a different stage of war on hand. Many dug-outs and trenches at present concealed will become visible and unsafe, and many will become impossible when rain begins.

I am busy writing, when I get time, something to help in the training and working of Snipers. If I could bring out something really useful before getting knocked out by climate or shells or bombs or bullets, I should feel happy and content. It has been healthy weather, and going about as a sniper is interesting, instructive, and an active occupation which suits me well. One of my jobs is looking after carrier-pigeons; we send four of them daily to test them, 15 miles in 20 minutes or so.'

In reserve for a Push.

25th September, 1915. – 'My Dear F., – We are awaiting orders to move, bivouacking in an orchard. For days guns have been going far and near. At 4 a.m. this morning the noise reached its zenith; and we knew the push had begun.

In the orchard the cows are making themselves a nuisance to various shelters and 'tamboos' rigged up by officers and men against last night's drizzle.

In the field beyond the natives are ploughing, apparently as indifferent as the cows themselves to coming events; while wagons (French and British), motor lorries, ambulances, pass up and down the crowded road. One of our Companies, in shirt sleeves, is doing Swedish drill; another formed up in hollow square, is being told by its Captain of coming events; another is doing steady drill; and soon breakfast as usual, and make a good one, for you never know your luck. It may be to hang on here; it may be to join in the strafe. Who knows? For miles and miles great guns are going and all each soldier molecule has to do is to wait and play his part – to acquit himself as a man, still better, as a *Rifleman*.'

Casualties.

Railway Wood, 8th October. – 'We began our tour in these new trenches with five or six casualties the first day. One gets reconciled to it all. How sad it seemed to me last night, as I groped my way back, in the pitch dark, from reading the service over two good Riflemen, just out from home, whose names I did not even know. At the next grave was a cross: 'To Five Unknown Good Men' – known so well, perhaps, and missed so much in some circle at home – and the kindest-hearted getting hardened to it all. It is sad; it is sad – and yet it is Heaven's decree, and part of some great unknown intention of Good.

Signallers.

Tell Jess I gave her parcel to the Signaller next door, for they have a 'worrying' time and deserve a treat, sitting all day and night squeezed up in dirty dug-outs, with instruments jammed to their ears. 'Hello, hello, can't hear you. A1 Trench, blown in by . . . yes . . . hello! Shake your instrument. Hello, that's better; is that you? Don Ack? Yes, buried, buried, what? Six-inch shell, what? Casualties; no casualties,' etc., etc. – a harassing job, and a job to keep smiling at times, and yet, on the whole, they do.'

'Straffing' at Railway Wood.

11th October, 1915. – 'Here we live high in a wood, or what is left of a wood, in a dug-out 6 yards long and 4 wide – darkness lit up by candles, and cooking done by Leather with a primus stove – wonderful man. The wooded height reminds me of a bald head, nothing but bristles for trees, for the Bosche showers explosives on it, day in, day out. This morning, from 8 to 9, he got busy, blazing away from three sides at all our communication trenches, and dumping trench mortar shells on top of us.

Lieut. Rider Bird.

Our snipers have been doing good work, but, alas, we lost a fine young officer, shot through the head by a sniper. It brought it very near, and somehow, though so near, it seemed to me nothing but a good end as far as he was concerned, keenly doing his best, knocked clean out, no pain, straight to the not very far beyond where men go who do their duty. It was his very keenness that ended his time with us. He had asked me to help to put in loopholes in a rotten parapet he was rebuilding that night, not 30 yards from the Hun crater. I had been looking round and talking over things with him; we had cautioned him about exposing himself too much. I was looking over the parapet with my periscope and talking to him; he jumped up and, without my noticing, peeped over just on my left. There was a crash and a smack, and I realised he had been hit. The bullet passed right through a rotten sandbag in the top layer and got him low down in the head. He died as he fell, without a groan or a word. The bullet passed on through a subaltern's cap and splinters of it hit my good Corpl. Scott in the face. The bullet (our first experience of steel-core bullets) had come from a well-concealed loophole 250 yards to our left, which has now been found and tackled.'

A Timid Rifleman.

'Our men are splendid, always a cheery look or word when you go round; though even Riflemen are sometimes "stumours." One poor fellow, who had not covered himself with glory, when invited to jump over the parapet on wiring duty at night, protested to his Captain (Frewen) that he seemed to intend him to go and join his wife. "Where is she?" asked the Captain. "In Heaven." "Heavens, man!" said the gallant Captain, "if she saw you looking like that she'd kick you right out at the door".'

Letter to 'Sentinel.'

October, 16th 1915. – 'My Dear Scouts, – I must send you a line, as I promised, for it is now two months since we met; ever since then I have been too busy to write properly, but now at last we are having a few days off. How one does enjoy getting back to a hut; how comfortable a wooden floor is after a muddy wet one; how grand it is to get a decent wash; what a feeling of liberty it gives one to be able to stand upright and walk in the open. You must do a fortnight in the trenches before you can realise it. And yet I have found it interesting and exciting at times, and the great thing is that any man who does his turn in the trenches can feel he is doing a wee bit more towards the winning day.

As for myself, I have been busy chiefly with the snipers, having ten splendid picked men, crack shots with telescope rifles. We lie in wait from dawn to dusk; there are always some of them watching with their eyes glued to the telescope. They become each day more cunning, and have great duels with the enemy's snipers. Sometimes we disguise ourselves by wearing a sandbag, sometimes a mask of brown or green gauze or with grass and bushes, or it might be a common masquerading mask painted like bricks or stone. We lie quite still for hours peeping cautiously out from some unexpected place behind the trenches.

We get some splendid views of the German soldier. The other day I saw a man take his jacket off and fold it up neatly, then he started digging; soon he got hot and took off his shirt; then he got still hotter and he took off his shorts, and there you saw him 'stark.' I think he would have been shy of exposing so much of his person if he had known I was watching so closely. 'Why did I not shoot?' you ask. Well, my boy, I was trying to find out what those slim Bosches were at, and there is a true saying that 'Dead men tell no tales.' I was scouting, you see, and wanted to find out all I could from him. But, of course, if he had been a sniper trying to shoot us, we should have had to take him on.

Then we have an elephant gun; I got it in London when at home. The German sniper has iron loopholes; you watch and watch, and at last you see the slot slowly opening, the muzzle of the rifle being gradually pushed forward. This is the time for your marksman to shoot, but sometimes he shuts up his port-hole quickly, like a snail going back to its shell. Now that's the time for the elephant gun – a steady aim and bang goes the great steel bullet clean through the steel plate, and Mr. Fritz does not bother you again that day.

But sometimes a poor chap on our side gets hit – for they have telescopes too. The other day I was looking through my periscope at a German loophole and telling an officer what I saw. He put up his head over the parapet to see; no sooner had he done so than he fell down, shot right through the head, killed at once. Such a fine young fellow, too, and a very great loss.

You see you must never despise your enemy. He is a very good soldier, the German, so do not listen when people laugh or sneer at 'Bosches.' When the newspapers talk so stupidly of 'Huns' not playing the game, etc., etc., as often as not these Germans are fine fellows doing their best for their country, and doing it better than most. They are standing all sorts of hardships; they are facing all kinds of dangers, just as much as our own good men at the front, an example to many who might do more.

So I give you the tip – always respect what is good in your enemy; it is part of the code of Chivalry of Scouts.

Well, as you know, we cannot send home full accounts of our battles. The Press Censor would object. Sometimes we have to face heavy shelling of our trenches and dug-outs – shells of all kinds whizzing or swishing or whistling past, or into our lines, with shaking noises and huge explosions often with sad results. Sometimes it is the trench mortar – you hear a report, you look up, and there you see sailing over towards you, high up over your head, then falling straight down amongst you – a clumsy, bottle-shaped shell like a rum jar. Down it comes. 'It's a dud,' some new hand exclaims (which means it won't explode), but the old hand knows better.

There is a pause, then a loud report, with clouds of dust and splinters, and you are lucky if you, or some poor fellow you are fond of, are not sent sky-high or buried alive. It may be the springing of an underground mine; it may be bullets from machine guns or from snipers; no one knows what each day may bring forth. You may be called on to set your teeth and charge barbed wire and gas and flame. You may have to hang on and stand up to a bombing attack and defend to the last. You never know, but this you do know – it is a life-and-death struggle now for the country, and for all you hold most dear. Happy the man who, at such a time, is enabled to do his tiny bit, bravely and wisely and well.

So then, my dear Scouts, play up and do your bit. If you are old enough and can be spared by your parents, lend a hand in helping to watch Britannia's shores, be thankful and proud that you got the chance. If you can assist the wounded, or help in any single practical way, then be up and doing at once. You may not be able to help in this, but I tell you there is this much each Scout can do – you can help the old country each day of your life; for each little thing that you do for others, giving up something yourself, your time, your games, perhaps, for a while, you are helping to build up true men, and that is what we want. A nation made of true men can never be beat.

Good-bye, and Good Luck to you all.

Yours sincerely,

F. M. CRUM.'

Railway Wood, 16th October, 1915. – 'Did I tell you of my birthday battle? About 6 p.m., as it got dark, the Germans suddenly opened with every gun at their disposal and bombarded our lines and Battalion Headquarters and communication trenches.

A tremendous doing; we expected an attack to follow. Some of the wires got broken by shells, but we were in touch with our guns and Brigade the whole time, and we gave them back as good as they gave us. The men were very good, and stood the strain of the bombardment very well.

The new General (Jeudwine) has just sent a note thanking the Battalion for splendid work and cheeriness and the way they mended the bombarded trenches in the night, repairing all damages. 'Purr when you are pleased' is a good motto, so I am very glad to find we have a man in charge who knows its value. So many do not. We had one officer killed and five wounded officers during our fortnight, a higher proportion than usual.'

Trafalgar Day, 21st October. – 'Still resting, my head is now far better; the noise of guns worried me a bit. One of the things that helped me was a 60-mile joy-ride to visit a training school, such a joy getting into the country and away from war.'

23rd October. – 'General Jeudwine has taken up my sniping keenly and asked me to train the Brigade snipers. As the Colonel came back today I am free to take it on . . . I finished up my week in command with a lecture, and a route march today, and have got on well, but I always feel that, though with health I could run a battalion, the strain of it would finish me sooner, so it is wiser not.'

25th October, 1915. – 'Very hard worked with Courts Martial and starting snipers. Very heavy rain yesterday, but clear again this morning, the sort of day in October when one looks out and sees from Stirling, Ben Ledi and Ben More. In this rotten country one seldom gets those fine dry mornings; it is damp and misty mostly.'

30th October, 1915. – 'My Dear F., – This morning I took my snipers over to see the model school of the 49th Division, where they test all the latest ideas. We had just tested and found very good a simple invention of one of my corporals, when General Plumer came along, so I showed and explained it to him. He made a note of it and said he would push the idea. Lucky we met at right time and place; it saves so much time and energy if you can get direct to the fountain-head.'

Prisons and Courts Martial.

'After training my men in a large room at Poperinghe, a decent Belgian woman gave us a good meal at one franc a head, and I spent the whole day teaching them how to make reports and what to report. Then I had to visit the prison, sad to think one cannot get on without that sort of thing, but there it is; discipline has to be strict, and men, unaccustomed to it perhaps in former days of 'British freedom,' give great trouble at times; perhaps it was sleeping at their posts, or absent when warned for the trenches, or drunk on service, or what not – anyway, I found a good few of them shut up when I paid my official visit. More than any other duty I hate most this side of soldiering. For two days I was on Court Martial dealing with cases, some upon capital charges, which is a trying responsibility.

But I may be giving a wrong impression. In such a huge army there are bound to be some 'bad hats.' The discipline and conduct of our men is, on the whole, exemplary, and I have never seen cheerier or more willing men, in spite of every hardship. We do all we can to make things more comfortable. To-night we have a concert. We have converted a large barn into a recreation room, and have a canteen with beer and stores and tea and coffee, which is much appreciated. The men get paid regularly, so that out of the trenches they are comparatively well off.

December 1915 proved a strenuous time in the trenches. Most of us will remember this time chiefly for its Xmas disappointment, when orders to move from mud and misery of Flanders to Egypt and sunshine were cancelled on Xmas Eve.'

9th December. – 'We have been passing eventful days in the

Scouts who helped in the war by guiding men to their regimental depots in August 1914.

Officers of 8th Battalion, King's Royal Rifles, Aldershot 1915.
F. M. Crum is in the front row, fifth from the left.

Blangy, Arras, where Crum was in March 1916.

Snipers at Acq, June 1916.

Imitation German trenches used for training.

Interior view of imitation German trenches.

Germans observing the British.

Snipers observing German trenches.

What they saw.

Training with black glasses
in night scounting.

Snipers camouflaged.

A moveable camouflage ruin for scouting purposes.

Curtain used at sniper's post.

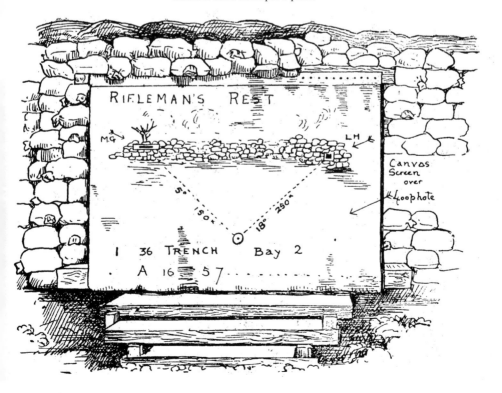

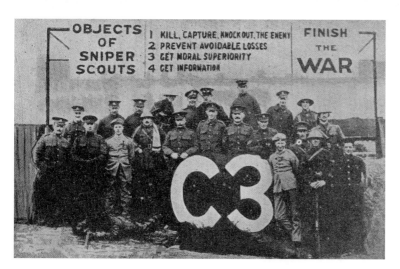

Aldershot Sniping
School staff.

Scouts' Victory Camp, Rosneath,
11th-25th July, 1919.

Parents' Day, 1922

trenches and are now out again for four days. Today it has poured and poured, and the mud which was 'the limit' before must now be beyond all words. The guns keep going through it all, and I suppose the troops of both sides are being put to as a high a test of endurance as ever is reached in war. My own occupation of late has been centred in supervising sniping and with visits to the trenches at night.

You can hardly imagine the mud. One squelches and struggles along in gum-boots, slipping, slithering and stumbling in the dark, saving oneself from a fall at the expense of covering one's hands inch-deep in mud, or, failing that, taking a pearler and covering oneself and one's clothes from top to toes with liquid filth, which one carries back to the dug-out, impossible to clean up self or clothes. I think I mind the mud far more than any shells or bullets, though I do not pretend to enjoy them either. As for the men, I suppose many of them do not feel it as much as I do, but their discomfort is far greater and they have far more to put up with than the Second-in-Command, with the excellent Matthews and Leather to help and look after him on his muddy return; far less space to live in, fewer clothes to change into, and long hours of sentry go and carrying rations and stores in the dark and mud. They are splendid in it all.

The other day I had to get some men to an exposed post by day; the only way was up a trench chock full of water. We crawled flat across the open till we got to the trench, then on our stomachs over the parapet into the trench. We all had 'thigh-gum-boots' on, which reach up to the hip. I planted the sides of my feet against the trench each side, supporting and elbowing up the trench; then it got too wide and down I slipped, down, down, over the thighs, so cold the water was as it poured in; now I am wet I do not care. I will shove along, but no, down and down, in liquid mud. This won't do for a man of 5 ft. 6 ins., I thought. However, it got no deeper, and on I got my party, struggling, till one of them lost heart and stuck. Leaving with him Liddiard, one of my best snipers, on I went with the other Riflemen to the isolated post.

An Exposed Post.

Shell holes in every direction, for this was a favourite 'cock shy' of the Bosche. One dug-out I found blown right in, some of the men's

225

packs buried in the debris of fallen roof and sandbags and, marvellous to relate, not a man hit, though some were shaken. There they sat, collected in the remaining dug-out, a charcoal brazier burning well, three sitting round it, four or five more huddled up just clear of the liquid mud, in a hole not fit for swine to wallow in. Here they had to stay all day, not a move for fear of aeroplanes, and every now and then a far-off report, then a sing-song sound and the cr-r-r-rump of some big shell bursting somewhere in the same parish.

These were some of the men who stand on guard barring the way to Calais. They had sent word to say they were being shelled, and might they shift to a flank. I had come to tell them they must stick it for 24 hours. I was wet to the skin, but for me there was a change of dry socks on return, but for them 12 hours more of waiting in wet and cold. It was difficult to swear at them, but it had to be done, for their orders were clear, and then I did what I could to remind them it was an important post, and that men who stick such things are the men no Kaiser can beat. Well, I did what I could and left them a bit bucked up; that afternoon a 'crump' carried away three of them, poor chaps.

Not all Heroes.

All Riflemen are not heroes, as I found on my return. There was Liddiard still struggling to get the other Rifleman on, but devil an inch could he get him forward, groaning and moaning and whining, all pluck and effort gone, a pitiful object he was. We tried persuasion, abuse, ridicule. He whined about cramp, he was 37 years of age, he was a married man, etc., etc. I saw he was useless; even if I did get him on, so we settled to get him back if we could. At the thought of getting back instead of forward his craven spirit bucked up a bit and he made some way, moaning and groaning, but hurrying after a fashion. 'A proud man would Colonel Green be if he led a thousand such as you,' said I, as Liddiard heaved him along by the seat of his pants and I gave a hand at the scruff of his neck. Somehow we got him back to Headquarters. Let us draw a curtain over such scenes. On returning I sent him to the Doctor, who said there was nothing wrong – alas, even Riflemen are not all heroes!

I had to get on for a Court Martial 3 miles off by 2 p.m., no time to change properly, so off I hurried, arriving just in time; the cold began to tell, my knees were burning with rheumatism and my body as stiff as a poker, so instead of returning to the Battalion I arranged to stay with the General. He was kindness itself and his servant, a treasure, a Scotsman. A good dinner, the General's underclothes, socks, trousers, and a bed rigged up in his own room, and I woke up next morning right as a trivet. I have made a long story of it, but I think you like my letting myself go occasionally; it lifts the curtain and shows you 'the kind of thing'.

I watch the war from a distance as well as from near; the end is not yet by a very long chalk; chiefly because we are not soldiers. If we *had* been and if we had had a Government which knew its own mind, and if we had one fixed international policy among the Allies, we should have had the Bosche stone cold by now. But we bungle along, with fresh time required to rectify fresh mistakes, and so it drags on. The Hun is efficient, unscrupulous, decided in all he does; he may deal us more sledge-hammer blows, but his cause is wrong and ours is right, and that must win in the end, even with us as its unworthy champions.

We improve, and are being beaten into shape, and they, with extending lines and swollen heads and endless intrigues and lies, they are bound to fail. Does any man with Faith say no? And what does it matter what happens to you and me so long as we mend our ways and grow worthy and win. For years I have felt unhappy about it all; it had to come, this chastening.

We may get much hammering yet, one must set one's teeth to it all; the gallant young fellows thrown away, the tears at home; it is troubles and trials, not comfort and money which make the man, and Britain will yet look the world in the face, stronger and better than ever before.

We are under orders to move. Where to? You know my love for the Salient, and will share with us our sorrow at parting. My love to you all, and may you keep strong and well and free from worries, for all is well.'

My First time in command in Trenches.

Same Trenches, 18th December, 1915. – 'We had expected to leave this 'lucky horse-shoe' some time ago, but we got word we were for yet another four day's tour. It was a keen disappointment; still no one grumbled, and being a move we had made before, we got off without trouble. It is a great help knowing the trenches, especially in dark and stormy weather. The hundred and one arrangements for sending up rations and water and coke, for greasing men's feet, for inspection of smoke helmets, all these things become a matter of routine, difficult to start in a new battalion, but easy enough in a well-organised battalion of old hands like ours, with a good Quartermaster, Adjutant and Staff.

We got off comfortably 4 p.m. and by 8.15 p.m. each Company had reported to us at H.Q. 'relief complete.' We were left in possession and I found myself for first time in charge in the trenches. Leather produced a good dinner after which Frewen and I struggled round, visiting the various posts, a fairly quiet night. Back about 2 a.m., I turned into my dug-out, and putting an old newspaper on the bed, lay full length in my dirty gum-boots, for one can't sleep on such occasions; any unusual sounds, rapid fire, a salvo of whizz-bangs, and one is on the *qui vive*. It was the same in South Africa, not 'jumpy,' but a feeling of alertness. It would be better, of course, to take things more easily and sleep, but there it is, I hardly sleep at all during my tour in the trenches.

These are noisy trenches, a lot of gunning, but as a rule few casualties, snipers went out and lit the usual fire in a deserted farm and successfully drew fire; the routine messages came in from the Companies and all went much as usual till 3 p.m. on 13th December when big shells landed a bit nearer. They shook the whole place, but it had often happened before, so we did not worry.

H.Q. Dug-out blown up.

About 4 p.m., six of us were sitting in the H.Q. dug-out when a 5.9 shell landed plumb on the top of us. Cullinan was standing at the telephone. I was at the door and Frewen near me. Miller, the Doctor, the R.A. officer, and Purdon, the M.G. Officer, were at the other end, just where the shell landed. The noise was terrific. Then a sound of tumbling debris and struggling. Cully and I were untouched and Frewen nearly so. We got the others out and found that only Purdon was seriously hurt and unconscious. More shells.

I got to the telephone dug-out and spoke to the Brigade. While I was doing so a shell landed in the signallers' dug-out. It rained shells for some time, great geysers of mud came tumbling down on us as we stooped in the trenches and all the time Miller, having extricated and shaken himself, was splendid in looking after others.

It was evident our position was now located and it was a poor look-out for the brains of the local defence! General Jeudwine came up and consulted, where to go? a conundrum. Every possible place was full up, water and rats were in possession everywhere else, nothing for it but to start and dig elsewhere, and so all night, in addition to their other work, our good men were at it.

The next day came and there was still no good covered way to our chosen cover in rear. When the shelling began again, we got all the men, skirmishing one by one, to a good place 300 yards in rear. Once there they were safe and we had the satisfaction of seeing crump after crump landing on our vacated dug-outs and trenches and of watching shells landing beautifully on the various dummy 'cockshies' we had erected, smoke fires, canvas screens, etc. But the cold was intense; thanks to Sergt.-Major Archer we got hot coffee and rum issued in spite of great difficulties, but, by jove, it *was* cold. We were not sorry when it grew dark and the firing died down, so that we could move back to our lines. Another night of good hard work found 5 good dug-outs finished and a trench to them, drained and boarded, a fine performance done with the help of some of the Kings Liverpool Pioneers. And so we got out of what looked a very unpleasant position. The bombardment was evidently preparatory to some attack. We had 5 or 6 dug-outs smashed in and 3 rifles hit, yet marvellous to say, only one man killed and one wounded during the whole of those stormy 4 days.

We have had a large dose of this salient, and the hope of getting away to warmer lands (Egypt) with a rest from shot and shell and mud is cheering us all up.'

19th December. – 'It was at this time that the Germans made a gas attack east of Ypres, and the Battalion which had just relieved us had a difficult time. We had expected it throughout our tour of duty, the wind having been from the east throughout, nor were we allowed to forget by the Brigade, Division and Corps Staffs who constantly sent reminders and cautions, till one – well – I won't say what.'

20th December. – 'We lose General Jeudwine shortly, getting Lord Binning as our Brigadier, I am very sorry he is going as he is a real friend now, besides being one of the best soldiers I have come across. During our trying time he was A1. In the middle of it he sent for me and began by saying he had been thinking over something I had said and that it was right, whereas we had disagreed overnight; and seeing I was tired he insisted on my lying down on his bed. I was soon half asleep, but not too far gone to be aware of his getting up from his work and putting a blanket over me, which I thought very good of him as I dozed off to the sound of the guns.'

Xmas Day, 1915. – 'We are nearly through Xmas Day. It began with the buglers playing Xmas hymns in camp on their key bugles. A Church Parade Service conducted by big Neville Talbot. Xmas dinner A1. A band concert at 3 p.m., conducted by Mr. Tyler, of 60th and Warren Hastings fame, and now there is another concert going on.

We are busy with plans for moving but all is still very uncertain.'

A Great Disappointment.

26th December. – 'We had a good Xmas for the men but it was spoiled by a sad knock last night. We do not move, and return at once to the old game. I find it hard to keep smiling. Oh, what a bore. The thought of sun instead of mud had bucked us all up, but we will plod along and try to be content. The men have been so splendid and full of the idea of a move, so that it is a keen trial. They looked so keen, alert and full of life at the Church Parade and Concert yesterday, and now I feel the dull drudgery feeling will have to be fought against. You see we never have had a proper rest since the start. We go back to new trenches (Lancashire Farm) very soon, so I must buck up and pluck up courage and give a good lead. I do not ever remember a more cruel disappointment.'

Elverdinghe Chateau.

31st December, 1915. – 'I think that few of my stays in various places in Flanders have left a more lively picture on my mind than

230

the three days spent in this fine chateau. How far is it wise to commit one's impressions to paper is a question, but I sit down in the Count's dining-room to jot down a few notes before leaving in the evening to start the New Year in the trenches. As I write, sitting at the dining-room table, looking up at the ceiling with its family coats of arms, one side of the hall sandbagged up to the roof, a fire burning merrily in the great fire-place at the other end, heavy 'straffing' is going on between the big guns, and splinter marks remind me that, if shelling gets nearer, we must vacate the ancient hall for muddy trenches.

After our Xmas disappointment we got orders to come to Elverdinghe Chateau, so did two other Battalions. We all turned up, only to find that the occupants (49th Div.) had no idea of any orders to turn out. Thus in a place not 2 miles from the Bosche, collected large numbers of men, new to their surroundings, giving their position away at night with numberless electric torches flashing like glow-worms all through the beautiful woods, swearing, slushing and searching for tents, shelters, dug-outs, tripping up, all in confusion. By day, liberties being taken enough to turn grey the hair of the cautious Commandant. Carts loaded with R.E. stores, white planks to catch the eye, parts of huts and what not; mounted orderlies in the open, formed groups parading, . . . goodness knows, what a show!

It is a beautiful Chateau, an artificial lake in front, great oak and beech trees in the grounds, thickly wooded towards the walled garden, greenhouses, fruit trees on the walls, stables, motor garages, and the village close by. The house a large grey stone square 'pile' – four stories high and built in 1874.

How the dickens it has so far escaped the shells, no one knows. The little ornamental bridge 100 yards north-east is blown up, a huge crater 20 ft. deep has formed a new pond on the green slope, not 20 yards from the Chateau itself. Splinters from the explosions have broken windows and doors, beyond a gash, and in the same line, more huge shell holes, it seems almost as if these shots were the long and short brackets made by some Bosche gunner, who had the Chateau for his mark. Or is it that the Count's wife is an Austrian?

At 1.30 p.m. we were lunching on the 3rd floor. What would the dear ones at home say, so many of their beloved living in this one chateau, as if we were in perfect peace, instead of being a registered target for 15-inch guns? No censor would pass this note if I mentioned the number of the Count's guests, or enlarged on the facts.

At 1.30 p.m. shelling begins, shrapnel bursting in the air, splinters flicking the lake in front, scattering and puzzling the ducks as they swim about, at a loss where to swim to next. Their wings are clipped, or they would surely fly; I would anyway. Then comes a noise as of a motor 'bus whirling through the air. We know it of old, in many parts, but here it comes, jolly near, just above our devoted heads, and then a crash beyond, and the whole Chateau trembles. We console ourselves with the idea that is is really quite a long way off and go on with our lunch. More shells flick the lake and the walls of the Chateau, then Rifleman Gambrell comes in and says some of them are tear shells and that all eyes are watering. We adjourn and walk down the staircase (poor Count, what a muddy staircase). In the front hall a badly-wounded man is lying on a stretcher. Everyone looks as if he was crying or had a very bad cold, but we know the 'lachrymatory shell.'

Just then another motor 'bus-like rumbling up above and then a crash. I push through to the front door, in time to see a cloud of debris. The Church Army hut which was – is now no more – gone sky high, all except a tricolour flag found fluttering as if to a mast.

Half-an-hour before the Sergeant-Major had reported to me that we had 'taken it over' games, gramophones, cups, etc., all correct – gone! What of the caretaker?

The men in tents and shelters had cleared into the trenches for cover, but not all, for the first big shell, the one which we had flattered ourselves was far away, had found a whole platoon of Monmouthshire lads, who had just fallen in, ready to march off, Altogether 5 big shells, 15-inch, landed in this part of the wood. Three of them harmless, two fatal to many a home in Wales. Once in a blue moon these big shells come off; this was once. One can never forget such a scene, one body was blown 200 yards over the tops of the giant beech trees – that is enough of description.

It fell to me that night to arrange the service. Like ourselves at Hooge, the outgoing regiment could not see to it themselves. Herculean work on the part of our digging parties, waggons commandeered to remove the remains, all in the dark, a large trench in a cemetery a mile away; an English and a Welsh padre (no one could say to what Church the good fellows belonged) and a single oil lamp lit up a sad scene at 11 p.m. that night; 35 men had done their bit for a side, for a cause which surely must win. God was with us as we stood at their graves. I walked back alone, somehow feeling at peace . . . . I came back to my room, the Count's best dressing-room, which I shared with Layton Frewen, and turning into my valise on the floor, warm as a trivet, felt thankful for so much comfort. If one comes to write one's story of the war, with a mind and body and spirit released from the strain, this account may help to recall three anxious days of bungling and bravery.'

21st January. – 'The first day of rest for ages, motoring to Army workshops, and seeing all the latest inventions. The *motor* drive! Seeing *cows* grazing, fields, houses not 'crumped' to glory, how refreshing!

Boy Scouts.

About your *Boy Scouts*. Do you ever pause and look back and see a fraction of the good you have done for all these boys when they are men? You should talk to a man out here who has been a Boy Scout. Why do people expect to see results at once? Why do they go about groaning about this terrible war? Only because they cannot look beyond their noses. If you or I passed away tomorrow, we could go with a smile of thankfulness that we had had the chance of helping on the Boy Scout Movement.'

29th January, 1916. – 'We have just parted with two splendid A.B.'s sent from the Navy to see trench life and report on it all to their Ships' Companies. They seemed to be much impressed and to have formed a high opinion of our men and the way they 'stick it.' Needless to say, there was great competition among the Riflemen to act as hosts and show them round. They put in 24 hours in one of the advance trenches and had quite enough, so they said, preferring their own element to Napoleon's fifth element, to say nothing of a shelling they came in for which, though a harmless one, sounded well and made an impression. It was only the Kaiser's birthday 'Strafe.' Fine fellows they were.'

6th February, 1916. – 'I got on very well with my lecture to Artillery Officers at Bailleul on 'Co-operation with Infantry,' a jolly drive, and lovely day. About 70 Officers present, the Senior Artillery Officer, an old friend also Gosling (60th, a Brigadier). They said it was just what they wanted; a friendly criticism and explanation of Infantry difficulties and discussion afterwards.

I found another 60th friend in Hugh Willan, once my subaltern now my senior. I meet a good many men who remember me of whom I have no sort of recollection, which is both stupid of me and clever of them, but having dropped soldiering like a live coal, I seem to have put many good friends out of my head as well as all my military knowledge.'

Last Tour of Duty in Salient.

12th February, 1916. – 'My Dear F., – It is some time since I wrote, for being in command during an anxious four days, I kept my eyes on the job. With the newspapers talking of great German moves on in the West, and of special cemeteries and hospitals being prepared behind their Ypres lines, you will be glad to know I am not yet an inmate of any of them. We got here (near Cassel) last night, I more dead than alive, but today again life is returning. Verdant is back, so all worry is off my shoulders. After six days' rest we returned to the (Lancashire Farm) trench; we found things more lively than usual, and it seemed probable that the Hun had some scheme up his sleeve. Shelling, shelling, shelling, and machine-gunning all day and night, but mostly away from our immediate sphere of usefulness. For the O.C. it is watch and watch, and keep on watching and wondering what is at the back of anything unusual. For the time he is screwed up, as it were, ready to do the right thing if it may be, and able to keep cheery and confident. He must be up and about, visiting sentries and snipers and bombers and working and wiring parties, and watching through the telescope from Observation Posts, an eye on the weather-cock for gas winds.

It was a great satisfaction to see the victory of our snipers. When we came away not a shot was ever fired by the Bosche sniper, and he had closed and sandbagged all his loopholes. Six weeks ago, when we took over the trenches, the Brigadier (Lord Binning) warned us that sniping was bad, and so it was.

Well, since we left the trenches, we have had hard marching for tired men; got in last night, some hitch somewhere, no very hospitable reception for me from an old Frenchman, alone in a biggish house, with his old wife ill. 'Soldiers make such a noise.' 'Must be in bed by 8.' 'No water,' 'No beds,' and what not. I flopped down, wet through and full of rheumatism, and dead beat. The hardest floor good enough; too tired to take any food. However, this morning I am better, and have moved to far better quarters. After moving back to Cassel, where the Battalion rested a few days and we were inspected and congratulated by the Commander-in-Chief, Sir Douglas Haig, and then sent South by train to an unknown destination, which turned out to be Amiens, thus ending a nine months tour of continuous duty of record duration in the Salient.'

18. IN FRANCE.

13th February. – 'We are very happy and comfortable by contrast, and we all begin to feel new men. 'There is nothing like putting a man into a dirty hole to make him contented later on,' said Verdant Green.'

14th February. – 'It is strange that we have now been relieved three times just before an attack came off; each time I have felt something was coming. Curiously, twice I was in command of the Battalion. This last time I sent a special private note direct to General Vic Couper Commanding the Division, telling him I thought it was coming, so I expect he now thinks me a bit of a prophet.'

17th February. – 'Today we were inspected by a distinguished Fifer. He was much pleased and called me aside as I passed at the tail of the Battalion and said, 'They march very well indeed.' So they do – the Key Bugles are a great feature in the 8th Battalion. I really think the Battalion looks wonderful considering all they have gone through in France.'

The Ruins of Arras.

March, 1916 to October, 1918. – It was among the ruins of the suburbs of Arras, in the village of Blangy, that we had our greatest success in sniping.

Set upon at Verdun, the French had called on the British for support. At very short notice, the British took over a large extent of line near Arras. This great move cost us our long-promised rest. It was a great disappointment, but so soon as the cause was known we took it smiling. The novelty of moving to France and meeting French troops also helped us to forget our troubles.

First Meeting with French Troops.

I remember going on ahead with Verdant Green and George Rennie, the two 60th Colonels. After calling on the French Brigadier and being received with great courtesy, we were guided to the Headquarters of the 111th Regiment (which comes from Marseilles), and which we were to relieve. It was evidently a big occasion – Entente Cordiale – a big lunch, and some flutter in the dove-cot. We were all introduced, and bowed and shook hands. Present: the Colonel, a fine old veteran from Algiers, with the green and white ribbon, a regular hater of Huns; the Port-Drapeau, a kind of cross between Adjutant and Sergeant-Major; the doctor, and one or two others. Here was the chance for Verdant and me to settle our long outstanding difference. He claimed to be the better French scholar of the two. His grandmother, he said, was French, and that, he held, was final, but I had always maintained that having had both a Swiss nurse and a French governess, that counted more in my favour. George Rennie, being more of an expert in horseflesh than in French was hardly able to decide the point.

The luncheon party passed pleasantly enough. It was easy to gather that Blangy was no health resort .... The Hun, two nights before our visit: had heavily trench-mortared our Allies, and driven them out of their advanced posts on the River Scarpe. They were not distressed to be leaving, but at the same time were anxious to make all as easy as possible for us and not to exaggerate any shortcomings these suburbs might have as a residence.

The conversation did not exactly flow. It was friendly, but laboured and spasmodic. The old difficulties of the Tower of Babel intervened. At times there were awkward pauses. 'Nous les avons,' said the French Colonel. 'Yes,' said I, sitting at the other end of the table, 'as we say, "We have got them on toast,"' and I called out to Verdant to put that into his best French. But the war had driven the word for 'toast' out of his head. His failure was complete, and the politely puzzled face of Monsieur le Colonel scored one up to me. When it came to speeches – well, I won't be hard on Verdant, for no one can compete with a Frenchman in putting things nicely on such occasions.

The French Colonel.

Then came the visit to the trenches. I remember hinting to the Porte-Drapeau, as we sailed down the centre of the main road to Blangy in full view of long, white chalk lines of German trenches, that we should never have been able to take such liberties in Flanders, and that the sight of three khaki and three light-blue warriors might give the coming relief away. 'Vous avez raison,' he said. 'Ni nous non plus – voilà le boyau; mais Monsieur le Colonel, il est trés conservateur. If you were to say to him, it is dangerous, he would reply. "Then I will go."'

Sniping was not a special department in the French army, and it took both Verdant and me all our combined stock of French to convey what a 'Snipair's' work entailed. The nearest French word seemed to be 'guetteur'(?), and I was duly introduced to a young N.C.O. who had achieved local celebrity by killing two Huns in a shot from the roof of a tall ruined house. The place was pointed out to me, and I gaily climbed up, the young Frenchman following gingerly. We got an extraordinarily good view, looking down into the Hun trenches, some 50 yards off, where all seemed wonderfully quiet. It was a foolish liberty to take. I did not realise at the time that my guide was too polite to tell me he had never been there since August, when the leaves were on the trees.

It was an interesting day. The French troops seemed as interested in us as we were in them, and I remember more than once standing arm-in-arm with my pal the Porte-Drapeau, to be 'kodaked' by some poilu. This struck me, because with us cameras were not allowed.

Blangy.

For the next two months and more Blangy became my hunting ground. When I was not prowling about or searching with a glass from some 'vantage point, I was studying maps, or aeroplane photographs, or dreaming of Blangy!

The Risks of Scouts.

We started badly. The very first day I went down to explore with Corporals Otterwell and Riches, my two best men. We climbed every ruined house at the back, which seemed to offer a view, and so, after a thorough search, worked our way forward to the foremost trenches and listening posts. Everything seemed still, and almost one might have thought the Hun had gone.

At a point where the Main Street ran through the village, the cobble stones had been pulled up, and a shallow trench dug to connect the foremost posts, on each side of the road. A few sand-bags increased the amount of shelter, but still a man had to keep down very low to avoid being seen from the opposite barrier 50 yards away. It must be remembered the French had only recently taken up this new line. Peeping over gradually, I got a general view and then proceeded to search the opposite breastwork methodically with my telescope for hidden loopholes. Suddenly it gave me a bit of a turn to see the silver outline and black centre of a rifle barrel pointing in my direction. It seemed so close. I kept quite still. Then, slowly, to my relief, it moved away from me. Keeping the glass steady, after noting the exact position with relation to a conspicuous pink sandbag, I slowly withdrew my head and showed it first to Otterwell and then to Riches. We all saw the rifle barrel move. Returning to cover, we considered our plans and noted the exact position on paper.

I then went back to warn the Sergeant on duty that he was to caution everyone who passed to keep down, and get the trench deepened that night. As I went, a shot rang out, and I turned to see both my Corporals wounded in the bottom of the trench. Otterwell died in my arms almost immediately. So, scouting the way for the benefit of his comrades, passed away as fine a young fellow as I have seen this war. He was awaiting his Commission at the time. Riches was not severely wounded. From that time onwards a special vendetta existed between the opposing Snipers at Blangy.

Letters from Blangy.

March, 1916. – 'I write from the dining-room of a prosperous oil merchant, mirrors and highly ornamental furniture, shell holes through the ceiling, the windows done up with sacking to keep out the wind, Frewen's, Miller's (the doctor) and my valises laid out in three corners; in the fourth corner a stove; in the centre your special correspondent, alone, having just lunched, sitting at a large table, surrounded by papers and letters, mess and canteen accounts, etc., sniffling and rather pulled down after three days' nasty cold, but the worst is over. Napoleon himself, with a cold in the head, so Ian Hamilton tells us, was but a moderate General.

Outside still snow and sleet and cold, and beyond, some 500 yards, the trenches, with Verdant Green going round, energetic as ever, occasional shots from guns or rifles. There you have the scene pictured. So many thanks for yours of 5th and Xylonite idea for range cards.

My dear Corporal Otterwell, as you will have heard, is gone, such a loss. I feel it every day. A fine young fellow, just going home for his Commission. I held his head up as he passed away, and realised as I saw him going what a useful young life was passing – no pain, a soldier's end, a gallant lead and duty done to the last. I felt no sort of feeling of revenge, and yet I tell my snipers it is their duty to do all they can to hit back.

New trenches, and difficult, in ruined, crumped-in suburbs and factories. At first, things incredibly quiet. But now we have war declared. Already we have most of their loopholes located and many of their steelplates pierced by our steel bullets. It is sad, the whole thing, but then I never looked upon it as anything else. When will it end? Verdun? All eyes are rivetted there now . . . may the French hold on and stick it. It is an all-important stand they are called on to make. May they be given strength. Our cause must win in the end, but we must show ourselves worthy champions first.'

15th March. – 'We have a big proposition in front of us with the gentlemen in the opposing ruins, but we will defeat them I am sure.

With war once declared between the snipers at Blangy we set to and brought all our past experience into play in real earnest. A good system of observation was established with a central post, connected by telephone, in the roof of a high red brick building, the shell of which was still left standing.

Hidden, camouflaged loopholes were so constructed that every part of the Hun lines could be kept under constant and close observation. Some of these posts were so near to Fritz that the work of building them took many nights. To excavate the stones, the snipers, in some cases dug them out laboriously with penknives to avoid being heard. The slightest sound drew bombs and rifle grenades and every change had to be gradual so as not to attract attention.

For a time the Hun was top dog; and, being newcomers, many casualties, as many even as 9 in one day, took place among our men from sniping alone. Every casualty which occurred was at once investigated; nine times out of ten it was an avoidable casualty, and steps were taken to prevent its recurrence. But the maze of ruins was so confusing that often a man would be hit standing at his post from what seemed to him to be behind, and this might well have caused that lack of confidence known to the troops as 'getting the wind up.'

I hit on the idea of drawing a plan of the trenches on a blackboard, and lecturing each Company that went into this tricky sector and explaining exactly how each casualty had occurred, and how unnecessary it had been. In this way men got over the idea that the Hun sniper did anything superhuman, and realised what *not* to do. It also gave them an interest in their work.

The Hun did not long have it all his own way. After long planning and watching, Otterwell was at last avenged by our left-handed champion, Sheehan, who killed his man and silenced all sniping from that quarter.

I remember one particular point of vantage from which we 'straffed' the Hun. We called it the 'Boiler House' for it contained the remains of the boilers of some huge ruined brewery. It was a tricky place to approach, and we had two men killed the first week. We had two bombers stationed at this point, where, peeping through a small hole in the wall, they watch for the Hun not 15 yards away.

One day, going to this post with Riches, I discovered that, by creeping forward like a cat and pushing a small ladder up on a platform above the bombing post, it was possible to look right down on the Hun, and occasionally catch a glimpse of the sentry. As I was looking my attention was attracted to earth being shovelled up at a point in the trench about 50 yards off. Presently the shovelling ceased, and a healthy young Hun emerged in his shirtsleeves, spade in hand, and smoking a cigar. He rested and leaned against the wall of the trench, looking up and staring in my direction. Fifty yards through a good Zeiss glass brings men pretty near. It was hard to keep still and realise he did not see me. I showed him to Riches who, trembling like an eager terrier, was all for a shot.

But I wanted to learn more. As I was watching, presently from a new direction six more Huns, carrying hods on their backs and large blocks of concrete, came up to this spot in file. I let them proceed till they all vanished with their loads down into the hole from which originally the thrown-up earth had attracted attention. What were they doing? Soon they came out and stood in a clump. This was asking too much! Riches fired and claimed to hit two, but the cloud of brick dust obscured my view. I only saw signs of some such struggle as that on the day when poor Otterwell fell. I remember clearly the expression of terror on the faces of those of them who did escape, crouching and running past us.

From that time until it was demolished by 'rum-jars,' competition to man the Boiler House was keen among the snipers, who claimed to have done much damage to the opposing garrison.

A year later I revisited this spot and found a comfortable, beautifully-built, concrete dug-out with a British subaltern sleeping inside. I have often wondered how many German lives it cost to build this dug-out under our noses, and still think of it as an example of the contrast between the two Armies. The Hun officer drives his men; his comfort comes before their lives. The British idea of leadership is very different.

I have said enough to give an idea of Blangy and sniping. We finished top dog, and casualties from sniping came to an end, and so, in due course, did our tour in this sector. For my services I was allotted by 'Verdant' the title of 'King of Blangy!'

Letter to Scouts.

Monday, 27th March, 1916. – From Major Crum to the Stirling Scouts, *per* Scout Henry Russell, No. 1 Troop. – 'My Dear Scouts, I was so glad to hear of your doings through the Scouts who wrote to me in answer to my last in the *Sentinel*, especially Nos. 1 and 4 Troops. One of them finished a very nice letter by saying: 'I hope you won't think me forward in writing to you, as I always find your letters in 'Scout Notes' so interesting.'

Well, now, I just sit down to write again because I want you to know it is just what one enjoys – to get a cheery letter from a Boy Scout, and know things are going along well while we are away. I got several letters, and they quite cheered me up when I was feeling a bit tired of this old war. I am so glad Miss Gilbert keeps the Scout flag flying. Scouts! what should we be in Stirling if it were not for the ladies? A full salute to them all, I say.

I write this from a swagger house in a ruined town bigger than Stirling (Arras) – very comfortable until the shelling begins. My bedroom, for instance, is fit for a princess – mirrors, candelabras, beautiful curtains, chairs, and wall paper. But in the ceiling a large gaping hole is seen, and the brass bedstead itself has a tell-tale dent on it, which reminds one that one's sleep might any moment be cut short and one might have to bolt to the cellars two storeys below. The old lady caretaker gets very wild, and talks very fast, and keeps a jealous eye on the property of the French Admiral, the owner of the house. I am afraid it does dirty the beautiful staircase when a soldier comes up with a message from the muddy trenches. But she generally ends up a long harangue each time with a good Scout smile and says: 'Mais – hélas! C'est la guerre.' I am afraid if some boys were here to see and hear her gesticulating they would find it great sport 'drawing her,' but the best way is, as the Chief Scout says, always to put yourself in the other fellow's place, and see it from his or her point of view. After all, the old dame is only doing her duty when she does strafe us for muddying the floor.

I see from the home papers that the cat is out of the bag as regards our having relieved the French in new trenches, so I don't suppose the censor will mind my telling you a bit about the French army. It was a new experience for all of us, and I think the French soldiers were as much interested in us as we were in them – anyway, they stared and looked round and all seemed very friendly. You would have laughed if you had seen us dressed up as French soldiers with light blue greatcoats and blue iron hats, going round visiting and learning all about the new trenches. I get on very well, and they are too polite to laugh at my bad French, and the men, too, get on, better than you would expect. The usual procedure is for the khaki hero to unbosom himself eloquently in English and end up with 'compris?' He then thinks that he has been talking in French. Usually a pot of jam from our men or a cigarette from a Frenchman starts the friendship. But if I were you I would try and learn French properly when you get the chance, because you may not always have a pot of jam handy; and even if the war is over soon, as we all hope it may be, the Frenchman should always be a great friend for long, long after the war.

I think 'Delta' will be angry with me, but I go further and say I hope we shall not go in for hating the Bosche after the war. We must hate all the cruel things that he has done, but as often as not it is the fault of those who taught him. The ordinary German soldier is a good fellow at bottom – a brave man, doing his duty as a good soldier. I think I see more of him than most, for, unknown to him, I am so constantly watching him, with a first-class telescope. The other day from a high point of view, not 800 yards off, I saw one leave the trench and run out to rescue a cat which was straying in our direction. Of course the cat knew better and wanted to join the British, but Fritz – you must put yourself in Fritz's place – thought it was far better to be a German cat, and so he risked being shot to save the animal. But it was stupid of Fritz all the same, for he showed us in so doing a yellow stripe down his trousers enabling us to tell what regiment he belonged to!

Yes, I see them doing all sorts of things – laughing and talking. Three days ago we had a fall of snow, and we saw them snow-balling each other in rear of their trenches. Well, well, the pity is that we should all be bombing and shooting each other instead of snowballing, all because that awful Kaiser is an ambitious blackguard, and he and his inner circle of Huns have so misled and misguided the wonderful Bosche nation that they seem almost past praying for. So then we have got to fight, and fight with every nerve. There can be no excuse for any able-bodied man now. It is a matter of life and death still, but we have not got to hate or despise.

And now I will stop. I have things to do, and so have you, I expect. Lessons or games – whatever it is, like Scouts, lead the way in all that you do, and good luck to you all. – Yours, as a Scout, F. M. CRUM.'

Sniping School at Acq.

In May we moved to Acq, and here, under General Skinner, I started a Brigade School of Sniping.

I was lucky enough to be billeted at the School-house, where M. and Mme. Astrua put their best room at my disposal, and lent me their schoolroom for lectures, out of the children's school hours. Six weeks under their hospitable roof and we became tremendous friends, and still we keep up the correspondence.

It is a pity more Britishers can't talk French, and more Frenchmen talk English, for 'bon' and 'no bon' and even 'Allemande no bon' go a very short way in expressing the admiration felt by us all for this heroic people.

Twice at intervals of six months I revisited this School. The children remembered the sweets and games, and Madame gave me a great welcome. She was bright and cheery as ever, doing her husband's work at the School, and as Town Clerk, while he, in spite of his age, had been called up to serve in the Artillery. To-day, I am glad to hear he is safely back to this Schoolhouse and garden and Madame; and the store of gas masks for the little scholars is only a part of a horrible dream.

The Sniping School.

My Sniping School was a great success. We were full of ideas, all of us, Hicks, Harman, Sherry, Cox, Taylor and others. The scandal of hundreds of men getting bowled over, simply from want of teaching and imagination, stirred us to great efforts so that in addition to building a range in a chalk quarry close by, and greatly improving our marksmanship, we were able to give demonstrations, to troops resting out of the line.

The methods of teaching are best understood from reading the small book which I wrote called *Scouts and Snipers in Trench Warfare*.

Education by Acting.

On one occasion we gave a special demonstration to the Divisional School. This was a great success except for one unfortunate incident. It was not that anyone was killed, though we did take many liberties which would not have been tolerated at Hythe. The trouble was this. In the morning we had rehearsed the demonstration. All had gone well. The actors ran through their parts and all was thought out, even to the audience – men being detailed to represent the Corps and Divisional Commanders (Sir Charles Ferguson and Sir V. Couper), 3 Brigadiers and 4 Colonels, all of whom had expressed their intention of coming.

It was part of a scene in the education by acting, that one of the snipers got hit through some foolish mistake of a 'Tenderfoot.' In coaching him I had told him to be a bit more forcible in his language and try to feel as if he really were in pain.

The afternoon came, and with it lorries and motors bringing a large and distinguised audience. The snipers were in great form; their shooting with rifles, telescopic and 'sniperscopic' was excellent. The targets, made as near the real thing as possible, were brought and shown to the audience riddled with holes.

Observation and other practices were carried out with men dressed up in German uniforms occupying a reproduction of the German trenches. Targets were located by observers working in co-operation with snipers and trench mortar officers, who at once opened fire.

Then came the acting, which caused great interest and amusement, combined with instruction. Some of the men had great talent that way, and their topical jokes went down – but when it came to the loophole scene————!

Education by Acting.

Two young soldiers were mishandling a periscope, doing everything wrong, when one of them saw a Hun showing his head in the German trench opposite. Getting excited he entered the loophole, sacred to snipers, loosed off 10 rounds rapid, and thus, after having clearly indicated the position of the loophole to Fritz, he retired from it leaving the shutter and screen open, and assuring his companion that he had exterminated the lot. Presently the sniper came along the trench and inquired what all the firing was. Being suspicious, after a lecture on 'giving away' loopholes, and the dangerous work snipers had in building and concealing them, he had just cautiously entered the loophole when a shot rang out from the German trench and a yell of pain came from inside. Out came the furious sniper. What he said – that was the trouble!

I had only anticipated such expressions as a Commanding Officer sometimes may hear when Battalion Headquarters have the Signallers' dug-out for neighbour, and the walls are not thick – but on this occasion the flow of abuse completely unmanned me. For a second I lost my head, and then I blew my whistle and sounded the 'cease fire.' A concluding lecture on the art of training and the scandal of unavoidable casualties, gave me the opportunity of explaining that strong language was not apart of my curriculum.

Some were shocked and some were amused. We all adjourned to a fine tea arranged by Sergt.-Major Archer at the Town Hall. The Captive Balloon Section provided a ripping concert; this, with the Divisional band and dancing up to 9 p.m., terminated a good day's relaxation, and few will forget that example of teaching by acting.

Letter to Scout David Finlayson, Stirling.

Somewhere in France, June, 1916. – 'My Dear Davy, – The country here is lovely; there are beautiful woods, all green once more, with beeches, and chestnuts, and hyacinths, and even lily-of-the-valley, growing wild, and all the birds singing away as if there never had been such a thing as war.

I got back after seeing you. You remember the house I told you of, where we climbed up, and looked down on to the Bosche? Well, it was too much for him. During my absence he sent back for a big trench mortar, and the morning I arrived he threw over 20 large shells – 'rum-jars' we call them, big tin cans holding 60 lbs. of high explosives. There was no house left, just heaps of rubble and debris, a few good Riflemen wounded, and 3 awarded the Military Medal. Then 'As you were,' and 'Carry on' much as before. One of my best snipers had a narrow escape; a 'rum-jar' landed at his feet; he stood there 'cut off'; he watched the fuse sparkling and spluttering and felt that his 'number was up,' and then, paralysed, he realised his good luck – it was a 'dud.' He has been wounded three times, but he tells me this was his most unpleasant adventure.

In this war you never know what old friends you will meet next. Just now we are resting not very far from where the 'Sons of the

Rock' are resting too; so I rode over – a jolly ride over an undulating fertile country, with large open fields, wonderfully cultivated by
the old people and children. Every man from 18 to 45 is away
fighting at the front. You would admire them, working long hours,
managing the horses and cattle, harrowing, sowing and rolling
large stretches of land, cultivating the rich soil – brave hearts as
any at the front. And, just beyond, a party of bronzed and
businesslike 'kilties' – men you might well feel proud of – farmers,
perhaps themselves, from the Carse of Stirling. What are they
doing here in France? Look at them throwing bombs, drilling and
shooting – fit and cheery, and as hard as nails. They are resting
from the trenches, and fitting themselves the better to hold off and
turn out the Bosche invader. My Riflemen, too, are a fine lot. I am
making good Boy Scouts of them all, and hope many of them will
have troops of Boy Scouts after the war.

You would laugh, if you could see my snipers sometimes great
big fellows, sitting on the 'wee kiddies' benches in the village
school, where I often get permission from the school-master to
lecture and teach them with the help of the blackboard. They look
a bit clumsy and cramped trying to squeeze themselves into the
seats and write or sketch at the children's desks. One of them upset
an inkpot – I could not find any strap in the dominie's desk, so we
let him off. The jolly French children, dressed in black smocks, the
boys mostly wearing their father's or brothers' light-blue uniform
caps, come peeping inquisitively in at the door, wondering perhaps
why grown-up men should go to school.

Fancy the poor schoolmaster! His assistants are all away in the
fields or at the war, and he is single-handed with 50 pupils of
various ages from 6 to 14. However, he manages. It seems a kind
of conjuring trick.

There you see three blackboards; on one pot-hooks and the A B
C for the infants; on another spelling and sums; and on the third,
for the more advanced, is written in French 'Anna is a good girl.
After school she assists the teacher; she cleans the desks and dusts
the forms; she rubs the windows and fills the pots with ink!' Anna
is evidently a bit of a Boy Scout doing her good turn – doing her
bit in the war. Anyway, I drew my diagrams of trenches and
loopholes on the other two boards. I rubbed out the pot-hooks,

the A B C and sums, and left the praises of Anna just as they were. It is well to write a good hand; it is very important, too, to get sums right; but, my dear David, it is even better to do good turns wherever you go through life.'

Acq, 3rd June, 1916.

Things continue to go A1. The model school, 3 Officers and 60 Riflemen, promises so well; and the MS. of book on Sniping is practically finished. I shall be glad when E.'s German sandbags and uniforms come, also I would like a false beard and a mask or two. I hope to give a display in a week or ten days. The 4th June is round once more (Floreat Etona) it finds me sitting in the schoolmaster's dining-room (writing my book on sniping). The sun comes in at the window, which looks out on to Monsieur's well-kept vegetable garden. At 6 a.m. each morning Madame brings me a very good cup of coffee, puts it on the window sill and, after some cheery talk, leaves me in possession. About 7 I get up and generally have a talk with Monsieur as I dress, while he busies himself with his garden. About 9 the children go into school, Madame taking the little ones. Her worst punishment is to make them stand up with a smoke helmet on! All of them have to carry smoke helmets. Monsieur Astrua takes the bigger ones upstairs, nearly all girls, there seem very few boys. At 11.30 if wet, I take my 'gros éleves' till 1 or 1.30; they listen like mice, except when they laugh and grow keen and encourage me. They make excellent progress, and will do well when the time comes.

Acq, 17th June, 1916. – I have just packed off MS. of book by King's Messenger. Am now safely through the training, of Brigade Scouts, the first thing of its kind, and having put my whole soul into it and pumped enthusiasm into the men for four weeks, I feel done up and shall be glad of the comparative rest. Everything has worked together for good and gone well, ending up with most amusing and, at the same time, realistic and instructive display to some 200 people, with glorious sunshine, and band playing during intervals; Generals and budding Generals; distinguished and otherwise – all very pleased.

Book on Scouting and Sniping.

Acq, 19th June – The school is now closed and we go to put into practice all we have taught.

About this time the proofs of my book on Scouting and Sniping being ready, and special permission having been obtained from G.H.Q. at Montreuil, where I paid a personal visit for the purpose, I wrote to General Baden-Powell, asking him to write me a few words of introduction for it.

To General Sir R. S. Baden-Powell.

24th June, 1916. – 'Dear Chief – The enclosed book having been written to try and help snipers to push on and end the war, I am bringing it out privately, one thousand copies. I owe so much to you that I am wondering if you would read it, and if you approved, write a short introduction. Your Boy Scout idea of teaching by acting the part has appealed to the snipers even as much as it does to our boys. I have trained them on Boy Scout lines all through, and found the results simply splendid; I began the first day by telling them all about the Scout Law and Movement, and ended by enlisting future Scout Masters! I read the *Gazette* regularly and am glad to know from it that you have not been arrested as a spy. I hope very much that you and Lady B.-P. keep well, only I hear you are both overworked.

Success to the Scouts. – Yours sincerely,

F.M.C.'

6th July, 1916. – 'My Dear Crum, – Mrs. Stewart has sent me the proofs of your book on Scouting and Sniping, and I must congratulate you very cordially upon it. It seems to me to put the whole idea of this new work most clearly and concisely and on very practical lines; and the training you propose should, I am sure, be popular, and at the same time effective. I hope the book will be widely read, not so much for your sake, as for the sake of the officers and men who will learn from it. – With best wishes, Yours sincerely,

(Signed) ROBERT BADEN-POWELL.'

On 41st Brigade Staff.

July, 1916. – About this time General Skinner, having succeeded Lord Binning, invited me to join his staff and run the snipers and Intelligence of the Brigade. The Brigade Headquarters were in Arras with two battalions in the chalk trenches north-east towards Rocquelincourt, where mining and countermining were an unpleasant feature. At this time the fighting further South on the Somme was beginning, and it was known that every battalion would take its turn sooner or later in the great push.

2nd July. – 'It goes on every day, such a row as no one has ever heard before; an inferno, and yet not much news. The British tail is up and of that there is no possible doubt whatever. The Lion is bound to suffer more wounds yet, but his tail is up; he sees the right end in sight, however far away it may be.'

Life in Rocquelincourt Trenches.

LETTER TO SCOUT HEADQUARTERS GAZETTE.

August, 1916. – 'My Dear Mr. Editor, – What am I to say to you worthy of the *Gazette*? My head is full of nothing but war, and sniping in particular. Nevertheless that glorious invention – the Boy Scout – is always at the back of my mind. I imagine myself back sometimes, and see him sitting all eyes, enthusiasm and sympathy as one tells him yarns of Fritz as seen in the trenches through a telescope – reflected, perhaps, in his own periscope. You may see him with fixed bayonet and baker's cap, standing on sentry or off duty – shaving, perhaps, or a cigar in his mouth, reading some *Zeitung* full of lies, or maybe a letter from Fraulein telling the truth. How interested the Scout would be in the various uniforms and badges, the different coloured bands and buttons on the caps. How breathlessly he would imagine himself crawling with you through the debris of ruined suburbs, or creeping disguised through long grass to reach some tricky vantage point. Yes, the life of a sniper is one which would appeal to the love of adventure in boys; but then one has to go easy. I hear someone saying: 'I told you so; it is a military movement.'

251

But, besides, sniping is only so small a part of this war. At sea
and under the sea, in the air, on land, and worst of all, to my mind,
underground, daily encounters take place. How little at ease we
feel when out of our element! We cross the Channel with a lifebelt
on – the sea looks very wet and cold. We go up in a balloon, and
shake at the thought of its breaking away and a parachute descent.
But, worst of all, to a sniper's mind, is the warfare underground.
Down a long dark shaft you find a man bending over a patent kind
of stethoscope. You take it and listen; pick and shovel seem to be
working just at your feet. You feel uneasy, then you hear a guttural
grumble. Your companion laughs. 'Bauermann,' he says, 'is always
a grouser; he has struck a hard seam, or perhaps he had no sausage
today.' For just as the British sniper knows Fritz, so the miners,
too, have their pals underground.

Then there comes a night – an earthquake shakes the countryside
– a pause of silence, then a hell let loose of guns and mortars,
'minnie-woppers,' bombs, and what-not. A crater has gone up.

Come with me down the long French boyau; the sun is up; the
larks are singing as before. Red poppies and blue cornflowers
waving in masses along the maze of white chalk trenches seem, in
the name of France, to defy Bauermann and all his evil works. You
push on down the narrow trench, squeezing past good fellows
being carried up on stretchers, the nearer you get to the scene the
more evident the signs of 'strafe.' Dug-outs 'crumped' in, trench
boards, and sandbags splintered and scattered, bits of shell and
signs of blood wherever you look.

Khaki gangs of diggers are repairing the damage, reopening
trenches and renewing cover. All night, by shifts, they have been
working hard in spite of shells and sniping. They look up, sweating
but smiling, as you pass; gallant fellows, all.

You pass along till there, before you, once a trench is now a
mountain of chalk. All around torn accoutrements, khaki
bandages, broken weapons, splinters, blood, and flies, and debris.

You crawl or bolt across the open, up the exposed hillside of
chalk, aware of sniping as you pass into the crater – No. 5 its name
is – there you see how busy officers and men, like ants, have been.
What a power of work they have put in! in spite of grenades and

whizzbangs. Alert, with swords fixed and bombs handy, gazing into periscopes, standing at their posts built in with sandbags, stand the look-out men in khaki – there they stand, 20 yards from the Hun, ready, as ever, to do their bit, whatever that bit may be. A blessing on them all. Truly the more you see of the British soldier out here the more your heart goes out to him.

But what is the British soldier to-day but the British nation in khaki? Moreover, whatever you say of the man at the front holds good still more of the woman at home. And yet there were times when many were feeling a bit uneasy. They only saw the man who seemed to think of nothing but self, or the spirit which seemed to be dead. But we who followed the Chief – or was it the boys themselves who urged us along? – we pegged away, and ever, according to orders, 'kept smiling.' Today we thank God. Our faces are beaming with smiles of thankfulness and confidence.

As for the *Gazette*, it has done far more than you know. Especially I like the 'Two Ideals.' Not being a man of words, I feel inclined simply to say 'Hear, hear,' as loud as I can. At any time I am shy – too shy, perhaps – of treading on sacred ground; but I feel with all my faith that in teaching our boys – our future men – religion, you are on the path too many have missed.

'We came of our own free wills; we came to say that this sort of thing shall not happen in the world so long as we are in it. We know we are doing right, and I tell you that on this mission on which we have come, so long as every man plays the game and plays it cleanly, he need not fear about his religion – for what else is his religion but that? "*Play the game and God will be with you* – never fear".' These are the words of a fighting Australian padre. Why were there tears in so many big Anzacs' eyes? Because a man had spoken as a man to men. His secret was out. Christ was showing the way. – Yours very much a brother Scout,

F. M. CRUM.'

Somewhere in France, 4th July, 1916.

Roland Phillipps.

20th July, 1916, – 'July is speeding past and an eventful month it is, one which will probably stand out in the history of this enormous 'strafe.' I can hear guns thundering at it again. Poor

Scout movement, we have lost the good Roland Phillips, who next to Elwes and Everett, perhaps, did most to help the Chief Scout in his great work. Lawrence of Edinburgh too, so strong and capable. We lose grand men on all sides, but we gain and push on, the khaki fights its way through Fricourt, Mametz, Trones, to the Bazentin line, struggling in the village mazes and woods, a couple of miles, perhaps; not very far on the road to Berlin, if you look at the map, and yet a very big stride in reality, a gaining of morale; a sort of turning point in this ghastly war.

Here, too, we have our part to play, mines and trench mortars and other tests of nerves and men, how long it may last we do not know. As for myself, I now only go up to the trenches one day on and one day off, for I find I have not the strength to do more.'

23rd July, 1916. – 'I am doing less because less able; in fact, the words I used to General Couper (14th Division) the other day were: 'The fact is, I feel more easily tired each day. The best thing is if you will write stating my qualifications or disqualifications and asking them to find me a suitable job.' Verdant has gone, and Frewen is now in his place, and no doubt Providence will arrange matters as may be best; who are we to say what is best? – leading a few good Riflemen in one of the waves that break on the heights of Thiepval, or returning, perhaps, to do a bit more in leading a few boys the right way. It is all one thing, and part of the rising tide.'

28th July, 1916. – 'We are shedding all superfluous kit.

I have a feeling of unsettledness about me just now, the sort of feeling a faithful dog has when it sees the household packing up.'

August, 1916. – From this time on, for the doings of the 8/60th and 41st Brigade I must refer my readers to the Regimental Chronicle. With Layton Frewen in command, the Battalion played a great part in Delville Wood, and the Snipers and Scouts did specially good work, but as for myself, alas, I fell out on the line of march to the Somme. Sad, but true. I had to give in, and come home; indeed, it was fully four months before I could again do an honest day's work.

19. THE TRAINING OF SCOUTS AND SNIPERS.

After three months' leave, while on a visit in Ayrshire, with still time before my sick leave was up, a telegram from W.O. called me back to work.

Letter to Scouts at Stirling.

1st November, 1916, Blandford House, N. Camp, Aldershot – 'Dear Scouts, – I was sorry to leave you so suddenly just when we were going to have a week-end together, but a telegram came from the War Office ordering me to report at once. Well, I was a bit surprised, for Dr. Moorhouse had recommended me for a further period of leave to get thoroughly well. Still War Office telegrams have to be obeyed, so off I went that night by train, reaching the War Office at 10.30 a.m. as ordered.

They took my breath away by saying that if I could pass the doctors, I was wanted to go down to Aldershot and help to teach 300 Colonels. Well, that is a big class, isn't it, of rather elderly pupils?

The thought of it rather made me fear the doctors might find me suffering from nervous shock, for surely it is more alarming to teach 300 Colonels than to charge any Bosche trenches. However, when they listened to my heart with that telephone instrument, which they call a stethoscope, they found it beating normally, they felt my pulse, and I put out my tongue, and hey! Presto! before you could say 'Jack Robinson' I was driving to Waterloo Station en route for Aldershot, passed 'fit for service at home.'

I must tell you about the Boy Scout at the War Office. The War Office is full of Boy Scouts buzzing about its endless passages, taking messages and making themselves very useful. One of them, dressed like No. 4 troop, led me up to the room for the medical

255

examination, and there handed me over to another Scout, quite a little chap, who was on day duty there. He was dressed in khaki, like Miss Lorrain's boys. He had been at this job for a year and a half, so he told me. Well, he took my papers and showed me to a seat. There were some 15 other officers all waiting their turn, and I saw to my regret that my papers were put at the bottom of all the others. No help for it, it was a case of 'first come, first served,' so I sat down and made up my mind to keep smiling like a good Scout.

'Never mind,' I said to myself, 'I will light a cigarette and the time will soon pass.' I had just lit up and settled down, when I heard a firm command, 'No smoking allowed, please, Sir.' It was my friend the Boy Scout on duty. I heard him stop a Brigadier-General soon afterwards, in the same way – very smart salute and courteous. So no one took offence, and we all admired the Scout. Isn't that rather a good show, don't you think? 'Quite right,' I said. I put out my cigarette at once, and then I showed him my Swastika Badge – the one the Perthshire boys gave me, you know, the one I showed you which had been my lucky charm all through the war. I said to him, 'What good turn are you going to do me now? Don't you think you ought to let me in a place or two earlier out of my turn?' But he was a good Scout; he looked me straight in the face, laughed, and shook his head, saying, 'That wouldn't be Scoutlike, and I know you wouldn't like me to do it.' 'Right you are again,' said I, 'I must tell the Chief Scout about you.'

There are lots of Scouts going about London, and some at Aldershot too, most of them are very smart, though occasionally one sees a slovenly Scout, who is dirty, and has his uniform badly put on, and doesn't salute officers. Probably his Scoutmaster and the Leaders are all away in France. It is a pity because people see him and say, 'How sad it is, the Scouts are not what they used to be.' I hope no Scouts in Stirling ever are slovenly, and that they all get a good name everywhere.

I must now be off. It means hard work, but I simply say '*Stick it*' to myself, and somehow I get along, and the work grows easier instead of harder. It is a good plan, try it and see for yourselves. I shall be busy till Christmas, when I hope to get two weeks, and will go up and see you again. So then, good-bye to you all for the present. If anyone likes to write and give me the news you know I am always glad to hear the latest. What about the patrol competition? I wish to give a prize to the best patrol in every troop. Each Scout should aim at making his own patrol the very best in every subject laid down for the competition. – Yours as a Scout,

F.M.C.'

Aldershot Senior Officers' School.

10th October, 1916 to 30th April, 1917. – From October to April I was offered a grand opportunity of promoting the cause of scouting and sniping throughout the Service, for General Reggie Kentish, an old Pretoria friend, having been commissioned to start a new school for training selected officers as Battalion Commanders, invited me to come and help. Originally his idea was that I should try my hand as a regular Instructor, but it was arranged that if this was too strenuous, I should limit my activities to the teaching of my own subject.

General R. Kentish.

I suppose that few men in the Army have done more towards winning the war than this indefatigable Brigadier. Before the war, he was best known in the Army for good work he had done under General Smith Dorrien at Aldershot, in connection with football, having diverted streams, removed several hills, and built some 35 level football fields.

With the Irish Fusiliers, both at Aldershot, and in the early days of the war, he had gained experience and rapid promotion, rising in a short time from Captain to Brigadier.

A man, so original, so pushing, so ready to put new ideas into practice, with such remarkable activity of mind, energy of body, and enthusiasm of spirit, was bound to meet many who shook their heads and disapproved; but, as a teacher of leadership and sympathy between officers and men, I think the good he has done, both during the war, and in days to come, is something any man might well feel proud of.

Let me give a sample of one day's work:– From 5 a.m., thinking and writing in bed, – about 7, his typist comes in, and between them they get through piles of correspondence. After breakfast and office, an energetic morning, visiting the various parties of officers scattered at their training over the district. After lunch he would rush off somewhere, perhaps to the military prison, give a good lecture and buck the men up, then in the afternoon you would find him in shorts and Brigadier's uniform, tearing up and down the field refereeing at some crowded football match, thinking nothing of blowing his whistle, stopping the game and cautioning some All-England player about some irregularity. After a bath and tea he would be off again to the Connaught Hospital, sitting down to the piano and starting a sing-song among the wounded men. Dinner, a cheery party at Blandford House, 2 glasses of port and big cigar! Then bed at 11 or 12, having put in an hour or two more of work.

I remember, as we two motored up to London next day, warning him that no man could go on indefinitely at such high pressure. 'Well,' he said, 'this war has got to be won and now's the time. It does not matter what happens to Reggie Kentish after that.' He was utterly out to win the war, and that is what I liked; with all his push and go, 'Kentish' came second.

As for my own work, finding myself very rusty in Military Law, Engineering, Tactics, Organisation, etc., and with too little strength to work up and teach these subjects, I gradually became more and more a specialist, taking over the existing Sniping School, building a new range on improved lines, as at Acq, and combining the training of classes to some 60 Officers and men, with demonstrations and lectures to the Senior Officers' School and others.

The method of training was new, the Aldershot and W.O. Staff were some of them old-fashioned, (the kind that says, 'It never has been done before,' or saves itself trouble by telling you that 'sniping is not the only thing in the world') so that one had to overcome many of the difficulties common to all pioneers.

New methods of Training.

I saw the whole thing 'in being' long before it took shape. I felt that by acting, and appealing to the imagination, by the imitation of German and British trenches, with men dressed up as Huns and as British troops in France, by the use of the cinema and lantern slides combined with lecturing, by the use of black goggles for teaching a man to work in the dark, and by the introduction of jiu jitsu and special training in self-defence, hundreds of lives which were being thrown away each twenty-four hours of the war, might be saved and turned to good purpose. I was lucky in securing assistance and encouragement from Sir Archibald Hunter, and from many up-to-date leaders who visited Aldershot, so that in the end we got together a capable staff (which included two of my good snipers from France) and most difficult of all, overcame difficulties of expense and establishment, and in the end we became a recognised institution.

Education by Acting.

It would be too long a story to give in detail the various scenes which we acted in order to teach. Suggestions and ideas were given at the time in various pamphlets which we printed and issued to every officer. It was very soon found, as at Acq, that the men showed talent in the acting and were able to reproduce the exact happenings and mishaps, often combined with much amusement. Large parties came from all directions and the thing being a novelty, soon became a popular 'show.'

Two hundred and fifty young soldiers, for instance, would be sent to me just before going to France. They would attend a lecture at the local cinema, illustrated with lantern slides and cinema films, and during an interval, sing a marching song, the words of which were thrown on the screen; they would next march to the ash ranges where there was room to accommodate them on the grand stand overlooking the trench. Then would take place some scene from trench life, men frying bacon over a brazier, making too much smoke, cleaning their rifles and making mistakes in doing so, which have too often proved fatal, or incautiously exposing themselves and so being hit and carried away on a stretcher; these and such like scenes, all commented on by the instructor, and acted by old hands, with their own language and jokes, whether they produced loud laughter or seriousness, left an impression which lasted far longer than any amount of ordinary instruction.

The programme was easily varied; when Artillery Officers came down from the W.O. the play was altered accordingly, *e.g.*, the

Snipers are seen with the forward Artillery Officer at some point from which they show him an enemy mortar, then plans are made, and the snipers acting as observers, telephone the results of each shell as it actually bursts in the German trenches opposite. The Battalion Commander comes up, and a friendly conversation takes place in the hearing of the audience, illustrating various points and requirements. Finally they go off arm in arm to breakfast, saying that after all, a good breakfast, friendship, and touch are the Chief requirements in 'co-operation between Infantry and Artillery.'

I remember that when General Baden-Powell came down with Sir Archibald Hunter we did a special 'stunt' in his honour called 'Be Prepared!'. In this scene the men were *not* prepared, they were collected round a fire, on a cold wet day, singing, cooking, tied up in waterproof sheets, mufflers over their ears, rifles left dirty, or with covers on, and out of reach. The Sentry got 'fed up' and joined the party. While all this was going on two escaped Germans are seen by the audience (150 Senior Officers and others) approaching across 'no man's land' to the deserted part of the British trench, they have their hands up and are shouting 'Kamerad.' Finding no one to surrender to, they enter the trench and hide – much to the amusement of the audience. Then an Officer comes along; he breaks up the sing-song, and puts the Leader under arrest, going off in a bad temper and saying how fatal it might be to be unprepared. His waterproof fits tightly over his revolver, his revolver is unloaded, he passes on. Rounding the next bay he finds himself suddenly confronted by the two Germans. He struggles to get at his revolver, . . . the Huns relieve him considerably by telling him they come from Alsace and are harmless.

There are always some who disapprove of anything new, and I remember on this occasion there were those who took exception to this scene, and said it lowered the Officer in the esteem of his men! However I was consoled when Gen. Baden-Powell told us, in speaking a few words to the audience after the performance, that he himself as a subaltern at Aldershot had got into serious trouble when through some original and amusing ruse he had outwitted an opposing Commander. His originality had drawn down the wrath of his Commander, but the approval of Sir Evelyn Wood.

'I am glad,' said the Chief Scout, 'to see that nowadays troops are not afraid to combine a good laugh with instruction.'

As I say, the show became popular. The Duke of Connaught, Prince Albert (King George VI), Sir Wm. Robertson, and other Generals, distinguished Admirals, and others came and all approved. A surprise visit from the Bishop of Winchester perhaps caused the greatest flutter among the actors, for they were not so sure of themselves before such an audience. I did not find that these performances, which lasted an hour or so, interfered in any way with the rest of the training. On the contrary they accelerated the training.

Black Goggles.

One night when lying awake, thinking of night patrolling and the numberless avoidable casualties which were constantly taking place through want of proper training, the idea came to me, 'why not train men with darkened glasses to give the effect of night, while the Instructor would be able to see and correct mistakes?' For the next week, all London was searched, but it was only possible to secure 12 pairs of black glass acetylene-workers' goggles. They were needed for other purposes. The Ministry of Munitions blocked the way. With the available glasses, the experiment was tried and found most promising; but the danger of a rough and tumble fight with glass goggles, the prohibitive price, and the difficulty of securing the glasses again blocked the way.

Field-Marshal Sir Wm. Robertson.

Sir Wm. Robertson was to visit my school next day, and I remember, as I was shaving that morning, looking at myself in the glass and saying – 'black goggles – see you get the idea taken up before I see you tomorrow.' The great man came. It was part of his official visit to Aldershot as Chief of the Staff. He had thousands of other and far more important matters on hand. He went up to the British Observation Post, and was given a look at the German trenches, . . . saw the Huns, reflected in their own periscope, visited the trenches, saw the Germans in their trench, saw the concealed British snipers' loopholes, nearly put his foot on a concealed camouflaged Sniper, watched some good shooting on the range, which was camouflaged to look like German trenches, then to finish up with, he watched a night patrol encounter between 6 Canadians and 6 others with the black goggles on. At any opening, I had been telling him I wanted him to see the idea, and at last, as he left, I put in a final word, so he turned to his Staff Officer, amused, I think, and told him to make note of it. As he left I remember in shaking hands and thanking me he said, 'It is all very interesting but there are so *many* things to teach.'

Time is Money.

The thought of *saving time* in war is a thought which goads the good soldier along. To me those goggles meant men. The next step was a visit to Sir Ch. Stuart-Wilson and through him direct to the head of the Optical Department of the Ministry of Munitions in London. How impossible it would be if every man with a fad of his own were to short-circuit and urge his particular scheme on heads of departments in this way! And yet, had one dealt through the post and proper channels, what sort of chance did one stand? In the end a good celluloid glass was evolved and thousands of pairs were sent out to France. It is a question how far one is right to push in such a case, I felt convinced that, on the whole, in this case it was right.

Letters.

It may be of interest to give a few extracts from letters during this period. They will show how many an officer must have felt at times during this long war and how in the end he was able to struggle through; there may be sidelights too on that excellent 'Senior Officers' School.'

15th October, Blandford House, Aldershot. – 'The Staff and instructors here are a splendid lot of fellows many of them old friends; you would have seen some long faces the first day when Kentish unfolded to us his syllabus. I drew a large pile of military books on many subjects. I can put my finger on only two or three in which I feel competent to teach anyone anything.'

16th November, 1916. – 'A great many letters asking for my book, but in meantime W.O. have written me asking on whose authority I wrote it – this after having made a special expedition, to G.H.Q. in France and got leave – anyway they say 'no more to be issued' – too late, for I have given away all the thousand copies. I am building a range, same as in France and overcoming many difficulties, all going well. Start to-day with 70, to-morrow with 200 men (in spite of there being 'no men available'). I have got Corporals Hicks and Elliott from France and Matthews; also Legard at W.O. and Kentish here, help me to push things; somehow I feel it will be a success,.'

December, 1916. – 'Towards Christmas the first course of the Senior Officers' School came to an end. The sniping range was completed and ready for two days of demonstrations by 22nd December. The demonstrations were preceded by lectures on Scouting, and cinema and lantern lectures on sniping in trench warfare, and jiu-jitsu. The course was voted a success, and it was very sure that the splendid body of budding Colonels who went back to command in every division would be more in sympathy with the art of Scouting and Sniping, so little understood or encouraged at that time by most Battalion Commanders.'

Report on Scouts and Snipers.

By May, 1917, we had completed another successful course and I had sent in the following Report, which led to my being appointed as Scouting and Sniping Expert at G.H.Q. in France.

PRESENT POSITION

'While we constantly miss chances of inflicting losses in men and morale on the enemy, we ourselves constantly incur avoidable losses.

We have no recognised system, or organisation, or training, and no one at the head to secure co-operation. The Schools at Home and in France are not in touch and vary. Men trained as Scouts are often not used as Scouts, chiefly because many Officers are ignorant of their uses and value, and may even be prejudiced against Scouts.

Co-operation.

Thus there is no co-operation between Scouts of neighbouring Battalions, or of Battalions relieving each other in the Line; nor do

Scouts work as they should in touch with Sentries, or with Trench-mortar, Artillery, and Intelligence Officers.

Waste.

There is considerable waste of valuable material, such as telescopic-rifles, periscopes, sniperscopes, dark-glasses, etc., issued often to men untrained in their uses; at the same time it is often difficult to obtain these articles, both for training and for use at the front.

Literature.

No official guide is yet available. Divisional Generals, Brigadiers, and keen young Officers are constantly enquiring for guidance. I forward herewith a printed booklet which has been commended by G.H.Q. France, and I could be glad if anything helpful in it, could be made available. Some such system and training with model German and British trenches; with teaching by acting, training in the use of telescopic rifles, dark-glasses, jiu-jitsu, camouflage, etc. would give valuable results.

Suggestions.

At present we are like some valuable war-ship without chart, course, compass, rudder or Captain. I suggest that some suitable Officer should be appointed, with Staff and Authority, to deal with the matter. That he should hold a Conference of Officers in charge of Schools, and that they should submit some sound scheme with an Official handbook to follow.'

G.H.Q. France.

17th May to 10th November, 1917.

The work for which I was now sent out to France was to carry out the 'co-ordination' for which I had always been agitating. There were (at the time) five schools of Sniping, one in each of the five armies; each of these Schools was working on its own lines, some devoting special attention to the scientific side of shooting and telescopic rifles, some making a speciality or observation, and some of camouflage. The wish of the Training Authorities was to introduce more night patrol work and open warfare scouting and sniping. The days of trench warfare seemed numbered and it was not considered advisable to keep a special staff merely for training in scientific marksmanship. The tendency at that time was to do away with the specialist and make men all-round handymen. How far it was possible to turn out men efficient both in sniping and scouting, were questions on which experts did not agree, any more than they did when it was laid down that an Infantry soldier must be efficient in bombing and Lewis gun as well as with bayonet, rifle, and the rifle grenade!

The 'powers that be' at G.H.Q. at the time were not in favour of sniping at all as a separate art; they were set on further training in Scouting, in which we had been found sadly deficient in those glimpses of open warfare afforded on the Somme, at Wytschaete Hill and further North. Thus at the outset one had to find out what was possible, and then how best to secure the soundest compromise in training.

One difficulty was that the authority of the Training Staff at G.H.Q., being newly established, old established Army Schools and Corps and other schools of all kinds often thought they knew better than G.H.Q. Possibly they did, sometimes, anyway. The process of co-ordination of all Education and Training was then at an early stage. My six months were taken up with four separate steps. Firstly, I spent two months visiting Army Schools, Corps and Divisional Headquarters, with occasional visits to Brigades and Battalions along the Front. In this way one came into touch with the views of all kinds and conditions of men. The next step was to hold a Conference of Experts in Scouting, Sniping and Observation at Boulogne, where the various views were discussed. Thirdly, at Bouchon, after training a dozen young soldiers with the help of expert officers and N.C.O.'s, I was able to work out and demonstrate to representatives of each Army H.Q. and Sniping School a suitable system of intensive training in Scouting.

The First Official Book on Scouting.

Lastly with the help of other experts and the experience gained, my time was taken up with the completion of an official book on 'Scouting, Sniping and Observation,' which became known as 'SS 195.' This was the first official book ever produced by the Army on the subject and is therefore of interest.

Extracts from Letters.

16th May, 1917. – 'Arrived G.H.Q. Montreuil 10 p.m. Met by car and found General Solly Flood and Gerald Dalby at work. They explained matters and received me very kindly. The General apologised – no extra pay, no acting rank, but held out hopes of a red and blue arm-band! I laughed. He seemed relieved I wanted none of these, only to help to end and win the war.'

21st May. – 'I write from 38th Welsh Divisional H.Q. The General, Blackadder, is an old South African friend. Yesterday I lunched with General Jeudwine, 55th Division, who also was very good to me. It is a little shy work, constantly visiting new messes with new faces, though all are very hospitable. Have visited many old haunts in the line.'

2nd Army Sniping School.

25th May, Mont des Cats. – 'Getting on well, Major Sclater and all his staff good friends. Have just completed a long report of experiences with 2nd Army.'

1st Army Sniping School.

Linghen, 2nd June. – 'Billetted in a farm, windows looking out on farm-yard one side, and on town-hall the other side. The way to my room is through the farm kitchen where a large family collects for supper about 9.30 p.m. after a tremendous long day's work in the fields, for they are all up at 4 a.m. From my window I see the children inspanning and driving off a big cart horse, and feeding the hens and rabbits and pigs. They make me feel ashamed to be seen in bed at 6 a.m. in pyjamas with a cigarette. Wonderful people, and so pleased if you just say anything to them. I am not really so idle as they probably think, for as I said to them, we were all helping to 'chasser les sales Bosches pour la belle France.' Here lives a sniping enthusiast, Major Hesketh-Pritchard. On the 4th I go off on a tour of visits.'

With 29th Division. General Broadwood, 9th June. – 'Just finished two days with this Division which I helped at Aldershot in training its snipers. It has been very hot, and my expeditions down to the trenches (and Armentières), though very interesting, are warm work. Many remembered me, and it was an entirely new bit of country to me. Tomorrow I go to Canadian Sniping School. The noise of the Wytschaete explosion was terrific. The night before last a Corps General (Haking) put me up, and the three days before that I was the guest of Generals Hordern and Holland, the one a brother officer, the other I used to play polo with at Malta. In fact it is difficult to remember where one has been and whom one has met. It helps me a lot with my work of course, meeting men who know, and are keen; and one sees things in truer perspective; but to be always a guest and overcome one's natural shyness in each new circle, is to me a little difficult. Many people would give worlds for the job I am doing. I am absorbing all the time, rather than giving out anything, but I expect something will come of it.'

Arras, Blangy, Rocquelincourt. – 17th June. – 'The visits to the old trenches most interesting and instructive, wonderful to see the work the Bosche had put in under our noses. A large concrete officers' dug-out built not 40 yards from our front line and all their trenches well built, with bricks and mortar and endless concrete sniping and observing loopholes from which they had shot many good Riflemen. The visit to Rocquelincourt was interesting too, I spent a day exploring craters and mines, and loopholes, emplacements, dug-outs, and forward saps and wire, all very instructive, then I went on (towards Oppy) and visited the beloved veteran Battalion of the War, the 1st/60th, where I had tea. In the evening I dined with Ian Stewart, now a Brigadier General on the Staff of the XIII Corps. Today should bring me near 8/60th, but my plans are uncertain, and difficulties in getting motor transport delay me. My report on 3rd Army shows I have learned a lot and not lost the exceptional chance given. I could never have written it a month ago.'

21st June. – '3rd Army School, Sniping School, Auxiliary and Army H.Q. at Albert.'

5th Army Sniping School.

23rd June. – 'Major Mickie (a good Scot). Tomorrow 14th Division at Marieux, and after that 4th Army School at Toutencourt.

Shall be glad when our tour is completed, so much in it all, new places and people each time. You see they do not know I am only working on one cylinder.'

Amiens, 13th July. – 'I asked them to look out for a younger and more vigorous man to carry on the system once started.'

4th Army School.

18th July. – 'I have a feeling the Conference 21st–24th will go well, though I personally feel little up to conducting it, for I have felt stupid and tired for a long time and feel like a ship waiting for a breeze, or a car waiting for petrol; however, I have the lusty Cozens Hardy with me doing Secretary . . . . A fine young fellow doing A1 work.'

Boulogne, 24th July. – 'Today finds me finished with Conference, a landmark in the story of sniping and scouting. All of them went away well pleased.'

4th Army Sniping School, Bouchon.

2nd August. – 'We expect to be here 3 weeks experimenting with a dozen young soldiers. I have Cozens Hardy to help and two keen and capable Sergeants, Hicks and Barry. Began preparing the ground today. It is a beautiful little French village in a narrow valley, off the Somme Valley. The steep chalk slopes act as good butts for our shooting.'

12th August, 1917. – 'I write this from bed, not the bed of sickness, but of laziness – 8 a.m. this Sunday morning, St Grouse's day, 1917 . . . . three years of war completed . . . A little room but a big and comfortable bed, the window open looking out on to the inevitable French farm yard, the hens and pigs and geese and manure heap, all complete. The sound of clogs and a cackle of *patois* French from an old couple in the kitchen next door. Matthews has been in smiling, as usual, and given me coffee, and a cigarette. Does that sound like the hardships of war?

I think our experiment here will prove a success. We are eliminating all but the salient points to be taught, and, with the help of the Amiens camouflage experts, introducing new dodges for teaching the use of ground. It is quite like old times teaching young keen Scouts, and reminds me of many a happy day in the

Himalayas and Scotland. Poor Matthews, to help in the training, he had one day hidden, disguised as a German. He never forgot how the natives with pitch forks gave chase!'

29th August. – 'All going A1 and a very good show, and just what is wanted. Three demonstrations very much approved by experts. Just finished showing round 5th Army School delegates, all very pleased, as also were 3rd Army and 4th Army Generals and Staff. On Friday G.H.Q. come to see, and on September 2nd our circus leaves for Linghem to demonstrate to 1st and 2nd Armies.'

2nd September. – 'General Solly Flood and Dalby came down from G.H.Q. and were delighted with it all, like others, keen to lose no time in spreading this training. They are also keen for me to get on with this book.'

Boulogne, 8th October, 1917. – 'Have worked without a stop for 3 weeks – 10 days at Boulogne, 4 in Scotland, 2 while travelling, 4 at Linghem and now the MS is complete.

When I asked for leave to Scotland on Boy Scout business, the General protested – Did I know there was a war on? 'Yes,' I said, 'and this is part of it'.'

Mont des Cats, 14th October, 1917. – 'Here by the old Mill, I sit perched up – away below are Poperinghe, Ypres, Messines, the whole salient spread out like a map; a band is playing popular tunes to some tired Battalion resting in billets, where all are rejoicing at the return of the sun after days of dreadful rain and mud, and far away beyond, the guns are booming.

Yesterday I revisited Hooge and away beyond. It is good for one to go. It reminds one of what our grand fellows go through in their terrible mud and shell-hole life. It reminds one that the Bosche has not run out of ammunition. We are apt to forget. It is good to have it brought home what a far more comfortable life one has led away from the line, for though one never forgets, one fails to realise.

I tried to visit Sanctuary Wood, where Wm. John Davies lies, and Zouave Wood, where Kenneth fought, but the place was being so straffed, it was impossible. There is nothing left of anything. Woods are but a name for a few stumps of dead trees. Where once I scouted and scrambled through fresh green forest of undergrowth, today there is no trace of anything – just a higgledy-piggledy jumble of shell holes and mud and ruins. Such a scene of desolation never was seen as these shell-swept areas. It makes one think; rather, it stops one thinking! This war is too vast to realise.'

The Scout Movement during the War.

November-December, 1917. – About this time my compass began to wobble. I found myself strongly tempted to return from the Army to my labour of love with the Boy Scouts. I seemed to have completed the work given to me to do – the five schools were now in touch and working on one system with an official Manual completed.

I felt no special call to go on soldiering, whereas in the Scout Movement the loss of leaders, absent at the war, had thrown a heavy strain on the Chief and those able lieutenants who were left to help him. They had kept the flag flying, but under great difficulties. And surely never had there been greater need for providing good leadership for boys. Fathers and elder brothers away from home, mothers working at munitions, and the boys themselves being in great demand and earning fancy wages, it was no wonder that complaints of 'youthful crime' and 'lack of discipline' were becoming serious. To those who looked ahead, the Scout Movement seemed to be called upon by Heaven itself to make a special effort, not only to stick it, but to go forward with increased energy.

In connection with this move I received many letters from the Chief, from Elwes and others, which, as I say, made my compass wobble.

'You have done your bit,' wrote the Chief (September, 1917) 'more than anyone could have hoped for when you have been so physically unfit for the strain . . . . If you ever return to Scout work, you can do so with a very clear conscience, and personally, I feel that you can do a bigger national work there, so take a rest now and save yourself, there is a grand job before you.'

Again in November: – 'I have been thinking a good deal since you saw me the other day. There are big things in my mind for the Scout Movement if only we can rise to the occasion, but we are tied down for want of Scout men, and yet the present moment is our big opportunity. It is little short of criminal to let it go by. There is such a vital need for a movement to get hold of the boys at this moment. We *could* do if we moved . . . . but all are tied by their other work. I cannot do the necessary visiting and giving the buck up all round, single handed.'

No wonder that the Chief, who was doing the work of three men, was needing assistance, and no wonder that I, having completed the work given to me to do in France, and feeling no definite call to any special usefulness with the Army, no wonder that I found myself in doubt. On the other hand, though the worst seemed over at the time, yet who could visit Paschendale, or live at G.H.Q., or come into touch with the continued calling up and training of men, and yet more men, at home, without feeling doubt as to which way duty lay?

The Italian Debacle.

Then, unexpectedly came the release of German troops from the Russian front, and the sudden Italian debacle. Doubt disappeared, and the compass again set steadily, pointing to the task of training men to kill, rather than to the happier work of teaching boys to live. It was up to every mother's son to do what he could to stand up against the Hun.

At Sheerness.

February-April, 1918. – But it was not for some months that I was able to take up work again, and after many medical boards, found myself at Sheerness with the 5th K.R.R. Depot Battalion under my old friend, Colonel Parker Jervis.

I do not think that the average civilian, or even soldiers themselves who only went through the war amid the more exciting scenes nearer the front, will ever realise the splendid work done by regular Officers and N.C.O's at these depot Battalions. To me it was an eye-opener, and I take this opportunity of paying a special tribute to Colonels St. Aubyn, Brownlow, and Parker Jervis, and to all their staff, for the patient, valuable work which they did in training, equipping and sending out a steady flow of good men to make good the enormous casualties of over 20 Battalions of Riflemen.

It was the training and spirit at these depots which alone made it possible to keep up the wonderful traditions of the 60th Rifles. The drudgery and constant grind of training new men and New Army Officers, in drill, shooting, bombing, gas, Lewis guns, rifle grenades, signalling, and in the Rifleman's traditions, was a very high test of efficiency and perseverance. But added to all this there were endless new orders, and changing regulations, and conundrums – questions as to classification of recruits, medical examinations, and conditions of discharge. Then on the top of it all there were constant bombing raids, and false alarms of raids, at night, so that life at Sheerness often meant for some of the Staff a twenty hour day of work for seven days a week!

I very soon saw that it would take a better man than myself, and a much longer time than I proposed to stay at Sheerness, to master the intricacies of mobilising and training and equipping and demobilising gallant Riflemen, so with every assistance from the C.O. I confined myself to establishing an intensive system of training young soldiers, so that they should go out to France and be some use as Scouts. The system included all that I had learned from experience in France and past experience in training. The young Riflemen were as keen as could be, and the results astonishingly satisfactory.

A course of 14 days was finally decided on, demonstrations and lectures were given, and the system duly reported to the War Office. I think, that though circumstances prevented this system of training being taken up, it was to me the most satisfactory piece of work I was able to do during the war.

The German Advance.

On the 23rd of March the threatened storm broke and the Hun burst through at St. Quentin. For the time being all training was at a standstill. Every available man who was fit was sent at once to France, and many were sent who were not fit. Many poor fellows, even those who had been wounded 3 or 4 times already, went off to do whatever they might be able to do. The young soldiers were splendid, what did they care for German shells or gas! they were going to France six months before they had expected and their keenness knew no bounds. Their enthusiasm was enough to start the engine by itself. It was a heartening sight to see such fine young fellows, so splendidly trained and fit, and bound to spread their own enthusiasm; and yet, I know I was not the only old soldier who felt moved when seeing them off to the front.

Lecturing for the War Office.

In April I was offered and accepted the task of lecturing on Sniping and Scouting to the various Officer Cadet Battalions scattered all over the country. It was work well suited to a free-lance like myself, for, while it gave me the chance of forwarding better work in this direction throughout the army, it also gave me the chance of improving and developing my experiments with the cinema as a means of teaching. And it gave me great chances of doing what I could to help the Boy Scout Movement wherever I went. Indeed, I had fallen on my feet.

Training in Leadership.

I hesitate to prolong these notes on the war, and yet some words should be added on training.

Who, when I was a subaltern, ever thought that we officers of the Old Army should be called upon to play such an important part as teachers? Indeed, I may add, which of my tutors, when I was a boy, would ever have looked on me as a possible Instructor?

And yet we Army Officers, having learned a good deal from mistakes and experience, in the end were able to do good work in this direction. As a subaltern, riding, shooting and sport were my chief training for war. There was a bit of soldiering to be done certainly, but that was allowed to come second. It was left to the average young officer on joining to pick up what he could. Certainly we were never taught *how to teach*.

Then came a time of more serious views of life, and the South African War. In the Regiments soldiering was made more of a profession. There was a stir-up all round and the Army Officer lived with promotion examinations hanging over his head, even till his hair had turned grey.

Yes, we had to work mighty hard and study a hundred and one subjects, but still the art of Leadership was never taught.

It is said that teaching and leadership are gifts, and no doubt the best teachers and leaders are born rather than made, but a certain amount of training will save much time and endless mistakes. Time and mistakes are costly in war. Therefore I think that for this, and for every profession, some training in leadership should be given.

The Boy Scout System of Training.

Personally, I had some practice in training both British and Native Scouts in the Himalayas and Plains of India, but what taught me most of what proved useful during this war was Sir Robert Baden-Powell's wonderful book *Scouting for Boys*.

I had read this book, if once, at least 25 times, and had spent three years putting the system of training into practice with a few Boy Scouts in Scotland. I do not think the Army Training Staff could do better than read this book carefully and then visit some good Troop of Boy Scouts.

They would be astonished to see how a good Patrol Leader sets about training the boys of his patrol, interesting them and making them keen; explaining and demonstrating, then making them do the thing whatever it is, for themselves, and finally sending them out into the world to keep their eyes open for opportunities of practice, combined with some good turns.

The Aldershot System of Training.

The system of training adopted at the Senior Officers School, was known as the 'Theory, Demonstration, Practice' system, and it was on those lines that we worked at our Sniping School.

The conditions were exceptional, there was so much to teach and so little time available. It was therefore only possible to concentrate on the essential points; one had to think out and teach a sound system, to interest the pupil and make the subject as simple and clear to him as possible, to inspire in him enthusiasm and the wish to excel, and all the time to bring on leadership and the art of training others as far as was possible. All talking was followed by demonstration and practice. Finally the pupil was launched out to the front, where, all too soon, the 'real thing' gave him every chance of further practice.

The use of the Cinema for Teaching.

Any good teacher will tell you that twice as much can be done by appealing to the eye as well as the ear.*

Where would the dominie be without his maps and blackboard and coloured chalks? In all my lectures I found it of the greatest assistance to show lantern slides with plans and pictures of real loop-holes made by my scouts at the front, with reports, trenches, disguises, aeroplane photographs, etc., etc. It was also possible to use the screen as a blackboard by means of specially prepared lantern slides; but *the* discovery to me was the extraordinary value of moving pictures as a means of appealing to the imagination and making things clear.

This I first learned from Sergt. Nuthall, of the South African Light Infantry, more commonly known by his professional 'jiu-jitsu' name of 'Osaka.'

Poor little chap (he weighed under 9 stone though he could toy with heavy-weight men) he was killed by a shell towards the end of the war. Like most of us, he had his faults, but he certainly had a genius for teaching his art. He was keen and made others keen, he was thoroughly master of his subject; he was quick, original, and full of humour. He had a gift for acting and showing by contrast the right and the wrong way of doing things. One good lecture with his film at the local cinema hall, then the class would fall in outside only too eager to experiment on each other. As ducklings take to water, so 'Osaka's' pupils took to jiu-jitsu – indeed my chief anxiety was lest some good fighting man should end his days prematurely on Ash ranges.

'A New Idea.'

With 'Osaka' and others we set about making new films and soon with the help of the 'Kineto' Company, we were able to reproduce on the screen all that we had found so useful in teaching by acting.

Then Lieut. Davies hit on a new way of showing the plan of ground with the Scouts moving over the map according to ground, and according to the movements of enemy Scouts. This moving

* 'Segnius irritat animos demissa per aurem Quam quae sunt oculis subjeeta fidelibus, et quae Ipse tradit spectator.'

275

diagram was followed by pictures of the Scouts of both sides actually carrying out the patrol, stalking, or running, or hiding according to the situation.

In April, 1917, we made our first film, but greatly improved on this later on. Many an hour did Davies and Wilson and myself spend in that dark room in Wardour Street, experimenting and working out those films. In March, 1918, at Sheerness, and in June, 1918, at Colchester, we were able to develop this idea, with other improvements, and in the end produced films which earned approval in all directions, as a valuable aid to training.

Lectures to Cadet Officers and Others.

Armed with my films and lantern slides and black goggles, I spent the time from April to October, 1918, touring all over the country, from Bath to Invergordon, from Sheerness to Gailes, seeing a good deal of the 'old country' as it was in war-time, and giving lectures in cinema halls and demonstrations in the open, to thousands of fine young fellows, the pick of the manhood of the Empire.

A look at my diary reminds me of much uncomfortable travelling, few trains and fewer porters. There were several visits to the Universities of Oxford and Cambridge, cadets in khaki deemed to have completely replaced undergraduates in cap and gown; Aldershot, Romford, York, Chatham, Cannock Chase, Wimbledon, etc., etc., were large military centres swarming with khaki. Scotland was full of khaki – everywhere khaki.

The audiences varied just as men vary. The Cadet Battalions seemed to reflect the character of their Commanding Officer, with some, one felt at home at once, some were stiffer and took more knowing.

I remember some 1,500 Guardsmen in London, seated in gilt chairs at the Victoria Palace of Varieties, rather stiff and 'on parade' at first, and how I felt the contrast at their Depot at Caterham, with an evening audience of 1,500 more of them, cheery and 'off parade' and less formal. It is easier to teach a man to think for himself, as Scouts must do, if you get him away from 'the position of attention.'

I remember too, at Aberdeen, a splendid audience of over 1,200 Gordon Highlanders. How they did listen and laugh and cheer!

At the end I told the Colonel it was one of the best audiences, and the best cinema hall, I had come across in my wanderings. At the close of the lecture he told his men this, and finished up with the comment which raised a perfect storm of applause – 'not bad,' said he, 'for a little fishing village.' – This puzzled me till the Colonel explained that some English Staff Officer had thus belittled their famous granite city.

Twice I revisited the Senior Officers' School at Aldershot, founded by Kentish, finding each time a new commandant and new classes of Senior Officers, but each time a warm welcome and much encouragement. On these occasions I was also able to fit in cinema talks to younger audiences – the Farnborough Orphan School, and the school children of Farnham. There were visits too to New Zealanders, Anzacs, Canadians, and every kind of British soldier.

One thing stands out in my mind and that is the genuine interest taken by old and young, and by all ranks. If you want to interest and grip your audience, try the cinema as an aid; and do not be afraid of a good laugh; these cinema films never failed to help me to teach by raising a laugh at certain points (a very good thing during the anxious days of March and April, 1918). It is a good thing too for the lecturer to be human and in touch with his hearers.

Thus from April to October it was given me to speak to audiences of some 25,000 men, most of them leaders of men. My subject was 'Scouting and Sniping,' but to me these were but a stepping stone to higher things – for who could speak to leaders of men at such a time without some word of leadership – and where is leadership without character?

At the War Office I had so many friends that in the end I could have found my way unaided by Scouts, or Girl Attendants, or Commissionaires, to almost any part of that rabbit warren, so that I was ever in touch and up to date with the latest news. The grave anxiety in April, the better outlook in June, or the retiring of Bulgaria in September. Thus in going forth to speak to thousands of men in khaki, who in turn would speak to tens of thousands of civilians, I was acting the part of a liaison officer. It was up to me to 'keep smiling' and give a good lead.

October, 1918.

In October good news poured in from every front, but at a terrible cost of gallant lives. In officers alone it was no uncommon thing to read of 450 casualties in one day's fighting, but the end was near.

On 1st November (together with General Ludendorf) I finally took leave of the Army, and returned to my Scouting in Scotland.

It was difficult to realise that my Army work was finished. Then, with the incentive of war removed, I seemed to collapse. The fact was that after these strenuous years my whole machinery needed a rest.

I was packed off to Miss Absolom's Nursing Home in Edinburgh, and there on November, 11th I heard from my bed the combined British and American Fleets announcing the armistice. There was plenty of noise and shouting, but it found me too tired to shout.

Then after weary weeks of resting, I returned to the outside world and tried to buck up. But I felt like a man counted out in the ring, trying to rise once again. It could not be done.

Again I returned to the Nursing Home. My old wound had gone wrong. For days and nights it had given great pain. The good Ian Bolton took charge and got me to Edinburgh, where on 6th February 1919, Sir Harold Stiles operated with great success. It took him some time, but in the end he dealt faithfully, casting out devils with many long names – Osteomyelitis, streptococus, staphylococus, and others. These, for a long time back, had been my undoing. Once they were gone, I mended quickly. Thus I was spared for another twenty years, the best years of my life, to get on with the work on which my whole being seemed bent.

Of these days I will hope, later on, to give some account which may help to promote the great cause. Meanwhile, let me wind up this part of my story with one word more about Scouts and happier days.

20. HAPPIER DAYS.

In the course of my War Office tour in Scotland, I was kept pretty busy, lugging my boxes of films and slides all over the country from Berwick to Dornoch. Trains were crowded and few, porters were scarce and cars often not to be had; however, before the end, I had lectured in Scotland to over 7,000 Officers and men in various cinemas and halls and in the open air.

Scotland.

July-August, 1918. It also gave me the chance of doing a bit for the Boy Scouts,. It was cheering to visit the Sea-Scouts and find them alert on Coast-Guard duty all along the East Coast. They were doing splendid work; also, here and there, in town and country some troops were still going strong, but after 3 years of war, with leaders like Lawrence and Stocks killed at the front, with others away on service, and very few left with time to help, there was bound to be much which needed attention. The wonder was that things were going as well as they were. At some points there were complaints, misunderstandings and friction. There was much to put right.

A turning-point.

On 28th September, we held an important Conference at Stirling. It went off well. A Rally, 500 Stirlingshire Scouts and 12 County Flags. At our opening session a fine spirit prevailed, and lasted right up to the final meeting on Sunday.

I see in my private diary – 'For the whole of last month my mind has been one steady prayer for the success of this meeting.'

This gathering was, I think, a turning point of our progress in Scotland. New men began to come forward and an energetic Committee tackled finance and supervision.

On release from the Army in August, 1918, my one thought was to get on with the Boy Scout Movement in Scotland. To me the whole of this ghastly war had seemed one big interruption; and now, with the ball at our feet we would soon get going again.

But it was not till May that I found myself completely recovered, and July found me back with my boys in as jolly a Camp as ever I knew.

June-July, 1919.

June and July were months of rejoicing all over the land. On 28th June came the signing of Peace. On 6th July the great Thanksgiving Day. Then came the crowning event – Victory Day, 19th July, 1919.

I had never been a Scoutmaster before, but when the boys pressed me to give them a lead and take them to Camp, I felt I could not say no. 'All right,' I said, 'We will have a great Victory Camp, but first you must do some training for camp, every man jack of you will have to qualify before I will take him to camp.'

The story of how for six weeks we carried out a cheery course of training, is given elsewhere.* We all had a great deal to learn and we made good progress all-round.

What a wonderful thing a first-class well-run camp of good Scouts can be when pitched on the shores of some beautiful Scottish Loch under perfect weather conditions. What other Movement can combine so perfect a holiday with such happy, practical training in manliness, handiness, and every variety of useful occupation?

Entraining at Stirling for Balloch with our trek-carts and gear we marched 8 miles along the 'Bonnie Banks of Loch Lomond,' then over the moors to Helensburgh, where we shipped for Rosneath. By 8 p.m. we had settled in camp on the shores of the Gareloch, and the cooking patrol had provided the evening meal. Thus we had had practice in travel by road, by rail and by boat. In loading, unloading, and dismantling their trek-carts, each boy had his job and knew what to do. They were all on their mettle to show what 'Sons of the Rock' could do.

* 'A Victory Camp.' Alden & Co., Ltd. (Now out of print.)

Arrival in Camp.

Any arrival in Camp, with so much that is thrilling and new, is of course an exciting adventure. Could they be off at once in the boat, bathing, fishing, exploring? The unwelcome answer is, No. Certain things have got to be done, an orderly meal, the issue of blankets, camp boundary rules, and rules as to bathing, boating and fishing. You may have to be stricter at first to establish a system where each does his share. It may take time, but once they tumble to the big idea, all will go well.

If 'Lights-out' and 'Reveille' are not exactly according to plan those first 24 hours, do not worry; they are all of them new to camp ways; if you tackle these things with a smile, by the fourth day fatigues for milk, firewood, latrines, a roster for boating and fishing, an inter-tent competition, all will be found running smoothly, and it will not be a harassing one-man show.

The second reveille will certainly find our young heroes less eager to rise. Ever since they arrived, these bundles of quick-silver have been on the move; if on Sunday you get them to the Parish Church Service by 12 noon, well fed and well turned out, that, to my mind, is quite good.

Sunday in Camp.

If the sermon is long and the windows are closed, it may very well be, after so much fresh air, that attention may falter. Once outside, they revive; but still they are not up to true form.

We take them away for the day with haversack rations along the lovely shores and woods to Rosneath Point. Here they can let off steam to their hearts' content and not shock those who would have them less active this Sabbath day. There are herons and gulls, and shells and flowers to discover, and tin-cans to bombard with endless ammunition. We can bathe and feed and rest in the sun and sea-air. We return in fine fettle to supper in camp, winding up a great day with our evening Scout Service.

The sunset and sky are magnificent, the hills outlined at the head of the Loch. The sea so still and reflections so clear. Someday, perhaps, in some far-away land when thoughts are of home, these scenes will return.

We lower the flag. The full moon rises, reflecting new glories. Our good host and padre (my grandfather's grandson) John McLeod Campbell, helps with our service. The boys sing well 'Abide with me.' How beautiful it sounds. So ends a happy day.

Reveille.

If you are a sound sleeper, take an alarm clock. But for me, well practised in such duties, it was no great matter to keep my overnight promise to that eager P.L. on cooking duty. He has made me promise on my honour as a Scout, to wake him without fail, in good time. The competition depends on it.

To me, indeed, it was yet another happy memory to have watched the dawn of another perfect day, the colours returning to fields and hills, heather and bracken, reflected upside down as in a mirror; to listen to the lapping waters, the gulls, the first to sound the bird's reveille, the splash of a diving tern, the cry of the curlew wading at half-tide.

Then comes the time to harden your heart and wake your two chefs. Without this experience the Scoutmaster's training is incomplete!

At the 'Bulldog' tent you find eight sleeping bundles of bulldogs in blankets. Which particular bundles did you promise to wake? This one here, with a cord tied to its leg and here is another, his Second in Command! What a position! His head is mixed up with his neighbour's knees. You pull. You pull several times. In the end, two sleepy smiling figures emerge and get on with lighting the fire.

Later the time has come to arouse the whole camp. You get hold of Gregor, the piper. Come, let us wake up and watch the 'Hounds.' Come, Gregor, right up to the door of the tent. Watch these eight bundles awake. Watch their expressions. Watch them turn over and stretch and rub their eyes as they hear 'Hey Johnny Cope.' Do they love Highland music, or is it a boot they would throw at the piper's head?

Eventful Days.

Truly it was a Victory Camp. Along with the daily routine there was always something new to enjoy and remember.

Each morning, after Inspection, we formed up round the Union

Jack and saluted its unfurling. We would sing the CXXI Psalm, 'I to the hills.' (It was our Padre who started this custom, one which we always kept up in later years). Then we sat round; a few verses, short simple talks which went home, then a short prayer.

After this there would be notices to give out – details of duties, and coming events. Scoutmaster, that is your chance, just a word, perhaps to hammer in the Padre's talk or perhaps some comment on something well done, or, may be, not so well done. It was Bacon who said, 'Praise in public, but find fault with individuals in private.' That is right for boys as well as men.

Today you went round the kitchen. It was ever so clean. The wood was ready, chopped, neatly stacked and covered up. All was ready, not for themselves, but for the incoming patrol. You noticed one particular Scout, you had thought him a slacker, but there he was doing specially well – well then, for goodness sake, remember to 'purr when you're pleased.' Give him a pat on the back. Here, standing round the flag is the chance of a lifetime, a word from you now may mean the turning-point in a man's career.

After the Service, as soon as duties had been done, there came boating and bathing and fishing arranged by turns and with due precautions. There were scouting games on the moors or in the woods. There were sports in the old Yew Avenue, expeditions and visits to other Troops.

There was Parent's Day when Mrs. Campbell of Achnashie welcomed us all in the beautiful grounds, and the boys, after giving an amusing display, challenged their fathers to races in rowing and running.

Victory Day.

But the best day of all was Victory Day, with the huge 30 ft. bonfire up on the Gallow Hill, 400 ft. above Rosneath Point. At 8 p.m. we were off, pipers, trek-carts and suppers. By 9 p.m. we had reached the bonfire on its commanding site.

The Zero hour for lighting was 11 p.m.

What a panorama! The Clyde, Dumbarton and Greenock, Arran and Bute, and Argyll's Bowling Green. The sun was setting N.W. The Loch Long peaks stood out in a blaze of gold. We put in the time of waiting with camp-fire songs. A crowd had collected and by 10.45 it began to get dark.

On distant hills all round us bonfires began to show, but we, less impatient, awaited the hour. Some local leader is speaking – The War. The German threat to our very existence. Our men, our gratitude to them and our humble thanks to God for Victory.

Then a small child is helped to start the lighting of this mass of pines and paraffin and tar. We cheer. Soon, driven back by the heat, the whole crowd presses back from the crackling fiery furnace. I never saw such a blaze.

Twelve midnight, it is time to be off. We sort out our laddies from the crowd. The night-march home is wonderful. The moon has risen in the East. I shall never forget that young piper playing the whole way down the hill, swinging surefooted through heather and bracken, and I – for all past practice in Himalayan hills and night-marching, my thoughts on war and peace, victory and defeat, on the triumph of Right over Wrong – was stumbling and tripping like a clumsy fellow. At the foot of the hill we halted awhile; then, winding round the lovely moonlit Camsail Bay, singing all the way, on through the beautiful woods, on past the famous giants, 'Adam and Eve,' on through the Clachan and back to our Camp at Achnashie. It was 1a.m. as we swung into camp to the tune of their favourite march. What was the tune? I could not whistle it now to save my life but some snatches I remember:–

'Come, all my comrades, raise high your voices,
Let us rejoice, while youth is ours today.
Brave be our hearts and strong our endeavour,
God keep us true and lead us on our way . . .
Heeding no fame, yet playing the game . . .
Going where duty may call us to go.'

But it was the way the boys sang it which helped to enchant the whole scene.

Thursday, 24th July. – The boys seem more cheery and indefatigable than ever. A wonderful sunrise. The whole sky as red as the rosiest sunset. What did that mean? Surely no shepherd's warning for this last day was the finest and best in all our glorious spell of grand weather. Bathing perfect. In the afternoon, sports and prizes. The wounded men in blue hospital dress were wheeled up from the Ferry to join in the fun.

The last camp-fire – scenery, sunset, singing, and laughter of boys – what more would you have? Just this – it was late. There was much to be done next day. It was close on 11 p.m. with an early reveille to come.

The boys were right at the top of their form; the shyest of singers had let himself go, lost in laughter at 'Cuddy's indiarubber nose' and the comic conductor.

Reluctantly I was about to close the concert, when a change seemed to come of itself. The comic song gave way to Poyser's March, And this in turn changed into our evening hymn, 'Abide with me,' then 'God save the King' and so 'Good night,' and all turned in.

It was the boys themselves who carried on and this was my reward.

I was happy and thankful that night. I had heard a clear call to press on after war, with peace and goodwill, through this practical training and friendship of boys.

As a Nation we had come through great trials. With 'backs to the wall,' our Freedom itself had been in great danger. It had been touch and go. Behind us now were these dark anxious days, explosions and noise, mud and mines, slaughter, and shattered remains. But with us survived traditions of Comradeship, of Faith, of Leadership.

Our goal must now be to build up a Nation of men trained to be worthy of Freedom. No longer must 50 per cent of our youth be left at a critical age to drift downhill to C.3 uselessness in body and mind and spirit, with never a word in their ear as to Duty and Honour, Service and Freedom. Is it freedom to let boys in their teens do just what they like? All must be given a chance to qualify for freedom and learn through self-discipline and comradeship and Faith to work, and work hard, towards the common good.

Would you have them salute the Union Jack? If so, then the Nation must give all a chance and win that devotion. God's plan is brotherhood: Here was a Movement bent on this plan. For us it was 'full steam ahead!'

MEMOIRS
OF A
RIFLEMAN SCOUT

PART IV

PART IV.

SCOUTING, 1919–1929.

CONTENTS

21. THE THREE JAMBOREES.

From 1919 to 1929 the outstanding events in the Boy Scout world were the three great Jamborees – Olympia, 1920; Wembley, 1924; and Birkenhead, 1929. There had been many Rallies before 1914, but the first Jamboree at Olympia was something quite new.

The spirit of the movement had been steadily growing. For many years the Chief Scout had had it in mind to hold a great international Rally. His idea was to assemble his boys and pledge them to friendship, and to practise friendship, in one happy camp. In his own happy way, with ceaseless hard work, he spread his enthusiasm from top to bottom, till it reached through and through, to the last-joined Scout.

The wonderful scene at the close of Wembley, when 10,000 boys of 26 nations cheered non-stop for a third of an hour, and acclaimed him Chief Scout of the World, was proof enough of success. Never was seen a greater ovation.

What did it mean, this new word. '*Jamboree*?'

> 'The Jamboree, the Jamboree!
> What does it mean to you and me!
> It means a vow, a pledge, a pact,
> To love, to serve, to think, to act,
> It means a league of boys – and then
> A world-wide league of full-grown men.'
>
> Anon.

The two Pipe Bands at Wembley.

In our Scottish display we had two Pipe bands. One from Greenock and one from St Andrews, both a credit to Scotland. A Pipe competition had just been held. A large crowd of young kilties were assembled, waiting and eager to hear the results. I was standing close to the St Andrews boys, among them the fine young drum-major from the Madras College. I knew all the Pipe Bands – they had camped together at Rosneath – many had fancied St Andrews as winners. We listened intently for the verdict – Greenock had won! I watched my young friend of St Andrews. For a space his face fell. Then at once he pulled himself up and his face was as bright as could be, while he called for three cheers for the Renfrewshire boys. Bravo St Andrews! You gave a good lead towards friendship at home as well as abroad.

The Tug-of-War.

Another great moment stands out in my mind. It was at the close of the International tug-of-war.

In the semi-finals, amid scenes of wild enthusiasm, America had beaten Sweden and the Scots had defeated the Swiss. Now Scotland was facing America. Never, perhaps, in any arena were seen two finer teams of young fellows, so highly trained, so intent on pulling together to win for their side.

There was in the air a feeling of sympathy with the American lads, 3,000 miles away from their home supporters, so far from the yells of Yale and Cornell; one felt a wish in the air for fair play in the cheering. But, in spite of that, the Scots were evidently the favourites with the vast audience.

What a fine lot of young fellows they were! Strapping young giants in kilts and white vests; the pick of some 7,000 Glasgow Scouts, fit and trained to a tee by the champion Glasgow Police. Scotland might well feel proud. The Americans, too, were a picture of muscle and fitness. No one knew how it would go.

Then followed a contest which no one who saw it will ever forget. Each team won one pull. One final ding-dong pull and Scotland had won.

What did the Yankees do? They took me, for one, by surprise. Running together and forming some kind of a rugby scrum, they gave what sounded like a Red Indian war-cry, an 'are-we-down-hearted?' kind of yell, and before the Jocks knew what was up, they were being embraced as brothers by their opponents. Then, arm in arm, all together, they left the arena.

The cheering had been frantic before; now it was frenzied.

In the camp from that time on, Yanks and Scots were special friends and heroes to all.

How pleased the Chief was with such happenings!

The Wembley Jamboree, 1924.

In 1924 the great British Empire Exhibition was held at Wembley. All the Dominions and Colonies were represented. For one week in August we had a huge Scout Camp of boys from all over the Commonwealth. Each afternoon the Scouts gave displays at the Stadium which attracted thousands of visitors. Scotland was there; it took 60 special trains to bring our contingent. It was a huge camp, run entirely by voluntary work, no Government help. The Scottish display was a popular item, and the boys did well and made many friends.

One picture stands out in my mind. It was Sunday. A great Empire Service was to be held in the Stadium. I was asked to lead the Scottish Contingent, but by then I was tired; instead, with the Padre, I climbed the zig-zag stairs to a height of 100 ft. above the large green oval lawn, one of 50,000 spectators.

It was an astonishing sight. The order, the colour, the thousands of boys and their fluttering flags. It was like some bright garden plot in the sun, with tier upon tier of spectators all round.

Then I noticed a tap. Where was Scotland? Were they late in spite of that early reveille? Then we heard the pipes. On they came, one hundred strong, followed by five divisions of kilties, 3,000 Scouts in sections of eight, swinging along in perfect order, and yet, no shouting of orders, no hesitation. Like clock-work and punctual to time, they formed up in their allotted position. With Scotland's arrival the pattern was complete.

With the organ playing the hymn, 'O God our help,' came a long procession of flags from all over the Empire, then the Chief and Prince of Wales and lastly the Archbishop of Canterbury. The Service was most impressive, the singing, the archbishop who spoke moving words, and Prince Edward of Wales, who overnight had danced a reel at the Scottish Camp, he too made a great impression.

There was now a pause of expectation, then the Chief stepped down to the rostrum. His first words were a bit unexpected. 'Scouts,' he said, 'Sit down.' So natural, just as if he were a Scoutmaster at an ordinary camp-fire circle. One could almost hear a smile as those 25,000 boys settled themselves down to listen. Slowly and clearly the Chief went on – 'You have just heard the Archbishop telling you of your duty to God. You have just heard your future King telling you of duty to your Country. Now I bid you pause and think.'

Then after a pause – 'Lower your flags.' It was a great moment. Flags from all over the world, flags of all colours, Union Jacks, distinctive flags of England, Scotland, Ireland, Wales, and of all the Empire, hundreds of Scout flags, bright green and yellow, hundreds of Scottish flags, each one a trophy won by merit – all these banners and flags rose slowly together and then drooped down,

'Lower your heads,' came the quiet command of the Chief and 25,000 heads were bowed.

'I want you to think of your promise' (a pause).

'I want you to go out from here eager to serve God' (a pause).

'Those who will – Tell me!'

The sun lit up the scene as a great forest of Scouts' bare arms shot up, and a great shout went up – 'I WILL.'

Words give little idea of such moments as these. Their measureless value is that they carry us on through less spectacular days. Tens and tens of thousands of boys are now better men because of the Chief and the lead that he gave.

The service over, after the blessing, the great assembly of Scouts dispersed in perfect order. We stood up above looking down on the endless columns marching away. At last came the turn of our five Scottish Divisions, and last of all, but far from least in my affections, came a compact party of 40 young hopefuls with dark blue shirts, Argyll scarves and kilts. I nudged my companion and said with more calm than I felt – 'Padre, that is my crowd.' These were lads who helped me far more than they knew.

They were part of my vision of great days ahead.

And now the arena was empty. We had just begun to move off, 50,000 of us, when out ran some 300 Scouts, a skirmishing line in full cry. Ten minutes later no vestige of litter was left.

The Birkenhead Jamboree, 1929.

Olympia in 1920 was good. Wembley, with experience gained was better, but the Arrowe Park Jamboree at Birkenhead was the best of these three Jamborees. It was a landmark of progress, of increased support and prestige. If in this account I focus too much on Scotland, or Stirling, or 'Self,' it is because the whole affair is too big to report.

The Objects.

First, let us see our objective. Here are the Chief's stop-press last words to his Leaders –

'Remember to impress on your Scouts that the objects of the Jamboree are for them –

(1) To make friendships with Scouts overseas.
(2) To show the Public how smart, well-behaved, and helpful Scouts can be.
(3) To have a good time.'

He knew very well that for us, his Leaders, it would mean a big effort, calling for all the forethought and work we could spare; and as for us, we who had seen the wonderful force of enthusiasm available on such occasions, it was up to us to guide this keenness aright. It was largely a matter of Faith. Only so can I account for the smoothness with which the vast camp was run, with its feeding, transport, health, and display arrangements, all on so big a scale; the good name won by the boys; and the good time that they had.

For eighteen months before the event we were busy, as a few extracts will show –

Liverpool, 26th August, 1928. 'A big reception to the Chief in Town Hall. Enter four Lord Mayors (Manchester, Chester, Birkenhead, and Liverpool) in formal procession. The Chief spots me in crowd and leaves procession quite informally, to welcome me back from New Zealand. Lord Derby takes the chair for Lady Mayoress who has lost her voice. Visit Arrowe Park with I.H.Q. Leaders. Arena is a rough stubble-field. We have made a good start, well ahead of time.'

'Encouraged on return to Scotland. Talks with all Leaders at all levels on Birkenhead plans.'

From this date on, my log has a steady series of notes on the coming Jamboree. Visits to H.Q. in Edinburgh, long meetings in winter and drives home in the fog and dark. 'A fine lot of Leaders – Calderwood, Glentanar, Julian, Howie, Dodds, the two Macs and others, and Ian Bolton, of course, all keen and helpful. Have secured John Robertson and Taylor for Band and other good men.'

On return there were letters and circulars and personal contacts to be made all over Scotland. There were broadcasts and articles, and at home in Stirling, a fine lot of Leaders and boys with whom to try out ideas for massed dancing and Highland games.

25/2/29. – 'All day at Jamboree, formations, spaces, etc., correspondence, telephone. Archie Stirling (Garden) and Q.V. School a great help with dancing and Bob Starkey with caber, etc. Our own boys, too, encourage, so keen. My brain is too active, but all will go well.'

24/3/29. – 'Parents Easter Display in Territorial Hall. 150 boys. Pipe band and 9 eightsomes.'

11/5/29. – 'Grand day up the Wharry to shake off Jamboree.'

26/5/29. – 'Elections turmoil, no time for. Our own boys now well set for Jamboree dancing and games. They won County Flag.'

1/6/29. – 'Sunbath on moors, recovering from Peebles Conference. Cuckoos, curlews, best time of the year. All shaping well.'

10/6/29. – 'Rehearsed County Rally at Falkirk (itself a preparation for Jamboree), but sad accident on return. We lost 'little Mac.' Rally cancelled.

'Little Mac.'

Never had our happy family been busier before, with camp training, and the coming County Rally; the prospect of the camp at the Lake of Menteith; and always the great Jamboree drawing nearer and nearer. Then suddenly the blow fell.

We had started off at 7 p.m. on Monday, 10th June, with all our impedimenta, gymnastic plant, dancing gear, pole and standards, hammer, shot, and caber. Some 70 Scouts in two buses and a lorry – as cheery a party of boys as ever was seen, bound for Falkirk, where we had a successful rehearsal.

One of our party was little Duncan McLeod Campbell. It was still an open question (with him a burning question) – Would he get to Birkenhead? He was a born gymnast, a very neat fling and sword dancer, and a general favourite, but just three months below the age.

It was late, nearly 10 p.m., when, after the rush of the rehearsal, this party started for home, cheering their way through the crowded streets of Falkirk, Carron, and Larbert; and many a man in the street stopped, turned round, and waved at the sight of the boys.

On nearing his home, the lorry on which our dear Mac was travelling slowed down nearer to his home than was the next ordained stop. He jumped, but, active though he was, he slipped, and, falling foul of the lorry, to the horror of his mates sustained terrible injuries.

Dr. Wilson was soon on the spot, and all that skill could do was done. 'Yes, I will be brave,' said little Mac and never a sign of pain did he show. Two hours later at the Infirmary, after a long distressing wait, all were advised to go home and come next morning.

But by 4 a.m. 'little Mac' had 'gone home.' Without pain he passed suddenly away. The shock had carried him off.

Who can describe the dark cloud which comes over close friends at such a time? All so united in a common sorrow. You feel it. You cannot describe it.

We 'carried on' as Scouts. So much to be done, so many details to see to. As usual next evening our camp training went on. Five small camps, each with its kitchen and oven and gadgets. To the outside observer all might have seemed as usual; but to us who understood the whole Troop was different. It was as though our little Mac had left each one of us a special legacy of greater kindness to each other.

Then came the funeral. The small coffin covered by the Union Jack, with Scout hat and wreaths, carried by six big fellow-Scouts. The Scouts salute. The long procession. The Pipers' sad slow march. At the grave the Minister, Rev. Wm. C. Charteris, an old Scout friend. His words are beautiful. How hard it is for our young comrades, this mystery of death, so new to them. So great a puzzle to us all. He thinks of all, the good Scout brother Alex, far away in Canada. There is an uplift in his words, almost he reconciles. This chosen corn of wheat shall bring forth good. Such wounds are healed by time alone, but through the clouds as rays of light, sympathy from all comes streaming through and helps.

From Scouts both far and near, from Boys' Brigade friends, the special thoughtful deeds of neighbours, the kindly looks of unknown friends – all these are rays of light. The love which passeth understanding may be love which chastens us.

From that day on for many a day, at least I know, we were a better and a more united Troop.

Bannockburn Day, 21/–23/6/29. – 'Visit of Pipe Band. 85 boys put up by Stirling parents and friends for week-end. Marked out the ground and explained to all with blackboard. Many experts and Leaders from all over Scotland at rehearsal. Sunday, fine address by Rev. A. M. Johnston, then display at Burgh Buildings. They have a fine spirit and excellent Leaders – (the stalwart John Robertson, 16 stone). Glorious day. After the Service spoke to Band – Robert the Bruce, Bannockburn Day. Pipers to lead 3,000 Scottish Scouts, who in turn would lead the Scouts of the world. A new kind of contest. A contest in making friends. All Stirling pleased with Band. The boys did well and had a great time.'

1/7/29. – 'Sun shines, but indoors all day, writing. Wingate splendid, has worked overtime to get out 3,000 copies of our 'book of directions' to all concerned. How far can one make things clear, and stir up enthusiasm in cold print? A rare feeling of having all now well in hand. All has gone well.'

30/7/29. – 'Just before first performance, asked to explain Scottish Display to some 50,000 spectators and 30,000 Scouts. Felt quite at home after previous broadcasts and keen on my subject. Made small joke. 'Aberdeen, rival cabers and camp-fuel shortage.' Strange to hear ripple of laughter all round the vast crowd. Later – pride followed by a fall. Next time, some nuisance nearby was talking. I raised my voice to drown his – result, broadcast a 'flop'.'

I will not dwell on all that went on at Birkenhead – the trying journey down from Scotland followed by strenuous hours of settling down in camp and a great massed charge of 50,000 boys. The boys stuck it well and before very long were mixing and laughing and swapping and making friends in the Jamboree way, with 36 Nations to choose from.

At half-time a big change over of half our contingent took place without any hitch, a big extra task for John Crawford and Malcolm Speir and all our H.Q. Staff.

One thing all will remember is the Arrowe Park mud. The morning of our first display, it had rained overnight. I slushed nearly a mile through the mud to survey the arena. Somehow I never felt more confident. At the arena I met the Chief. 'What about Scotland?' he asked. 'Scotland will not let you down!' I answered, 'We will dance a massed mudsome!'

But the sun seemed specially kind to Scotland. We gave our display three times, and each time he came out and dried into clay our muddy dancing floor.

The Scottish Display.

The Scottish display consisted of Highland Games, Procession of Flags, Pipe Band, Massed Dancing, and then a final March-past. It lasted 25 minutes. The boys had come from all parts of Scotland, meeting each other for the first time, scarcely time for rehearsal, and yet on 10th August, at our third and last display, the show seemed to run of itself. It was a case of massed individual effort.

Twelve hundred Danes had just marched off the ground after a magnificent gymnastic display; Indians and Greeks had also won great applause. Then Scotland came on the scene. First came a new version of Highland Games. The novelty was that instead of lasting all day, it took only five minutes. From opposite ends of the arena, 100 young athletes marched to their positions, caber, hammer, shot and wrestling, pole jumping, hop step and leap, dancing and piping competitions, and in the centre a tug-of-war. All these events went on at the same time. Tossing the caber roused special interest.

Then at a beat of the drums the athletes withdrew with perfect precision, the Pipe Band entered the arena, advanced to the centre playing, then counter-marching formed one big circle, 60 pipers, 40 drummers and a splendid drum-major.

Meanwhile, with equal precision, a long succession of Scottish banners and flags, spaced at 3 yards or so, took up position round the arena. The scene was set. A short pause, then, to the roll of drums, came pouring in from opposite ends torrents of cheering boys; on they came, and still they came, and then, there they were in position, standing, waiting, quiet and still.

Then the Band struck up 'Mistress McLeod of Raasey,' four bars, and all together, away they went, a great swirl of swinging kilts and shouts and pipes; a dancing mass of extra happy Scottish boys; and all the while the Scottish Flags circling round the dance add life and colour to a thrilling scene.

Six minutes, then the dance is ended. The Band forms up to face the Stand and play young Scotland past. Beyond the Band the Flags have formed one long straight line. The bearers stand as rocks, only their banners fluttering seem to wave 'Scotland the brave!' 'Scotland for ever!'

Meanwhile Athletes and Dancers have converged and now await the signal to march past. The Band strikes up 'Scotland the Brave,' and, marching well, on they come. As they near the Stand, now comes the great moment as they raise their hats and wave and cheer and cheer – a wonderful salute. The Flags wheel round and follow, colours flying. Lastly comes the Band, no check, no pause in pace or time – how well they deserved that final great ovation.

So Scotland passes on, soon to be merged in all the fun and friendship of the camp.

22. THE SECRET OF SUCCESS.

Scouting gets touch.

I have given these glimpses of the highlights which helped us some 30 years back. I have often marvelled and wondered, how was it that with all these thousands of boys assembled from far and near, all went so well, no hitches and no mishaps? Surely 'B.P.' and his ways had some special blessing?

In the Army a Commander has his trained staff, his Colonels and Captains to pass on his wishes to all concerned. If one falls out, another trained man is there to fill the gap.

In Voluntary Movements, in the very nature of things, this is not so. There are bound to be gaps and weak links in the chain of leadership. Here, no Scoutmaster; there, no Commissioner; in another place no local Secretary. How did we bridge such gaps? What I found was that wherever I went there was always some moving spirit, in touch with the spirit of Baden-Powell. Age and standing might vary. It might be a soldier or a lawyer, a padre, a butcher, a teacher, or a miner; a man or a woman or boy, who took up the torch, got others to follow and got things done. Initiative and enthusiasm, leaders who got down to the job (often more than one job) all went to make one team with a spirit which leapt over gaps and won through. In a unique way true Scouting 'gets touch.'

The Chief.

From my privileged position I saw this was so. In London on the Council I came into touch with the Chief, with Everett, Elwes, Green, and Morgan and others at I.H.Q. where I was always made welcome.

As an example of touch with the Chief here is just one sample which tells of this Leader who got things done –

301

I was once in London for a Conference. Overnight the Chief had summed up with great effect. I had slept at the Reubens Hotel. So too had the Chief and Lady B.P. Next morning I sat at breakfast alone. Suddenly my table was invaded. Regardless of waiters and others, more staid, the Chief Scout, the Chief Guide, and old 'Uncle' Elwes swooped down in a raid and my plates, knives and forks, tea-pot, tea-cup and tea-spoon, sausages and all, were swiftly and deftly transported the length of the room to a far-away table, where I found myself making a fourth, one of as jolly a party as ever could be.

Scottish H.Q.

At Scottish H.Q. too we also worked as a team. There had been times when our 'Scottish Constitution' and 'litigiousness' may have caused surface ripples; but with the arrival of men like Calderwood and Glentanar at the head of affairs; we soon learned to take 'litigiousness' less seriously.

What was an 'Office Bearer?' We listened patiently. In the end our experts agreed – An 'Office Bearer' was 'one who held office.' We gave them a cheer and got on with Scouting.

At Scottish H.Q. we had our 'triumvirate' – Crawford, Crichton and Crum; all three mad keen and yet best of friends. There is a saying that all Scout enthusiasts are either 'Crocks,' 'Cranks,' or 'Criminals.' Crawford was the brains of the Staff. Crichton spread keenness wherever he went. Crum of course was the 'Crock'. The other two may both have been 'Cranks,' but 'Criminals,' no! They did great things for Scotland. It was they who with McIntyre and others founded our Training Camp at Wemyss Firs which did the pioneer work of passing on the spirit of Gidney and Gilwell to hundreds still serving today.

In the Counties too we made good progress. I will only say here that with men like Jock Neish in Angus and Ian Bolton in Stirlingshire there was never much fear of our losing touch.

As for myself, always in touch with our own local problems and doings in Stirling, this helped me and kept me in touch with similar problems further afield. I certainly did hold a unique position. One day I might be at tea with our County President, the Laird of Polmaise, discussing his tartan and two Polmaise Troops; next day it might be sharing a billy-can up the glen with his garden-boy discussing the pit boys on strike at Polmaise. At one time I had 15 boys in my Troop who had lost their Fathers. With letters of thanks from Mothers for keeping an eye on their lads, I need say no more of the touch which a Scoutmaster may have with his boys.

23. A PERSONAL STATEMENT.

At this point, speaking of touch, I feel that perhaps it is up to me to get touch with my readers and make some personal statement, however much one may wish to avoid all mention of 'Self.'

Always a bit of a pioneer, on leaving the Army I found myself free to get on with ideas. With my pension and £400 a year, by living carefully, as a bachelor, on £150 a year, I was able to keep a small car and was able to get everywhere at no cost to the Movement. I had no extravagant tastes. Bridge and cross-word puzzles, dances and parties took up none of my time.

My work was the organisation and training and spreading of the gospel of Scouting. My chief recreation was contact and outings with boys. It was no case of self-denial. 'A very dull dog' you might say, but I never felt dull. I found life exciting.

My tendency was to overwork. I would gladly have kept hard at it the whole year round, but past breakdowns had taught wisdom. Moreover, each winter the Scottish climate got at my throat and pulled me up short, so, often I had to slow down.

Occasionally there were special events. Jamborees, fetes, speeches, or conferences, which called for special effort, and then I often had to sail near the wind, but by nursing my strength, with an occasional day alone on the moors, or a holiday outing with Scouts, I found myself helped and able to do quite a bit. Or, if need be, I could give myself leave and go right away from it all and recoup. In all this I was fortunate indeed, but my chief blessing was that at Longworth in Berkshire, my father and sister, and various permutations and combinations of children and grand-children and friends under his roof, were always ready to give me a welcome and change.

My father passed on, alert and kind to the last, within a few days of 90. With my very dear mother (Jean Campbell), they lie in that beautiful spot. Two beautiful lives, but over far from the beauties of Scotland.

Having made this personal statement to acknowledge my many advantages I will now proceed.

For ten years the routine of my life in Stirling did not greatly vary. It was always the future we worked for. With each new season came new preparations for coming events. With my Troop it was training and camps and 'Scouts' Owns.' Further afield it was visits to cities and towns with functions, speeches, rallies. After each step came follow-up letters, reports, pamphlets and books, and hatching new schemes for a further advance. Then we wound up each year with our Xmas good-turn which merits some mention. So under this head, I will now continue my story.

24. XMAS GOOD TURNS.

'We must get at the young. We must tackle the youth of the better-to-do and teach them sympathy, duty, and service in a practical way. We must get at those less fortunate and give all a fair chance.'

It started in quite a small way. I had long been interested in the Whinwell Home where for 60 years Miss Croall had rescued children from disgraceful conditions. She was a pioneer; religious, and devoted to children, she fought through and won a fair chance in life for hundreds of bairns.

Whinwell Home.

At a 'Scouts' Own' Service in June, 1919, I told the boys about the Home and we 'adopted' two little chaps, age 6. In the afternoon we went up and were introduced and shown round the Home.

Six months later my next entry is – '23rd November, 1919'. 'At Scouts' Own spoke to the boys about slums.' And again a year later – '13th November, 1920. Spoke of S.F.C.C. work. We decided to give a Xmas Concert at Whinwell.' From that day to this, for 30 years, the Scouts have kept up this connection.

These concerts were jolly affairs. In the big schoolroom, on one side of the screen, wee kiddies on tiny forms in front, the older children in rows behind, all neat and expectant, whispering and wondering. On the other side, Zulus, Red Indians, Fairies, a young 'Paganini' and a budding Reubinstein, and others ready to play their parts with songs, recitations, dances and conjuring. At first the Scouts had to be helped, but in later years the boys ran their own show.

After a good tea Father Xmas arrived, handed out parcels to all and soon, Scouts and Cubs and the bairns were mixed up in one happy jumble, opening parcels – Teddy-bears, dolls, books, and balls, with clock-work toys careering in all directions, shouts of joy!

In 1920 we went one better. We added a Xmas dinner for 127 children chosen by Mr. Reid. In 1922, this number rose to 400, and in addition parcels were made up and taken to 44 'necessitous' homes, an idea which came to us from the Aberdeen Scouts. Lists of children, with names, ages and sex, and details of each home, were made out, and the Scouts chose suitable presents for those allotted to them. This was a big job, but Miss Nairn and Henry Russell had a good system and all went well.

At the start we wondered what the Scout Parents would say. Would they allow their young knights errant to visit the slums and risk vermin and infection and what-not? And, just as important, how would the boys be received?

It was here that the tact and enthusiasm of Alex Reid (himself the father of a King's Scout) came to our aid. As Inspector of the S.P.C.C. he knew every home. For 40 years he did wonderful work in Stirling. They called him 'the cruelty man' for short; but it was really a term of endearment. He was kindness itself and loved his work. He did all he possibly could to forward our scheme.

23/12/1923. – 'At 'Scouts' Own' Reid spoke to the boys on conditions at top of the town. All volunteered to fetch holly from Airthrey in afternoon. The dinners are up from 400 to 510 this year and 56 parcels. Pipe Band and Scouts raised £35 with torch-light processions etc.'

In 1925 numbers reached 650 dinners and 90 parcels and in 1927 (the year I was away in New Zealand) the peak of 865 dinners and 150 parcels was reached. Parents and friends did wonders with sales and the Pipe Band and Scouts worked well displays at football intervals and torch-light processions. In this way £82 was raised to meet expenses.

24/12/1925. – 'Coming away from cheery Whinwell show found big crowd of Scouts and Parents at Hall doing great work. Took charge of one cart, a dozen boys, Scouts and Cubs. Our destination – a dozen homes up Castlehill, some of which I knew. Conditions shocking, poverty, cold, damp, rats and overcrowded homes. May this work of educating the young help later on. Home 8.30 p.m., hot, tired, but happy.'

Xmas Parcels.

Yes, the Scout Hall in Princes Street on Xmas Eve on such occasions was a hub of activity. The Committee had been preparing for months. Parcels were being sorted and checked, in some cases added to. Trek carts were loaded and packed according to streets and destinations, bunches of holly in every cart and holly in each Scout hat. When all was ready, off we went, each party bent on its separate mission – a cheerful sight.

Through the well-lit streets and holiday-shopping crowds we went, then up the hill to dark closes and turrets and old narrow stairs in our search for attics not easy to find. Groping our way we knocked at the door. (Here my confidential list says – 'the dirtiest house in Stirling'.) We enter. In honour of Santa Claus (and maybe due to a tactful hint from Reid) the room tonight is clean, but crowded and bare. A good fire is burning and we receive a warm welcome. Some of the kiddies are shy and hide, but not for long. The Scouts play up and soon all are at home. While I talk to the parents the boys get busy with holly and paper festoons and parcels are all undone. So, with good wishes for Xmas, we pass on. All are touchingly grateful.

In each house conditions vary. In one, I remember, a keen wee Cub had brought his own big jig-saw puzzle. How eager he was to show how it worked! But here was a puzzle for him – Where could he put it? What should he do?

By 8 p.m. the last of the Scouts was back, all the more ready for Xmas doings at home. One boy was so much impressed that on his return he told his Dad of all he had seen and insisted next year he would save up and do a bit more on his own, and he did!

I will not attempt to describe the dinners or the concerts we added in later years. At these concerts the boys ran their own shows. They seemed to know better than we did what would go down. Each Patrol gave its own sketch or display.

Nor will I dwell on the hectic business of feeding those crowds of children, such scenes are common enough. The Scout parents were grand, and the boys distinguished themselves as waiters, rushing to and fro, eager to see all fed and fair play. One little tough, I remember, shoving and using his fists, regardless of size or sex, to make sure of his share; in contrast a girlie of 12, acting as 'mother' of quite a big brood.

By 2 p.m. the banquet was over, oranges, tissue paper, crackers and all. What a glorious mess! Who would come back after dinner to help to clear up? In the King's Park, toboganning was at its best. What about it? By 5 p.m. some 30 Scouts had helped to sweep and tidy up both halls.

By 1932 (the peak year of desperate unemployment) the Boys' Brigade and Girl Guides had joined to help in these Good Turns. At the same time conditions began to improve. Slum clearance and new housing schemes were taking shape. In addition others such as the British Legion, the Miners' Welfare, and Co-ops, had entered the field. The need for this venture grew less, but by no means the need for the practical character-training of youth.

25. THE 1ST STIRLINGSHIRE TROOP.

I hope that some veteran of the 1st Stirlingshire Group will one day feel it a duty to write some account of this good old pioneer Troop. It has won a good name, let us pass it on; but I have not space to do them the justice deserved.

I expect that Ralph Common, Donald and John McEwan and others who started as High School boys in 1909, using a stable near the Golf Club, would have been surprised had they known that their venture would one day grow to nearly 200 boys – Cubs, Junior and Senior Scouts, and Rovers – united in one keen Group; not to mention our B.P. Guild of Old Scouts who are doing so much in the district today.

It is not large numbers that count. A small Troop may do wonders, a big one may even do harm. Nor do I suppose that in 1909, any more than in 1850 or 1950, boys bothered their heads overmuch about 'mental, moral, and spiritual welfare.' This was a new game, its code was part of the game; the code was good seed and the boys were good ground. I do not claim more.

From 1924 to 1931, as Scoutmaster, I brought out each year, fully illustrated reports, giving more detail than most would have time for. This was to pass on ideas and help future progress. Later, less detail was needed.

In 1919, as I have said, the boys pressed me to come to the rescue and help to run their Victory Camp. After that, for 2 or 3 years we found Leaders and all went well; but in 1923, two Scoutmasters had to go and again it fell to me to decide as Commissioner for Scotland, had I the time to act also as Scoutmaster? On the other hand how could I boost the good cause all over Scotland with events at my base disproving my case?

With a solemn promise of help from the Patrol Leaders, and

with Henry Russell and John Forsyth as assistants, this Rubicon was crossed. I consented to give what help I could. As it was not in me to take charge of 50 Scouts without getting drawn into their keenness, I was soon a whole-hearted Scoutmaster.

Training.

It will be seen from old Reports that we drew up each year a complete syllabus of meetings and coming events, with times, dates, and subjects for training according to seasons. Our year was divided into three distinct seasons – Winter, October to Xmas; Easter, February to April; and Summer (all out of doors), May to September. With so many boys and such varied activities this was essential.

The training was based on a progressive advance from Tenderfoot up to First Class, with games, gymnastics, dancing and badgework thrown in. At the end of the year we had 57 boys, 6 King's Scouts and 32 2nd Class.

After one year it was time to reorganise. At a Court of Honour we decided to make 2 distinct Troops, meeting on separate nights. Seniors (14–18) on Fridays, Juniors (12–14) on Tuesdays. Up till then we had had professional Instructor for gym and first-aid. From now on, only the Seniors got this help, and the best of them passed on the training on Tuesdays to the Juniors. Moreover, the Junior Leaders attended with the Seniors on Fridays and so kept ahead as leaders. Only so was it possible to cope with large numbers.

Before long many keen boys were arriving from the Cubs and elsewhere. At the same time some became too old and some had lost interest, so, like Bruce before Bannockburn, we gave out that only the keen need apply. We made 3 good patrols out of 4 Senior patrols and parted with the rest.

By 1927 we had 40 Seniors and 40 Juniors, and Scouters. Miss Nairn with her gift for small boys was doing wonders with 80 Cubs, while 18 Rovers, well led by David Finlayson, were full of ideas of Service. Thus, before long, we had good Instructors. The Rovers also 'adopted' the 4th Troop with Jas. Hutchison, John Nelson, Ramsay Hynd and Alex Dunsmore and others whose names stand out in our records.

Leaders.

At one time it had seemed to me that no one would take responsibility, that duty and honour had never been taught, that to put oneself out for the good name of the Troop came as a new idea; but I soon found out that, given the chance, most boys would play up.

Difficulties.

At times of course there were difficulties. For a while the whole Troop would be bursting with keenness on passing tests, winning badges, and on inter-patrol competitions; then there would come lulls and rival attractions or duties – exams, home lessons, music, continuation classes, church soirees, parties, school football and cricket, or tennis or golf, to say nothing of mumps, measles and 'flu! Such events might thwart our best-laid plans, but we made it a point to back up the School, urging more *esprit-de-corps* than some of them seemed to show. We backed up the Padres and Homes, and we found that it paid.

When things go wrong, you have got to look wide and not worry. It is none of your job, Scoutmaster, to aim at perfection in stalking or knots. Your job is to give a good lead and keep smiling. You cannot do more than your best. Tact may be needed. It may be a case of hard work or hard lines, but, taken all round, there is no better or cheerier service than that of helping to set these eager young hopefuls on the right track.

The right use of leisure.

Over and over again I find in my log complaints that boys, when left to themselves, have so little idea how best to spend a holiday. With the increase of leisure, surely more training was needed in that direction? Among teachers all the world over our Movement has had its ardent supporters, but still there are those who say that Scouting prevents success in exams, or may clash with School games, yet time after time we proved the opposite.

In 1927, out of 60 Scouts, 32 excelled in school work, while 18 had won prizes at School Sports. In 1932, the Dux of the School and the runner-up were Scouts, also the Junior School Dux and the School Sports Champion.

But as to the right use of leisure – in the Scouts we train the boys to run their own games. Watch some Troop in an inter-patrol competition, say a relay race. Each patrol takes its turn selecting what type of race it shall be. They have thought it out and got all ready themselves. The Leader stands out in front of the Troop and explains the game. The rest of his patrol assist as umpires and in getting all ready. The P.L. gives the sign and off they go. Each Patrol has its turn. Which game was the best? It is put to the vote. They enjoy it far more. So, too, in football or cricket or outings, in treasure hunts, flag-raiding or nature-study, Leaders are trained to think for themselves, to make arrangements and 'be prepared.'

In School P.T. Classes you see games, agility, dexterity and all that, often a very smart show, but should the boys not also be trained to want to run a good show of their own, when right away from the school?

And here, lest I give a wrong impression of teachers, I insert a quotation from one of many Headmasters who approved and encouraged our work. Speaking at our Parents' Display in 1929, Mr. J. M. Taylor, a Larbert Headmaster and father of Ian,* said – 'Year by year the group seems to go one better, and what strikes me most is that throughout the programme, carried out so efficiently, no one seems to be giving orders. Each seems to have his job and to know when and how to do it, the young leaders especially seeing that all went smoothly.'

---

* Ian Taylor, one of our best Scouts, later killed as a Chaplain with the R.A.F.

26. OUTINGS AND CAMPS.

One of my favourite ploys was 'Outings' with boys on Saturdays or School holidays. We would go right away from the town, high up in good air, up the various glens, to the woods and moors within reach; wonderful all-day explorations, boys from various troops mixing as friends, a dozen perhaps, or three dozen, or more.

Each Scout had his rucksack and rations according to fancy, sausages, mince or stew, spuds, dripping, and tea, sugar and milk and billy complete. En route to the rendezvous, there might be some boys sent ahead for an ambush, or scouting game. On arrival, in parties of twos and threes, the Scouts had soon settled down with fires lit, and cooking in progress. After this would come some special activity such as building a bridge or a dam or perhaps two Scouts would set a treasure hunt. Some would prefer to explore trees, flowers or birds. Occasionally we had a find – a dipper's nest under a fall, a capercailzie with eggs, woodcock, snipe, peewits, curlews with nests or with young, a young cuckoo fed by a pipit, all these we had seen and learned not to touch. When the primroses were out, we used to tie them in bundles and take them to the Infirmary on our return, always sure of a welcome from the Matron, a good friend to all Scouts.

Wherever we camped, the rule was: no sign of our camp to be left. On such jaunts there were endless openings – tracking, signs and codes, observation, judging distances, camouflage, map-reading, reports, etc . In a hundred and one ways it was first rate training; it was also very good fun, and the boys made great progress as Scouts.

You would see the new-comer, his haversack loaded with buns and a bottle of milk, maybe, a tin of pineapple chunks. In spite of the heat you would see him fully-clad, shirt-sleeves down, woolies and scarf, stockings and boots; but before very long he was quite the old hand with billy and rations and axe; stripped and bare-footed getting the sun and the air, his well-laid fire with well-chosen site and wood, quickly set going in spite of the breeze. He soon came out of his shell, a picture to show the value of training.

As for myself, I enjoyed it as much as the boys. In my kit I carried coloured wool for arm-bands in games, and always a podex ball, a great game in which any number could join on any ground, with any old stick as a bat.

On the November School-holiday, ('the Teachers' rest') we used to get further afield. Travelling by train to St Fillans, or Strathyre, or Callander, we would cover long distances, making for some other railway station, exploring and cooking and games on the way – we spent glorious days, returning home in the dark in high spirits.

On Sundays, too, at the 'Scouts' Own' we would often fix on some rendezvous in the afternoons and carry out some ploy, a visit perhaps to the Field of Bannockburn, or exploring and measuring the Forth; or a visit to Whinwell, or the Castle, or the Boys' Club to see how the work was progressing; and often Mr. Chisholm, an expert in trees and geology, would join us and conduct a nature ramble.

A New Venture.

In June, 1925, we made a new venture. With trek-carts and stores, we took some 30 small boys from the top of the town, collected by Mr. Reid, for an all-day outing 'up Polmaise.' There were Scouting games and camp-fires and cooking and paddling in the burn, ending up with a sing-song and a happy march home. It was this first summer good-turn which led to our good-turn camps at Malling later on.

Camping.

Camping for Scouts is *the* great event of the year. I only wish I had space to say more on the subject, but my aim in these notes is to interest, and maybe attract, others outside Scout enthusiasts.

After our Victory Camp in 1919, my mind was set on furthering this branch of Scout training. From 1921 to 1925 at Rhu in the Gareloch, and from 1926 to 1938 at Malling on the Lake of Menteith I had standing camps. In these 17 years over 3,000 boys passed through our hands.

So far as our own boys were concerned, these camps were a training ground for younger boys, and also an opening for service for our Seniors. As the Scouts grew more experienced they went further afield. There were hikes and trek-camps and in 1926 and 1927 we went on two tours by charabanc. There was also Mr. Harold's camp in France in 1930. From 1926 to 1938 the Troop each year ran a good-turn Camp at Malling, which later became the Annual Boys' Club Camp.

In 1922 and 1926 I wrote two books* in an effort to help, so far as books can. In his preface the Chief wrote – 'full of practical suggestions and helpfulness . . . but a camp may be faultlessly organised in its catering, discipline, recreation, Church parades, hygiene, etc., and still may miss the spirit . . . . It is because many practical steps towards getting this all-important spirit are suggested, that I heartily commend the book.'

Training at Viewforth.

In our training at Stirling we had a special blessing, for from 1919 to 1932 we had free use of the Viewforth grounds, next door to my rooms at Pitt Terrace, and also the use of the stables as a Club and Storeroom and Summer H.Q.

In my books I have given more fully our system of camp-training. For one night in the week, for five weeks in May and June the Patrol Leaders were trained, on a progressive system, in all that makes for good camping. On the next night they had their own patrols to practise – inspection and flag, tents and cooking, clean dixies, hygiene, blankets, axes, etc. Points for the best patrol. A buzz of activity, all busy, all happy.

Then came the June School-holiday, a whole day spent on kitchens, ovens (mud-pies of clay), pitching and striking tents, loading up carts, gadgets, games, supper, camp-fire. and sing-song – a glorious day. Next came a weekend practice camp, within easy

* 'Camp and Character Training' and 'Camp and Charabanc Touring.' (Brown, Son & Ferguson, Ltd., 52 Darnley Street, Glasgow.)

reach of shops and homes, each P.L. had time to think out his needs. Things forgotten had to be fetched and so were better remembered next time. If the boys did not sleep the whole of those short June nights, at least they got over that phase of their training, were well turned-out, and had the camp clean in time for the Sunday Service next day.

Finally came the Display, an ordinary Troop night, all on their mettle. A new Scout is enrolled. Tea, games and camp-fire. Parents well pleased and now know a lot more.

Camps at Rhu.

Thus it was that when we went to camp, the Scoutmaster's worries were not such as befell those less fortunate who perhaps had no decent chance of training their boys. At Rhu and Malling there were many different kinds of Troops. Some were old hands with lots of Leaders and all went well. Others were less well placed, but what struck me was the quick progress made in every Troop even in seven days.

Take this sample – 'On arrival, excited. They do not talk, they shout, and shout all at once; Poor Scoutmaster, short-handed and so much to see to. His Leaders are willing enough but have not been trained. But now is the Scoutmaster's chance; he has got them together and soon you will see a great change.'

At first meals may be late, too much may fall on too few. They have not all learned each to do his share. Perhaps, without due warning (it may be a false alarm), someone shouts – 'Dinner's up!' What a scramble, a rush of ravenous boys; but with time such scenes are put right.

Or, here is a lad in long trousers, a 'working man.' He looks lost and helpless. He does not yet know what to do. He does not yet know there is work to be done. He is grousing. He came for a holiday. Find him a job and explain. Before very long, by doing his bit, and doing it well, he discovers what makes a Scout happy in camp.

Or, here is another, smothered in sweaters and clothes in the heat of the day. Before long you will find him stripped, sea- and sun-bathing along with the rest. At the end of the camp you won't know him.

Meanwhile at the Flag each day you see steady improvement in smartness and manners, sportsmanship and comradeship, and in duty and all that makes a good camp.

All too soon it is time to go. All are sad to leave. All are full of plans for next summer. They have learned a great deal, and their Scoutmaster too he has both learned and earned a great deal – Next Year let us hope that part of his plan may be a Gilwell course and some chance of training his boys before he takes them to camp.

And if here and there he comes on a dud and has his set-backs, tell him to smile! Why should he worry? Why should he take all the blame? There are bound to be lapses. We are training for freedom. We want 'Self-discipline.' This is not learned without practice and risks. No boy is an angel. No Scoutmaster an Archangel. But, granted all this, it is the Home, the School or Workshop, and the Church which deal with nine-tenths of the time of the boy. We have only to do with one-tenth of his time at the most, and that is the time of all others when Youth kicks his heels. It is up to Parents, Employers, Teachers and Padres to help youth to learn that *in all that they do character must come first*. Would that more of them saw the great value of camping and games, and a right use of leisure as a means to this end.

The 'Empress' Experiment.

In our camp at Rhu we had all kinds of Scouts, but the best camps of all were those in which the 'Empress' boys shared. These boys had been sent to the Training Ship for various misdeeds, faults mostly due to bad home conditions. In the old black and white wooden battleship, Captain Denny, D.S.O., R.N. in command, had enlightened ideas, he wanted a 'Happy Ship.' We worked out a plan for mixing his boys with our Scouts in camp.

In 1921 one patrol of his boys camped in charge of a Scoutmaster, as an extra patrol with each successive Scout Troop. In 1922 we went one better. Every Scout Patrol of each visiting Troop adopted one 'Empress' boy as one of their patrol. Friendship became a tradition. To us all it was astonishing. On leaving, the Scouts would part with badges, whistles, belts, as souvenirs, and many as they drove off were, as their Scoutmaster said, on the verge of tears. I too was surprised. More than once I saw those young sailor boys weeping as though their heaven had come to an end.

Then came two final 'Empress' camps, 50 at a time, each with 6 or 7 good Scoutmasters as Leaders and the boys we had previously trained as Patrol Leaders.

The camps were run on Scout lines; the mornings were spent on camp duties and learning the Promise and Law. At the Flag a new Leader each day would give a short talk which got home. The rest of the day they were free, boating and bathing, Scouting and games, ending up with wonderful camp-fires. Friendship seemed part of the air and the singing still sounds in my ears.

We had hoped for great things and had started a Scout Troop on the ship, but, alas, it was not to be, for one sad day in 1923, the old 'Empress' was towed down the Clyde to be broken up.

The Story of 'Monkey' and the 8th Scout Law.

I have told elsewhere of those days, of the Captain's 'Well done!' and of the Committee's official approval. I will close with the story of 'Monkey' to give just one glimpse which speaks for itself.

You never can tell. You may think over and work at some talk to your boys at a 'Scouts' Own' Service. The meeting comes and goes with no apparent result. On the other hand you may find some unconsidered act or word of yours has got right home. But there can be no doubt that if you talk to your boys at the Flag about everyday happenings in camp they will listen. Here is an example –

A new Troop of Scouts had arrived in camp at Rhu, also a new party of 'Empress' boys. It was my first introduction to 'Monkey' as they called him. 'Might he go into town?' 'No,' I said, 'it is out of bounds.' But he would not take 'No,' he hung about and returned to the attack. Again I refused. He persisted – 'No,' I said finally, 'You can't get, and that's that.'

Never off the stage have I seen such a villainous frown as that boy gave me. He knitted his brows, clenched his teeth, and lowered his head; his eyes scowled up at me with an evil expression till they were all but hidden. Then he turned his back and walked slowly and sulkily away. This was something quite new to me. It interested

319

me. What would a psychologist do? Sack him? That would be easy. Smack him? That would not be Scouting. To do either might foster some latent murder germ; so I did what is often wise when in doubt – I did nothing. I waited and figured it out.

Next day at the Flag, I took the 8th Scout Law (Keep Smiling) for my talk. It is my favourite, for it stands for three things – (1) A good digestion. (2) Good will towards men. (3) A good conscience before God.

I told the boys of a Scout with an invalid mother, who painted the words 'KEEP SMILING' in large type, and placed them on the entrance door of his bed-ridden mother's room, so that whenever he came back from work or play he was reminded, and so cheered her up with a smile as he entered the sickroom. I told them of good men in the trenches and mud of France who kept others in good heart, and how infectious their cheerfulness was –

> 'Smile your smile, in a while
> Another smiles,
> And soon there's miles and miles
> Of smiles,
> And Life's worth while
> Because you smile.'

Then, without mentioning names, I described the scene of yesterday, how one of the boys had looked like this – my efforts at scowling tickled them all, and especially I noticed my friend, the hero of this story, beaming all over. 'Now,' I said, 'if any one feels like that let him try the 8th Scout Law.' From that day on, for the rest of the camp, wherever we met, 'Monkey's' face would light up. His smile was a thing to cheer one up for the rest of the week.

'Monkey' did well in camp. He was one of the first to pass in the Scout Law and Tests and to wear the Scout badge on his jumper. He was good at games and seemed to have good friends among the Scouts. When time was up he went back to the ship and wrote me some weeks later –

'I think you will be pleased to know I have turned over a new leaf since I have been back from camp. Please tell me what I need to pass for my 2nd Class Test, and would it be too late for me to join the Scouts when I leave the Ship? – Your obedient Servant, MONKEY'

A month later when we had two lots of 'Empress' boys in camp, each for 10 days, 'Monkey' was one of the chosen Leaders in charge of a tent. He did well, and wherever I went, there he was smiling broader than most.

On the last day I took his photograph. 'Now,' I said, 'Scowl at me, 'Monkey,' like you did the first day. I want a photo of what you used to be like.' He often wrote after that from the ship and always some joke about 'When I pulled that long face,' but now he signed himself 'Your affectionate Scout.' I never got the photo of that scowl!

Malling Camp, Lake of Menteith.

On 27th May, 1926, with the good 'President Wilson,' I discovered Malling. The farm was to let for the summer months. We got a good welcome from Mrs. Johnston, saw the big field at the back of the farm and climbed the Gallows Hill, a conspicuous knoll just beyond. The view and the country were at their best. What a wonderful panorama, The Lake of Menteith below with its three Isles – Inchchuan, Inch Talla, and Inchmaholm – the Fintry Hills to the South, Stirling Castle and Rock 18 miles east, then the Ochils and round by the hills of Menteith, right round to Ben Lomond due West. A lovely burn ran through the grounds to the Lake, with a boathouse on the shore. It all seemed too good to be true. What would Farmer Johnston say to our proposed invasion by boys? What would the neighbours and fishermen say about boats and boating?

All went well. In Mr. and Mrs. Johnston we found friends who were fond of boys and joined in our sing-songs and games. Sir Norman Orr Ewing gave us leave to land and bathe on that perfect silver strand; and permission was given for boating. The neighbours at Rednock, Cardross, Glennie, Arntomy and also Will Joynson, all were helpful and kind. As Scouts we were trusted; it was up to us to win a good name.

Very soon we had transported from Rhu our cookhouse and

store-hut, two boats, and the 'Empress' ship's bell, and soon our 20-foot flagstaff stood conspicuous for miles around on the knoll. And so for twelve happy summers hundreds of boys from all parts saluted our big Union Jack and learned a great deal which helped them throughout later years.

I will not dwell on these camps. Malling was a blessing to many a local Troop. The youngsters got practice in camping while the older hands gave splendid service in helping many a short-handed Scoutmaster. There were Troops of all kinds, from Scotland and England, boys from the Fens, strange to hills and towns, boys from London, Belfast, Edinburgh, Glasgow, and visiting Scouts from overseas. I will only tell of one camp, our own first 'Good turn' camp, which led later on to the Stirling Boys' Club at the top of the town.

The Good Turn Camp, 1926.

In 1920 we started our Xmas good turn. In 1925 our Summer Outing proved a success. In 1926 we arranged that after our Touring Camp and Junior Camp we would wind up the season with a week-end Camp for 60 boys selected by Mr. Reid. To run this Camp we had 10 scouts and 10 Rovers, Duncan (the Army Cook) and the indispensable Alex Reid. You will say that looks easy enough – 3 men, 20 Scouts and Rovers to handle 60 small boys of from 10 to 14. Yes, but on Friday only the younger Scouts were free; as a matter of fact, the start proved a pretty tough job.

At 6.30 p.m. on a Friday late in August, two charabancs drove up to Malling, the boys cheering and full of excitement. At the farm a few Scouts and the Cook had got all ready. The visitors were arranged in 7 patrols with Scouts in charge. Soon they were 'Lions,' 'Swifts,' 'Hounds,' etc., full of team rivalry.

Once that first night was over the Camp was a huge success, but few will forget that first night! By 10 p.m. after tea and games and supper, the boys were shown by the Scouts how to arrange their blankets. The novelty had its appeal, so much so, that many were soon rolled up in their blankets and looked like settling down for the night. To us who knew more of first nights in Camp, this seemed too good to be true. We encouraged the idea and retired, surprised but on guard.

It is enough to say we were soon undeceived, and at intervals we had to read the riot act. Boots and plates, blankets, bottles, and bad language went flying about throughout the small hours.

On the whole the situation was well handled; once the boys had had their fling, things quietened down. Each boy had been given a towel and piece of soap. At the burn we had dammed up a washing pool. At 2 a.m. this was discovered and vigorous washing began. By 8 a.m. it was an extra clean and hungry queue that lined up for porridge and milk from the farm.

Tent inspection and Flag were quite good, but games were not so good. Why are boys not taught how to play games? The Scouts did their best but at cricket no one would field, all must bat or bowl. At football, rows and wrangling, shouts of 'foul.' Their games seemed practice in battle and murder!

Then came dinner. Here again the Scouts had to step in and stop fighting and pushing for places in the queue. By 3 p.m. the sandy silver strand across the Lake with 80 boys disporting themselves in the sun was a happy sight. By this time we were joined by the older Scouts. This reinforcement clinched our success. A great sing-song in the barn. The Rovers were well-known entertainers and the little chaps too played their part. At 11 p.m. we closed with one verse of 'Abide with me.' All was peace and good order that night.

Sunday 8 a.m. Reveille. Breakfast 9 a.m. Inspection 10.30, all goes wonderfully well. At the Flag, with mixed denominations, we only discuss the Flag and Scout Law. The rest of the day we stoke up with meals and let off more steam with bathing and games. By 7 p.m. we are all great friends. They are all off again, two cheering charabancs.

As we lower the Flag that night, the distant view of Castle and Rock stand out as we ask for God's blessing.

Charabanc Tours, 1926 and 1927.

To me our charabanc tours in 1926 and 1927 were far more than mere joy-rides. They entailed forethought, preparation, detail and hard work, but results proved them well worthwhile.

In the early 'twenties these open charabancs, with their novelty and exhilaration were not always a source of good-will wherever they went. Indeed for a time, certain bottle-throwing, church-disturbing, litter-leaving charabangers got a very bad name as they careered through towns and country-side, an object lesson in how not to behave; but at least they gave me an idea.

As Commissioner for Scotland I had seen a need to send out good Scouts to show the idea and ideals of Scout training.

Here we had well-trained boys, old hands at camping keen to go further afield. They had hiked and trekked and run good Scout Camps, Why not now add this 'novelty and exhilaration' and cover more ground, making more friends and maybe, incidentally, act as a contrast to show up the value of training?

I will leave out details of planning, and cost of equipment and feeding; all this was given elsewhere to pass on the idea. If in our case it was thought too much of a 'one-man show,' the answer is that pioneers may have to plead guilty of this. Once we had launched the idea, for six months beforehand, all worked hard to prepare. All were in it. It was not a one-man show and that is why it went well.

Our objects were – to see the world; to forward the cause of Scouting, making friends on the way; and, as 'B.P.' would certainly have added, 'to have a good time.'

Before starting, each Scout made the following promises –

(1) I understand that a touring camp means extra work to be done on arrival and departure, in pitching and striking tents and packing and unloading equipment.

(2) I undertake to practise cooking the dishes allotted to me, so as to make a good job of it when my turn comes.

(3) I realise that the good name of Scouting depends on the impression made by the Troop during the Tour and I undertake to do my best.

On 16th July came our final rehearsal. With charabanc packed and all in good order we drove off at 7.30 p.m. Viewforth to Craig-forth. On arrival we timed ourselves pitching and striking Camp.

It took us 4 minutes to unload and pitch 7 tents and break and salute the Flag. After a talk with the Laird, always a good friend to the Scouts, we struck our tents and lowered the Flag and packed up again. This took 3 minutes and we were all back at Viewforth by 9.30 p.m. It made quite a good game. It had also been a chance for a word in season.

The boys were all so keen. Here was a younger Scout who had boarded the 'chara' unbidden and seized the best place. He was stamping his feet and keen to be off. What of that other fellow sprawling on his back below the chassis, helping to stow away tents on the carrier? or those others roping up bundles of blankets, or packing stores and equipment? Now is the time to make sure of your men and, like Robert the Bruce, to 'fall out the slackers.'

Some one has ventured an idle remark – 'By the time we get back, we shall be so fed up with pitching and striking tents, we shall never want to see one again.' Was that so? If anyone felt like that he could fall out. To the old hand pitching and striking tents was nothing, a 3 or 4 minute job. The packing and roping must be well done. All must feel responsible. Camps must be left clean. They would come back real Scouts and proud of themselves. As for the man who bagged the best place, the best place for him was behind the exhaust pipe! A few words in this vein at the start save trouble later on. No one fell out.

We will skip our first four days. The route through Dunfermline, St Andrews, Perth, and Dundee to Blair Atholl had been fixed with Scout Commissioners on the way, so that all had a great time of sight-seeing and friendships.

Perth to Blair Atholl, 20th July.

11.30 a.m. 'After visit to glass-works, sun in full glory. Scotland looks grand. The road-menders halt at their work, they stare, then wave and cheer. We are gone, we are off to the Highlands!'

6 p.m. 'Our camp looks well spread out among Scots firs on the bank of the Garry. Lord James Murray shows us over the Castle, broadswords, targes, and arms, long passages hung with antlers and trophies, and in room after room pictures, china, tapestries, four-poster beds. His grim joke about the Campbell Clan causes a shiver.'

8 p.m. 'After good dinner, pipes are playing. From a neighbouring camp a big heavy-weight Army boxer visits us. The gloves are produced. One after another our champions fall. Wee Donny emerges in pyjamas to slay Goliath, but is carried off kicking under Goliath's left arm.'

Laggan Bridge.

21st July. 'We are now well into the Highlands . . . . our stores and milk waiting, we camp near the Spey in full flood. All friendly and kind, drying wet clothes, augmenting our rations and dabbing Scout faces with various midge cures. The whole village comes to our sing-song – 11 p.m. (still light). Our hosts ask again for the 'Road to the Isles.' The piper plays well and we all join in. We have come by the Tummel and pass by Lochaber. We return via Loch Rannoch. The Minister, Dr. Neil Ross, a piper himself, says a few kind words and closes with a blessing. So ends another, perfect day.'

Laggan to Fort William.

22nd July. 'Cloudy and threatening. Good breakfast in spite of rain, bills paid, camp tidy, we salute the Flag, thank our friends and are off. At a halt Clan McDonald less friendly, our Argyll tartan perhaps? 9d a bottle for lemonade! At Spean Bridge Hotel another McDonald; we ask him for shelter. At the sight of 30 dripping-wet Scouts, poor man, he shakes his head,

'No,' he says 'We never do that kind of thing.' On hearing we only ask for hot water and the shelter of a shed, he relents and shows us into the garage. We give him some tunes on the pipes; this softens his heart, but he is fonder of pipes than of boys. 'The pipes are all right,' he says as we part, 'but I wouldn't be you with that handful so full of life!'

3 p.m. 'We push on, and, singing and dripping, arrived at Fort William 3 hours early. Here an extra kind welcome awaited us. Padre McMichael had cancelled our camp in Glen Nevis because of the storm and put his Church Hall at our disposal. But, arriving so early, we caught our kind host in the act of kindling a fire in his own vestry. This sanctum he handed over to us as a cook-house. 'Stay as long as you like,' he said. We soon settled down, a good dinner, tables and forms a luxury now.'

9.45 p.m. 'They are hungry again. The vestry, now our cook-house, store-room, and drying-room, reserved for cooks and Scoutmasters, is besieged by hungry Scouts.'

10.15 p.m. 'Hunger satisfied. In the big hall, some reading, some sparring with gloves, or wrestling in pyjamas, some rope-spinning, others have got a spare motor-wheel and are spinning it round the hall. At the harmonium our Gilwell friend Marr has a few singers, others join and swell the chorus. The Minister looks in and invites us into the Church through a side door in the hall. It is no formal church-going. Dressed or in undress, just as we are, we take our seats. The Padre sits at the organ and plays the evening hymn. A few words of welcome, then the 'Lord's Prayer' and we retire. Good-night all round and 'God bless.' Outside it still pours a deluge.'

23rd July. 'On Friday the storm had passed. The boys attacked and conquered Ben Nevis (4,400 feet). With James Kerr who helped me to master the words and tune of 'The Road to the Isles,' I took on the job of cook for the day; haricot mutton, 50 potatoes and salad for 30. At this task we were joined by the Padre, who was caught by his Church Officer in the act of peeling a pailful of spuds in his shirt-sleeves and in his own vestry! By 7 p.m. our young mountaineers were back, full of their adventures. Too tired to eat? Plates, knives and forks, rattling, give you the answer. Stew and salad voted A1.'

'By 8 p.m. the hall is empty. Football outside on the green is stopped by the "Cop" who shows the boys where to go – the game continues till dark, then follow boxing and vigorous games till supper at 10 p.m. At 10.15 the Padre helps us again and so closes another great day. I have never seen boys more happy or known them less trouble.'

24th July. 'Another wet day. Visit to aluminium tunnelling works. Marr and Toc H and local Scouts join in final sing-song. "Auld Lang Syne." A word to the boys – "Tomorrow Sunday – the vestry wanted for Service. We would rise early and make a push to have all in good order, and the "chara" loaded and ready to leave after the Service."'

Sunday, 25th July. 'Wind veers to North, a spell of glorious weather sets in. 10 a.m., cookhouse now transformed. It is again the Minister's sanctum. No muddy waterproof sheets on the floor, no grimy pots and pans, no stores, no boots and socks drying, no noise! A carpet covers a (fairly) clean floor. On a chair is a black gown laid out with purple hood. On the table a large Bible. The hall too looks clean, though the charwoman may shake her head tomorrow. Outside the 'chara' is loaded and ready, and Scouts, extra tidy and clean, stand around in groups awaiting the Service at 11 a.m.'

After the Service and an inspection by Cameron of Lochiel, and a real happy stay, we left for Ballachulish. Here again good Scouts and great kindness, and on to Bridge of Orchy, where we soon settled down with some friendly Glasgow Scouts as neighbours. It was good to see how quickly our boys fixed up their camp and made friends as a matter of course. Each Scout had his job and set about it at once in a cheery and businesslike way. Tents were soon up and the various fatigues – firewood, water, latrines, kitchen, and store-tent – all know what to do. Two Scouts have helped me to pitch my small Tinker-tent. Close by runs the Orchy in spate. On each side of the river are towering heights of 2,000 feet. Down the steep slopes run torrents cascading into the Orchy. Not far from our camp, in one of these tributaries., the waters converged in a narrow granite channel to a point where they shot down a 10 foot drop, into a foaming pool below.

The Salmon Leap.

Guided by our Glasgow friends, we scrambled up to this point to watch the salmon leaping. Seated, or sprawling, or lying flat face down all round the pool we watched a wonderful sight. Every now and then a great shout went up from the boys as a salmon made a spring. The fish were trying against the stream to leap the 10 foot fall, but each in turn was hurled back into the pool. Some did better than others and were duly encouraged, but so far, all had failed to clear the leap. Suddenly out of the eddy a monster salmon appeared. Up he goes, with a slow heavy-weight spring, he seems doomed to failure – but he keeps on rising and rising steadily upwards, We hold our breath as he reaches and tops the bar, then with a swish of his tail, changing his course, he dives forward, gliding through the rapids into the shallows beyond. The boys are thrilled. Some of them rush to welcome and congratulate him, but he does not wait to shake hands! We do not see him again though the water seems shallow and clear. I do not know where he got to, but he got a great cheer from Glasgow and Stirling – a 'Hampden-Annfield roar.'

Red Deer.

But my story is growing too long. Next morning again we were lucky. Porridge had just been served, when the mist rolled away from the hills and red deer were seen on the heights. A gallant stag was standing apart on the sky-line. An eager queue lined up for a look through my little Zeiss spy-glass. In the end 30 or 40 of the noble beasts paraded for our inspection.

Then came the business of voting by secret ballot for the best cooks and the best all-round Scout. The 'Lions' were champion cooks. Robert Burnett, a good unselfish King's Scout, with 16 votes was duly elected and cheered as best Scout.

We salute the Flag, and now it is 'all aboard' for our 60 miles final run back to Stirling. After halts at Lochs Dochart and Lubnaig for meals, our chariot, now smothered in garlands of heather, speeds on its way like a horse which pulls at its bit all the way home. From this point on cheering seems the order of the day. The roads are full of holiday traffic, folk enjoying the bluebells and heather, the sun, the air and the views. Wherever we pass there are smiles and cheers and waving of hands and handkerchiefs and answering smiles and cheers and pipes, and waving of hats and flags from the Scouts.

Cheering non-stop the last 20 miles right up to Viewforth Gate. Here we find proud parents awaiting our heroes' arrival. Dutifully they stand apart till goods and chattels have been disposed of. Then comes a great reunion. We have had a great time 'with all that handful so full of life.'

I have said enough to give an idea of our venture. We had covered 312 miles in 11 days at a cost of £1 per head, plus for the 'chara' earned by displays. The whole crowd were keener than ever to try it again next summer.

In 1927 we combined an invasion of England with a tour of southern Scotland. 432 miles in 11 days. Wherever we went again our chief impression was the kind welcome we got.

In crossing the Border near Gretna, unknown to me, on in advance in my car, the 'chara' was halted, and, headed by 3 Pipers and the Banner of St Andrew, the whole Troop marched in triumph over the Border; some of the younger boys surprised to find the roads and milestones were much like our own!

At Carlisle, Hexham, Newcastle, Bamburgh, yes, wherever we went, we had a great time, and learned at first hand that real Scouts are sure of a welcome wherever they go.

27. DISPLAYS, RALLIES AND CONFERENCES.

I do not propose to say much about the many conferences, displays and rallies which helped on our progress during those ten years. Today the tendency is to limit these efforts, and, so far as may be, to combine them with camps.

Our Parents' Displays at Easter were cheery events which brought us together and bucked the boys up in their training. Our County Rallies, too, in Summer showed the Flag had helped the training, with a minimum of rehearsals.

We varied the programme each year and these gatherings were quite good fun for all concerned. There were processions showing the various Scout Badges, displays of International Flags, massed reel dancing with the Girl Guides, fire fighting, gymnastics, camping, etc., and inter district events, and the Cubs were always a popular item. We never drew big crowds such as football attracts, but after every display we were always pressed to give a repeat performance. Little they knew what an effort it was to assemble the Scouts and forego even one of our precious Summer week-ends.

There were also special occasions when thousands of boys were assembled in Glasgow or Edinburgh; but to get boys there and back in one day was a rush, and the large numbers entailed much waiting about, so that, as a rule, the boys were better in camp. In later years these rallies grew to still larger numbers. In 1938, I saw two magnificent rallies at Ibrox. In May, 20,000 Boys' Brigade, and in June, 30,000 Boy Scouts. Each in its own distinctive way was a very great credit and most inspiring. As a veteran and friend of the 'high heid-yins' in both great movements, I felt greatly encouraged, but the sight of the undisciplined, jostling crowds next door, desperately scrambling for a flutter at the adjacent dog-races was, in contrast, a wholesome check on any complacency. It is good indeed to see 50,000 clean-living boys, but what of some 200,000 more left out and far too often completely neglected?

Boys' Brigade and Scouts.

Ever since 1911 when Captain Turnbull used to mix his well-trained St Ninians Boys' Brigade with our Tenderfoot Troop of Scouts at Auchenbowie, I had always wished to see the Boys' Brigade and Scouts work well together.

At first there were bound to be misunderstandings. They were the old Guard, we were new-comers. They were the Guardsmen before the days of Guardsmen in Jeeps! We were the Scouts, with still much to learn, but pioneers. Our tactics might vary, but, by working together, this fact would strengthen, not weaken, our joint assault on youth neglect.

In Stirling our mutual friendship had always been a strong point because our Leaders were friends and in touch. In 1922, after a friendly interchange of correspondence in the B.B. and Scout Gazettes, we took a step forward, sending delegates to each others' Conferences. George Harvey was welcomed by us at Callander, while I received an extra kind welcome from 250 B.B. Officers at Swanwick. We seemed to have so much in common that often I quite forgot it was a 'B .B.' and not a Scout Conference. A fine lot of fellows friendly, united, and out for the good of the boy; men with no cant, who yet made it quite clear that they took their stand on the Christian Faith and good discipline.

At one session Earley, from Oxford, was to speak on Badges. He did not approve of badges and had given a friendly warning that Scouts might come in for some of his chaff. The drift of an amusing speech was that if he were C.-in-C. of the B.B., as to badges, he would 'scrap the lot.' When it came to pulling my leg, he did not mention Scouts; he only spoke of Girl Guides, with a side glance at me. 'But sauce for the goose,' he said, 'may not be good for ganders.' In my turn, I explained that our badge was a reminder and pledge of service, that we had no use for badge-hunters, we called them 'badge-hogs,' that all our geese were not swans, still less were our goslings, and (in confidence) that even some Scoutmasters were geese. It was all in good fun and I think it was Leonard Bilton who raised a loud laugh as he told of 'one of our goslings.' It seems he had made some friendly advance to a boy who wore a Scout button-hole badge. 'What is the object of Scouts?' he had asked the boy half in joke. 'To smash the B.B.!' was the prompt reply.

I still have letters about this mutual friendship from both our Leaders, Sir William Smith and Lord Baden-Powell. I know they would like me to pass on these views.

28. THE CHIEF SCOUT.

Auchengillan.

On 11th July, 1926, the Chief paid us a visit to open the Camp at Auchengillan. No wonder he came away pleased. As usual he got a great welcome from Glasgow's vigorous Leaders, Robert Young, Malcolm Speir, and others, and from thousauds of boys.

This camp was a great step forward, a step full of vision and promise. Here was an ideal camping ground of 195 acres, within 10 miles of Glasgow, high up on the Moors, with good air and wonderful views. Well was it named Auchengillan, 'the Field of Youth.' Since then it is reckoned that some 150,000 boys have camped on the site.

Lord Glentanar.

It was on this occasion that Glentanar carried us off, the Chief and myself, for a happy week-end on his yacht in the Kyles of Bute. In him the Scout Movement in Scotland had found just the Leader we needed, a man of vision, strong as a horse, and full of energy; a man of business who knew what was wanted and got things done with tact, and above all, a good Scout and a good friend.

As we sped on our way through Ayrshire to Largs, to join the good ship 'Pleiausaurus,' suddenly the wind dislodged our driver's Scout hat. I caught it and handed it back. Later, again the hat flew off, this time to leg; but the chauffeur was there and fielded it well. I suggested this time we should keep it in store. 'No,' shouted Glentanar, 'the Scout Hat is part of the Scout' 'Quite right,' said the Chief, who all this time, head down, had clung like grim death to the lace at the back of his head.

The Scout Hat.

At the time there had been some question of bonnets for Rovers and Pipers, and the Chief had fears that this might lead to bonnets for all Scottish Scouts. Myself I was fond of my old Scout hat. It had helped me so often to blow up the fire. It had even served as a bucket, and yet, scrubbed with soap and a nail-brush, it had never let me down on bigger occasions. It is true there were times when together we had caused amusement. At Pitt Terrace one day, I did not quite know what amused two toughs as they passed till I heard one exclaim___*' 'Wha' a ha'!' Then there were the Dundee mill-girls, miles and miles, it seemed, of mill-girls, together we had faced the whole lot with a smile.

It may not be a good hat for a speed car, but after all, it is the Scout hat. Like 'B.P.' I would say – Scouts, stick to your hat. Do not discard it lest with it you throw great traditions away.

On the yacht we had glorious weather and the time flew past, the Chief and our host in good form. The Chief had his sketch-book of course. In the evening, Glentanar entertained us with music. On the Sunday morning we went ashore at Tighnabruaich where the Chief called on a friend. On the hill above we had spotted a neat Scout Camp, but the Chief and all of us, including the Captain, had agreed that this should be 'tabu.' He needed a rest; we would leave it severely alone.

When the Chief came out from his call, he suggested a stroll. 'Which way?' we asked. 'This way of course,' said the Chief, and, in spite of mild protests, we headed direct for the camp. It was up a steep hill, so that when these three civilians emerged, they came on the camp by surprise. Facing us, in front of their tents, were some 20 boys, smart and ready for Church. With his back to us, the Scoutmaster was quite unaware of our presence, till the looks of his boys made him turn round.

'Good morning, Scoutmaster,' the Chief called out, and then as if to explain our intrusion he added – 'This is Major Crum,' when this drew no response the Chief added – 'And this is Lord Glentanar,' But still the Scoutmaster seemed puzzled. 'And I am a

* 'What a hat!'

335

Scoutmaster' added the Chief. By now we were quite close up to the boys and I heard whispers – 'It is the Chief!' At last it dawned on their Leader who duly welcomed this invasion.

By this time the Church bells were ringing. The Chief bucked the boys up with a word and we saw them depart. We returned to the yacht where the Captain and crew with glasses had watched all our movements. On Monday the Chief was due in Edinburgh.

As for myself, I spent the next two days' heat-wave at the Lake of Menteith – 'no clothes on all day, enjoying a perfect rest.'

Two days later we were off on our charabanc tour.

29. THE STIRLING BOYS' LEAGUE.

When I first came to Stirling in 1912, it surprised me to find how little was done towards helping boys in their games. Whenever I sallied forth from my rooms in Pitt Terrace, every boy seemed engaged on some sort of game. In the closes one came on boys bouncing or heading a ball. In the Terraces, they were dribbling tins or balls of paper; you even found message-boys, with their baskets as goal posts, engaged in keen contest. In the parks groups of boys were kicking a football with jackets as goalposts. It was quite the exception to find a decent game going on, with some good B.B. Officer, or School Teacher, leading his boys towards fitness and playing the game.

At school to me as a boy, and later in the Army, the value of games as a means towards health and character, had seemed a matter of course, and yet in Stirling on holidays the parks seemed empty of boys' games, while grown-up games were often so rowdy and rough as to become a public nuisance.

Formation of the S.B.L.

In the King's Park there were no facilities for shelter or stripping, no washing or lavatory accommodation. Nothing was done to set aside pitches for boys though there was room for double the number of pitches. As I came to know more of the boys I found that most of their talk was of football. Why did no one seize this opening and encourage this manly game?

It was not till February, 1921, that together with Mr. Forbes of Sterling School, Captain W. Hardie of the King's Park F.C. and Dr. T. Adam, the County M.O., we took up this matter and started the 'Stirling Boys' League' for boys under 16, with its printed rules, its motto – 'Play the game,' its shield, and league of 16 Clubs, its office-bearers and 7 referees.

We had our ups and downs. There were squabbles, 'objections' and rows. Teams failed to turn up, players let down their teams and so on, but, with Captain Hardie giving all a fair hearing and with talks to the boys, good progress was made and much was done through friendly games, e.g., with Q.V.S. and Edinburgh teams.

Peter Craigmyle.

In March during the Students' Campaign, the Rev. R. Morris gave a splendid talk on the game with lantern slides; and later the famous Aberdeen Referee, Peter Craigmyle, spoke to a full-house of boys and received a tremendous ovation. After speaking of fitness and team-work, he said that 'not knowing the rules' was the source of most of the rows.

Then with the help of diagrams he would describe some situation and set them a problem – 'As Referee, what would your decision be?' How eager they were, these cock-sure young experts, as they shouted their rival solutions – 'A goal!' 'A foul!' 'Offside!' 'A burl up!' And often no one was right! He fairly opened their eyes.

Again in December he spoke at another big meeting and told of great successes in Aberdeen where Councillors and Education Authorities had united to help the boys. Mr. Wm. Brown, a well-known Stirling educationist, spoke in support and advised the League to approach the Town Council.

Petition to the Town Council.

In January 1923 our committee drew up a petition asking the Town Council for support and facilities. It was also signed by eight other Leaders – B.B. (Jas. F. Marshall); Scouts (Thos. Wilson); High School (Alex. Third); Education (Wm. Brown); King's Park F.C. (W. Stevenson); Hurst Grange (L. Plant); the Rev. A. M. Johnston and Sheriff Dean Leslie. Our five points were:– (1) Rearrangement of pitches; (2) Provision of goal-posts; (3) Shelter and lavatory facilities; (4) An official in charge; (5) The support of the Town Council.

On 10th April our deputation was kindly and courteously received. We all had our say, and they all had their say. Dr. Adam wound up our case with a special plea as to health and delinquency, But little came of this meeting.

Looking back now, I think the cause of our failure was that we had not first approached and convinced our highly esteemed Town Clerk, Mr. D. B. Morris. It may even be that in our approach we had stressed what was done in Aberdeen too much for the liking of this loyal Son of the Rock. However that may be, the well-known historian of our ancient Burgh noted though he was as one of Youth's most kindly friends, certainly did not come down on our side as a champion of football for boys in the King's Park.

The right use of increased leisure.

In those days of transition, with the arrival of increased leisure and charabancs, too often it was true that rowdy crowds did not enhance the good name of football. Thus, difficulties were raised. The provision of shelters and lavatories and supervision would mean extra expense. Councillors were busy men and had more pressing claims on their time. Boys could run their own games as they always had done before. Alas, our plea for character-training through games had carried little weight. Thus it was that six months later in November, 1923, at the start of new season, little had been done.

10th November, 1923. – 'Visited 3 joiners and got sawdust to mark out 3 pitches. A jolly morning with a whole crowd of boys and 3 trek carts. We have now got 3 pitches in good order, but too much falls on me, and I so much else to see to. Young fellows are not free from their work and have no time to see to these things, and the boys seem lost without Leaders. We were lucky to get a present of goal-posts from the old 'Empress' and I bought two more sets on my own, to save time. With boys so daft on football, it does seem daft to neglect them and their games.'

However the League went well, with McLaren (Y.M.C.A.) and Donald McEwan and others helping, there were at times as many as 4 or 5 good games going on at the same time in the Park. The Shield was won by the Fallin boys after a good sporting game with the Methodist team.

With my Scout duties taking me all over Scotland and a Jamboree in London and a training course at Gilwell and Scoutmaster's duties in Stirling, often running two troops at once, and with camps for hundreds of boys in the summer and trouble with the winter climate, it will be understood that during these 3 years I had not the time desired to further the League, but at least we had helped to launch the idea and later, the torch was carried on by the Boys' Brigade and Y.M.C.A. The cry was always for leaders – 'How much more could be done if we brought on boy-leaders to run their own show, and had more men to lead all these boys.'

Fourteen years later I found myself pleading once more with the Town Council for support of Youth in their games, but that belongs to another part of my story.

30. 'SCOUTS' OWN' SERVICES.

Before passing on from Scouting days to Boys' Club and other activities, I would close with some word of our 'Scouts' Own' Services, an important part of our training.

In the early days of Scouting there were those who shook their heads and said the Movement could not last – 'it was not on a religious basis.' The fact is that in 1908 the Chief offered the idea to help religious training. It is true he did not expect all his Scoutmasters to conduct Bible classes, but he did from the first wish his boys to have some Church connection. His genius was that along with their Scouting and games he gave boys a code which also appealed, and put it in language which all understood. His secret, along with his fun, was his example and friendship. No one who heard him sum up at the close of a happy conference could have failed to be moved by the faith that was in him.

In those days the hold of the Home, the Church and Sunday School was such that the average boy got some instruction in Christian Faith. But today this is, too often, not so. Conditions have changed. I have read the latest reports of Scouts and Clubs on this subject. Both agree – 'There is now a dangerous gap which has got to be filled.' 'The problem,' they say, 'is how best to interest, inspire, and guide all kinds of youth towards the Christian Faith.'

In speaking of these things our reticence is natural. We who are, ourselves, so far behind, who are we to be giving a lead? Sincerity may hold us silent, but this silence must not be misunderstood. How often have I heard some good fellow exclaim – 'That's the spirit!' 'A Scout,' we say, 'is no Scout at all without the Scout Spirit.' But this practice of brotherhood is nothing new, we have no monopoly! We are right to do all we can to get this spirit, but our secret must be that we see beyond this. It is God's command and Christ is the way.

To get touch, that is our great need. Touch with our boys, touch with the Spirit that guides. At times the way will be hard, boys must be taught the Faith of their fathers and the value of prayer. This is the task of the Church. It has never been claimed that a 'Scouts' Own' Service is more than an aid in the right direction.

The 1st Stirling 'Scouts' Own' Services.

In 1909 the 1st Stirling Scouts were started by a few High School boys. Later a smart ex-cavalry sergeant, John Logan, took charge and the Rev. John Arnott was keenly interested. When war came in 1914, Mrs. Howie, a missionary lady, home from Africa, and Miss Nairn, kept the boys together throughout the war. I suppose it was due to these two good ladies and Mr. Arnott that, when I first helped in 1919, I found myself detailed as a Leader, not only in Scouting, camping and games, but also for quite a new role as their Leader in Sunday meetings.

At this time the influence of 'Uncle' Elwes, Roland Phillips, and others was inspiring greater attention to the spiritual side of Scout training. In Scout camps and church-going there had been an advance, and the 'Scouts' Own,' (a Service in which the boys did more for themselves), was becoming a well-known feature.

I have notes of such meetings dating from 1919 to 1948. Meetings where, overcoming diffidence, I spoke to thousands of boys in Glasgow, Manchester, and Nottingham; notes of meetings of one or two hundred boys in camps. I have also notes of our own 'Scouts' Own' Services in Stirling, which after 30 years, I am thankful to say, are still doing well. I do not know how far to go into detail. What I want to do is to convey some idea of our progress to friends who may be interested. We certainly learned a great deal.

At first I did too much myself: We all had to learn and someone had to begin. It is true we made the boys responsible for music and hymns, for readings and repeating the Promise and Law, but the details of duties and arranging for speakers, which latterly was seen to by the Patrol Leaders, was originally worked out by the Scoutmaster. At first we were apt to lean too much on 'experts' and make claims on Ministers who, though generous in their support, were busy men on Sundays. As speakers we also had great help from School teachers and Officers of the Boys' Brigade. As time went on and Scouts grew into Rovers, many of these turned out among our best speakers to boys.

And so tradition grew, till in due course, during the war, you would find some 50 boys, with boys under 18 in charge, conducting the whole Service, and always a quota of ex-Scouts on leave from the Forces, glad to be back among us and sure of a welcome from all. As for those who were older, we too were welcome and happy to join in the Service and help or guide, or add a few words as occasion required.

To convey some idea I propose to give extracts from my log; and if here and there, I let out some secret, which at the time it was written, was never meant for cold print, I let it out now only because as a friend, I want to 'get touch.'

Notes on 1st Stirling 'Scouts' Own' Services.

For 15 years, until our New Scout Hall was ready, we were made welcome at the South Church Hall where the Ministers always encouraged us. Our Services started at 10 a.m. and were over in time for the Services of the various Churches to which the boys belonged. Some had other classes to attend, but the average attendance was from ½ to ¾ of our total numbers. We started in 1919 with some 20 Scouts. By 1931, with the 4th Troop added, there were some 60 or more. It would fill a large book to tell of the excellent talks given by so many speakers during those 30 years, but my purpose is rather to give a general impression with as few extracts as may be.

12/10/1919. – 'Scouts make me a birthday present (48 today). Told them best present would be to get a good name for the Troop, Spoke about slums and S.P.C.C. work.'

(And here I will let out just one secret note never dreamed of for print some 30 years back.) –

23/6/1920. – 'After a strenuous week preparing for Olympia Jamboree and Rosneath Camps, sat for an hour 'up Polmaise,' stripped in the sun, glorious day, glorious views. The flag at the Borestone below is flying in honour of Robert the Bruce and of Freedom. As I sat there thinking of the coming camps and Jamboree, and the talk to the boys tomorrow, how lovely it was! Last visit was blue-bells, now it is dog-roses, pink and white; soon

343

it will be fox-gloves. Knelt down, as often before on such occasions, after prayer, came away happy and knowing that all was well.'

25/6/1920. – 'Last and best meeting of season. Spoke of the Practice of Friendship and the coming Olympia Jamboree.'

After Scout meetings, on Sunday afternoons, a few of us often foregathered and went for walks with some objective, e.g. to visit the Castle, or to visit the Infirmary.

13/2/1921. – 'The boys are certainly good listeners. We all find it the same. In the afternoon with 12 Scouts visit to Whinwell where we adopted two more bairns. Then a practice in night stalking with black goggles on the Gowan Hills. Later returned to Whinwell with J.F., a case for first-aid to both kilt and bare knees.'

15/2/1922. – 'Glasgow – 5, 000 Scouts. Constant throat troubles have kept me indoors since Xmas, but determined to go. Left Stirling 1.30 p.m. with Ian Bolton (my stable companion) and 5 Patrol Leaders. Hall packed with eager boys, galleries filled with parents and friends, and on the platform tiers of Glasgow folk behind us. The Service inspiring, especially the singing. Spoke 10 minutes only. A separate word to Scouts, to Scoutmasters and to the Public – 'Look wide. The Spirit which makes a Nation great. The Scout Movement a stepping-stone towards the way.' To the Scouts – 'The Chief, his birthday (loud cheers) just play the game. You will find the way and bring great happiness.' In spite of throat (no amplifiers then) no difficulty at all. For me a landmark on the way.'

For the next few years our Services went well. In 1923 in liaison with the 1st B.B. Coy. we started annual joint services (home and away), a custom which is still well maintained. Later with the 4th Troop added and Scouts from Menstrie, our numbers increased. It will be understood that all this time, with Outings and Summer Camps, touch and comradeship were helping to build up tradition. About this date my spare-time hobby was, with Thomas Miller, to explore the battle-field of Bannockburn, with all its many sites. Often after Sunday meetings, Scouts and Boys' Brigade would join me and explore the New Park boundaries, the Gillies Hill, or the fords in the Carse.

22/2/1925. – 'Good Scouts' Own-Chief's birthday. Walk with 8 Scouts to Crook's Ford in snow. Snow-balling. Counted 15 different kinds of birds.'

1/3/1925. – '1st B .B. and Scouts joint Service. 80 boys sang well. Talk on 'Pulling together.'. Boys invite me take them round the battlefield. Walked Steuarthall and Forth.'

26/3/1925. – 'Walk Earl's Hill alone, reciting Nottingham speech to curlews and peewits – and prayer. Sang all the way down hill!'

20/6/1925. – 'Week-end camp at Auchenbowie. Sunday Mission Service. Over 100 from Denny, Torwood, Stirling. When I look back to 1911, thanks be for progress.'

And now I skip such entries and pass on to 1935 when I find a sample service given in more detail.

1/4/1935. – 'A lovely Spring day, primroses and daffodils, took my Menstrie 'bodyguard' in from Gogar. Felt I had something which I wanted very much to say. Found assembled in Scout Hall 20 Rovers, 40 Scouts, an informal coming-together of friends, all pleased to meet. The good Harold and Steel and McNaught of the older brigade are there as usual. Glad to see 'Joe'* from the Club now a pit-boy.'

'Today the Peewits are on duty. Their Patrol Leader in the Chair; on his left his 2nd, who has the 'reading' and 'order of service.' The other Peewits are in charge of repeating the Law, issuing hymn books, and taking round the hat for Whinwell collection. On the right of the young chairman sits the Speaker. In front, some two dozen younger boys of 12 to 13; graduating back in age, a fine lot of lads, alert, fit-looking. Bruce Wallace, our pianist starts a Psalm. Then comes the prayer. Sometimes. the Leader reads a prayer from the 'Scout Book of Prayer.' Today he looks at me and I stand up. 'I want you to give me your closest attention', I said. It felt quite natural; there came an atmosphere of prayer.

'After a hymn a younger Scout repeats the Law and does it well. He is prepared. He does it thoughtfully, with confidence. Next comes the Reading. The 2nd has had notice for a week, it is Mark x. 32–45 – he reads it from Moffat's version, but before he starts, I say a word. With the help of a map I speak of Jesus' three visits

---

* 8/12/34. 'Joe sat between two 4th Troop boys. C. my only Scout success so far, is one of them. Each presses me to share his hymn-book. They sing like larks. Told C. afterwards to get Joe back. Joe, his pal, had left school, deserted the Club and Scouts, and was now unemployed, looks the other way if we meet, instead, of the 'cheerio' that used to be.'

to Jerusalem, A.D. 28. October? December? April? Three times He foretells death. Three times His team show poor team spirit. Arguing which is first. Three times Jesus teaches Service and Leadership. Then the 2nd reads. He too does well. Another hymn and then the hat goes round. Then comes 'The Major's talk.' The Chairman with his usual smile, stands up to introduce the speaker.'

A Talk at 'Scouts' Own.'

'I give them my story of Rifleman Egan, not new perhaps to older lads, but this does not seem to matter. I could feel the younger boys settle down in their seats as I started – 'I am going to tell you a story,' and as I spoke I seemed to see Egan and the veld and bullocks and wagons, the Boers and the ambush. The boys seemed with me, seeing it all; then turning to the Rovers – '25 years ago,' I said, 'I took up Scouting – Why? – because it seemed to me the finest practice of Christianity I could see. I was younger then and full of zeal and went all over Scotland thinking to get Scouting going everywhere . . . . But found 50 per cent could not afford . . . .' (Here I gave the story of a visit to a Club boy's home)* 'What about touch with the 50 percent?' I asked. Since 1911 the Scouts had helped – Xmas, Whinwell, parcels, dinners, outings, camp, and now in the Boys' Club the Rovers were helping with boxing and gym, and the Scouts with football. This was good service. In other ways they could help. At home and elsewhere. We were not all called on like Egan to be heroes and 'stop the bullets,' but all are called on to serve in some way or other.'

'And so we closed with the blessing. A few notices and a kind word from Mr. Harold, the Commissioner, commending the Peewits, with a special pat on the back for the boy who repeated the Law, I was pleased when his friends promptly gave a spontaneous. round of applause.'

---

* 'Club-boy, "Tweedledee," deserts B.B., reported to me by his Captain. I visit the home to find out why. It seems no boots and "shabby suit" is the trouble. He will go back "shabby suit" and all, but not before Friday. Why? He likes B. B. and wants to be back, but not before the "Party," lest others think it was the "Party" which enticed him back.'

The Boy Leaders take Charge.

5/11/1939. – 'I see that in November, 1939, our meetings had reached a high level as we passed our 20th milestone. Then with the 2nd World War came hard times, but to me the way the Patrol Leaders rose to the occasion was the most encouraging feature of all.'

15/3/1941. – 'Living at Gogar, 4 miles away, and short of petrol, I had not latterly been in close touch. On 15th March, 1941, a time when the war outlook was as grim as could be, I groped my way through the black-out to Stirling and visited the Troop, in their darkened hall. There were several keen young Leaders, Jim McNab was in charge, but I did not know the younger boys as in old days. They asked me to speak at the 'Scouts' Own' that Sunday. I went and found only 6 boys. The two Leaders were much distressed. We had quite a happy natural meeting, after which we decided that something must be done. We decided to make a special effort next Sunday, which happened to be a special 'Day of National Prayer'.'

23/3/1941. – (Armageddon at its height) 'The best 'Scouts' Own' for many a day. Three good Patrol Leaders ran the Meeting. Ronnie McPherson in the chair. Geo. Lunn the Reading and Jim McNab's address on this 'Day of Prayer' was quite first class. Ian Robertson at the piano, 32 boys, also two Service Ex-Scouts, one of them Kenneth Clough from Yorkshire, who proved a very great help at this time.'

8/4/1941. – 'The last meeting of the Session. All went well, spoke to the Leader about his prayer, it had been so natural, the boyish way he asked that, by being real Scouts, we might help to win the war.'

27/10/1941. – 'A new session and new Leaders. Boys are called up at 18 and, before you can say 'presto!' they are Airmen, Soldiers, or Sailors. Some 30 boys and the Graham twins, ex-King Scouts, on leave. Explained about 'Scouts' Own' Services to the 'Court of Honour' afterwards. I found few went to Church. Why? Glad to get touch again but we must get the boys to run their own show. This may mean preliminary launching, speakers, duties, etc.'

16/11/1941. – 'The new Patrol Leaders ran their first 'Scouts' Own.' Piano. Chairman. Reading. Law – Address by Alastair Lamb, so good. They had all been anxious a bit, and were relieved and pleased a good start had been made. They were now a team and had something accomplished, something done?'

24/11/1941. – 'Visit from 1st B.B. Small mistakes, but let them make mistakes and point them out later. Submit, Commit, and Carry On.'

15/12/1941. – 'All goes well. The Leaders want an extra day, 28th December.'

18/12/1941. – 'Miss McJannet and Alex. Reid speak on Whinwell – visit with subscriptions later. Callum Stark, age 17, fills the chair with much assurance. Some 30 boys and my Menstrie boys.' (The gallant Callum, bomber pilot at 19, lost in North Sea not long after.)

29/11/1942. – 'Real progress with new Session. Leaders, 1st and 4th, good friends and work together on their own, with no word from me they have now all prepared for opening session 12th October, and ask me to speak on my 70th birthday. 24 years since we started. I send a word of 'well done' and say I hope to speak on 'The Spirit that wins.'

The Menstrie Scouts.

And here, at the risk of being too long, I would say a word about the Menstrie boys, a country Troop, because it also shows how boys will take responsibility when given the chance. After two years at Gogar I took over the Menstrie Troop in 1934. In reviving the Troop, visits to the four Stirling Troops played a great part. It was good for all concerned.

On 28th October, 1934. – I took 3 Menstrie Scouts in to attend a 'Scouts' Own.' At first there seemed trouble about getting away, owing to milk and Sunday papers. In 1935 I always had half-a-dozen or so in the car and the mixing did much good.

29/11/1936. – 'Five weeks away due to winter throat troubles but the Menstrie boys rise earlier and go on their own by bus.'

7/2/1937. – 'Robert Nelson gave an excellent talk on Birkenhead Jamboree. (He must have been a very small boy at the time.) Seven Menstrie boys, good to see them coming on so well.'

4/12/1938. – 'Took my "bodyguard," eight Menstrie boys all back in time for Dr. Boyd's Service.'

2/4/1939. – 'Talk to 7th B.B. Took my Menstrie bodyguard and on to Holy Rude. A fine service, and Church full, but they found us a good place and made us feel welcome.'

15/2/1942. – 'Menstrie boys took charge of running 'Scouts' Own' and did it well. On the way in some seemed a bit anxious, but returned with more confidence.'

15/11/1942. – 'Menstrie Scouts in charge. Though they have lost four Scoutmasters called up in succession, they still do well. A silence for George Miller killed with Argylls.'

18/4/1943. – 'Closing Meeting. Silence to remember very gallant Willie Murray. Menstrie boys in charge again, did well.'

The Boys' Brigade.

So too I have entries about our touch with the Boys' Brigade. In James Marshall, John Campbell, Jas. Ingram and others we had many good friends, but I will only give one entry and that to show progress.

23/3/1943. – 'Joint service with 7th B.B. On their own initiative the two Troop Leaders, E. Robertson, 1st, and Ian Burnie, 4th Troop, spoke a special word of welcome to the Boys' Brigade.'

1943. – And so through all this anxious year of 1943, they carried on. New Leaders came and went. Guardsmen, Airmen, Navy, Merchant Service men would join us when on leave and often we had news of gaps – Jim McNab, a pilot now in German hands and Lexie Laing, Argylls, killed at the front, Callum Stark, and Billy White and Ian Livingstone, all these so recently among us, others too, older well-known Scouts, the brothers Davie, Donald Crawford, Angus McVicar, Milne Johnstone, Alex. Miller, H. Mathieson, Dan McDermont and so on, into 1944, and still with changing Leaders, services went well. In 1945 and 1946 again each year this entry – 'New Leaders doing well.' Yes right on till 1947, always this same finding.

9/2/1947. – 'Fifth week absent. I hear the boys did well. Today remember young Patrol Leader speaking for first time, a Dollar boy and keen King's Scout. It does one good to see these youngsters coming on. Just think if you at 16 had been asked to speak to 40 boys, or take the Chair with elders there, yet here we have these boys building up a good tradition.'

20/4/1947. – 'Founders' Day. Thankful for so much gone well. Renewed our promise and so closed a happy 28th Session.'

31. CONCLUSION.

When I come to this stage of my Memoirs, before I tackle new fields of Boys' Clubs, Games Leaders, 'Keep Fit,' and other such ventures – as I pause and look back all these years – I give thanks for wonderful progress.

I think of great days of sunshine and camps and friendships and boys, and my thoughts go back to a Hall, unique in its way, with its Scout works of art, its Clan tartans and trophies, with all the traditions and efforts they stand for. In my mind I revisit this home of good Scouting. I hear the Cubs' 'Woof!' the laughter of Scouts and the sound of their vigorous contests and games, or perhaps I join in some Rover debate.

I see the Scouts alert and saluting the Flag, or I find myself back at a 'Scouts' Own' Service. Meetings, Displays, Concerts and Plays come to mind, but what stands out most is the thanks that are due for a long succession of Leaders – Sixers, Patrol Leaders, Akelas, Scoutmasters, and all who by zeal and example have lived up to the law and passed on the torch. All these have kept up the tradition, the good name, and the Spirit of Scouting.

Here in such work there is no petty thought for the kudos of this or that Pack or Patrol, this Troop or Crew, this County or Country. It is part of the Founder's great vision of Service and world-wide good-will which these have helped to uphold. Did any, at times, have doubts on the way, wondering was it worthwhile? If so, my last message would be to give them this call – 'Every good Scout is a Leader.' Above all it is Leaders we need. Such work has God's blessing, yes, and it is ten thousand times worth-while!